ISBN 0-8373-2802-0

C-2802 CAREER EXAMINATION SER

## This is your PASSBOOK® for...

# Police Lieutenant

**Test Preparation Study Guide**

**Questions & Answers**

**NLC**

**NATIONAL LEARNING CORPORATION**

Copyright © 2013 by

# National Learning Corporation

### 212 Michael Drive, Syosset, New York 11791

All rights reserved, including the right of reproduction in whole or in part, in any form or by any means, electronic or mechanical, including photocopying, recording, or by any information storage and retrieval system, without permission in writing from the Publisher.

(516) 921-8888
(800) 645-6337
FAX: (516) 921-8743
www.passbooks.com
sales @ passbooks.com
info @ passbooks.com

PRINTED IN THE UNITED STATES OF AMERICA

# PASSBOOK®

## NOTICE

This book is SOLELY intended for, is sold ONLY to, and its use is RESTRICTED to *individual*, bona fide applicants or candidates who qualify by virtue of having seriously filed applications for appropriate license, certificate, professional and/or promotional advancement, higher school matriculation, scholarship, or other legitimate requirements of educational and/or governmental authorities.

This book is NOT intended for use, class instruction, tutoring, training, duplication, copying, reprinting, excerption, or adaptation, etc., by:

(1) Other publishers

(2) Proprietors and/or Instructors of "Coaching" and/or Preparatory Courses

(3) Personnel and/or Training Divisions of commercial, industrial, and governmental organizations

(4) Schools, colleges, or universities and/or their departments and staffs, including teachers and other personnel

(5) Testing Agencies or Bureaus

(6) Study groups which seek by the purchase of a single volume to copy and/or duplicate and/or adapt this material for use by the group as a whole without having purchased individual volumes for each of the members of the group

(7) Et al.

Such persons would be in violation of appropriate Federal and State statutes.

*PROVISION OF LICENSING AGREEMENTS.* — Recognized educational commercial, industrial, and governmental institutions and organizations, and others legitimately engaged in educational pursuits, including training, testing, and measurement activities, may address a request for a licensing agreement to the copyright owners, who will determine whether, and under what conditions, including fees and charges, the materials in this book may be used by them. In other words, a licensing facility exists for the legitimate use of the material in this book on other than an individual basis. However, it is asseverated and affirmed here that the material in this book *CANNOT* be used without the receipt of the express permission of such a licensing agreement from the Publishers.

NATIONAL LEARNING CORPORATION
212 Michael Drive
Syosset, New York  11791

Inquiries re licensing agreements should be addressed to:
The President
National Learning Corporation
212 Michael Drive
Syosset, New York  11791

# PASSBOOK® SERIES

THE *PASSBOOK® SERIES* has been created to prepare applicants and candidates for the ultimate academic battlefield — the examination room.

At some time in our lives, each and every one of us may be required to take an examination — for validation, matriculation, admission, qualification, registration, certification, or licensure.

Based on the assumption that every applicant or candidate has met the basic formal educational standards, has taken the required number of courses, and read the necessary texts, the *PASSBOOK® SERIES* furnishes the one special preparation which may assure passing with confidence, instead of failing with insecurity. Examination questions — together with answers — are furnished as the basic vehicle for study so that the mysteries of the examination and its compounding difficulties may be eliminated or diminished by a sure method.

This book is meant to help you pass your examination provided that you qualify and are serious in your objective.

The entire field is reviewed through the huge store of content information which is succinctly presented through a provocative and challenging approach — the question-and-answer method.

A climate of success is established by furnishing the correct answers at the end of each test.

You soon learn to recognize types of questions, forms of questions, and patterns of questioning. You may even begin to anticipate expected outcomes.

You perceive that many questions are repeated or adapted so that you can gain acute insights, which may enable you to score many sure points.

You learn how to confront new questions, or types of questions, and to attack them confidently and work out the correct answers.

You note objectives and emphases, and recognize pitfalls and dangers, so that you may make positive educational adjustments.

Moreover, you are kept fully informed in relation to new concepts, methods, practices, and directions in the field.

You discover that you are actually taking the examination all the time: you are preparing for the examination by "taking" an examination, not by reading extraneous and/or supererogatory textbooks.

In short, this PASSBOOK®, used directedly, should be an important factor in helping you to pass your test.

# POLICE LIEUTENANT

## DUTIES

Directs the activities of a patrol force, detective squad, or headquarters bureau when so assigned. Assigns tasks to subordinate officers and instructs them as to the methods of operations. Directs raids and makes arrests. Investigates crimes where unusual and/or difficult law enforcement problems are likely to occur. Prepares technical and administrative police reports.

## SCOPE OF THE WRITTEN TEST

The multiple-choice written test will cover knowledge's, skills, and/or abilities in the following areas:

1. State Law, which will include the Penal Law, Criminal Procedure Law, Vehicle and Traffic Law, and the Family Court Act;
2. Modern law enforcement methods and practices and the use of good judgment in solving police problems;
3. Preparation of written material;
4. Understanding and interpreting written material; and
5. Administration and supervision.

# HOW TO TAKE A TEST

I. YOU MUST PASS AN EXAMINATION

*A. WHAT EVERY CANDIDATE SHOULD KNOW*

Examination applicants often ask us for help in preparing for the written test. What can I study in advance? What kinds of questions will be asked? How will the test be given? How will the papers be graded?

As an applicant for a civil service examination, you may be wondering about some of these things. Our purpose here is to suggest effective methods of advance study and to describe civil service examinations.

Your chances for success on this examination can be increased if you know how to prepare. Those "pre-examination jitters" can be reduced if you know what to expect. You can even experience an adventure in good citizenship if you know why civil service exams are given.

*B. WHY ARE CIVIL SERVICE EXAMINATIONS GIVEN?*

Civil service examinations are important to you in two ways. As a citizen, you want public jobs filled by employees who know how to do their work. As a job seeker, you want a fair chance to compete for that job on an equal footing with other candidates. The best-known means of accomplishing this two-fold goal is the competitive examination.

Exams are widely publicized throughout the nation. They may be administered for jobs in federal, state, city, municipal, town or village governments or agencies.

Any citizen may apply, with some limitations, such as the age or residence of applicants. Your experience and education may be reviewed to see whether you meet the requirements for the particular examination. When these requirements exist, they are reasonable and applied consistently to all applicants. Thus, a competitive examination may cause you some uneasiness now, but it is your privilege and safeguard.

*C. HOW ARE CIVIL SERVICE EXAMS DEVELOPED?*

Examinations are carefully written by trained technicians who are specialists in the field known as "psychological measurement," in consultation with recognized authorities in the field of work that the test will cover. These experts recommend the subject matter areas or skills to be tested; only those knowledges or skills important to your success on the job are included. The most reliable books and source materials available are used as references. Together, the experts and technicians judge the difficulty level of the questions.

Test technicians know how to phrase questions so that the problem is clearly stated. Their ethics do not permit "trick" or "catch" questions. Questions may have been tried out on sample groups, or subjected to statistical analysis, to determine their usefulness.

Written tests are often used in combination with performance tests, ratings of training and experience, and oral interviews. All of these measures combine to form the best-known means of finding the right person for the right job.

## II. HOW TO PASS THE WRITTEN TEST

### A. NATURE OF THE EXAMINATION

To prepare intelligently for civil service examinations, you should know how they differ from school examinations you have taken. In school you were assigned certain definite pages to read or subjects to cover. The examination questions were quite detailed and usually emphasized memory. Civil service exams, on the other hand, try to discover your present ability to perform the duties of a position, plus your potentiality to learn these duties. In other words, a civil service exam attempts to predict how successful you will be. Questions cover such a broad area that they cannot be as minute and detailed as school exam questions.

In the public service similar kinds of work, or positions, are grouped together in one "class." This process is known as *position-classification*. All the positions in a class are paid according to the salary range for that class. One class title covers all of these positions, and they are all tested by the same examination.

### B. FOUR BASIC STEPS

#### 1) Study the announcement

How, then, can you know what subjects to study? Our best answer is: "Learn as much as possible about the class of positions for which you've applied." The exam will test the knowledge, skills and abilities needed to do the work.

Your most valuable source of information about the position you want is the official exam announcement. This announcement lists the training and experience qualifications. Check these standards and apply only if you come reasonably close to meeting them.

The brief description of the position in the examination announcement offers some clues to the subjects which will be tested. Think about the job itself. Review the duties in your mind. Can you perform them, or are there some in which you are rusty? Fill in the blank spots in your preparation.

Many jurisdictions preview the written test in the exam announcement by including a section called "Knowledge and Abilities Required," "Scope of the Examination," or some similar heading. Here you will find out specifically what fields will be tested.

#### 2) Review your own background

Once you learn in general what the position is all about, and what you need to know to do the work, ask yourself which subjects you already know fairly well and which need improvement. You may wonder whether to concentrate on improving your strong areas or on building some background in your fields of weakness. When the announcement has specified "some knowledge" or "considerable knowledge," or has used adjectives like "beginning principles of…" or "advanced … methods," you can get a clue as to the number and difficulty of questions to be asked in any given field. More questions, and hence broader coverage, would be included for those subjects which are more important in the work. Now weigh your strengths and weaknesses against the job requirements and prepare accordingly.

#### 3) Determine the level of the position

Another way to tell how intensively you should prepare is to understand the level of the job for which you are applying. Is it the entering level? In other words, is this the position in which beginners in a field of work are hired? Or is it an intermediate or advanced level? Sometimes this is indicated by such words as "Junior" or "Senior" in the class title. Other jurisdictions use Roman numerals to designate the level – Clerk I, Clerk II, for example. The word "Supervisor" sometimes appears in the title. If the level is not indicated by the title, check the description of duties. Will you be working under very close supervision, or will you have responsibility for independent decisions in this work?

**4) Choose appropriate study materials**

Now that you know the subjects to be examined and the relative amount of each subject to be covered, you can choose suitable study materials. For beginning level jobs, or even advanced ones, if you have a pronounced weakness in some aspect of your training, read a modern, standard textbook in that field. Be sure it is up to date and has general coverage. Such books are normally available at your library, and the librarian will be glad to help you locate one. For entry-level positions, questions of appropriate difficulty are chosen – neither highly advanced questions, nor those too simple. Such questions require careful thought but not advanced training.

If the position for which you are applying is technical or advanced, you will read more advanced, specialized material. If you are already familiar with the basic principles of your field, elementary textbooks would waste your time. Concentrate on advanced textbooks and technical periodicals. Think through the concepts and review difficult problems in your field.

These are all general sources. You can get more ideas on your own initiative, following these leads. For example, training manuals and publications of the government agency which employs workers in your field can be useful, particularly for technical and professional positions. A letter or visit to the government department involved may result in more specific study suggestions, and certainly will provide you with a more definite idea of the exact nature of the position you are seeking.

## III. KINDS OF TESTS

Tests are used for purposes other than measuring knowledge and ability to perform specified duties. For some positions, it is equally important to test ability to make adjustments to new situations or to profit from training. In others, basic mental abilities not dependent on information are essential. Questions which test these things may not appear as pertinent to the duties of the position as those which test for knowledge and information. Yet they are often highly important parts of a fair examination. For very general questions, it is almost impossible to help you direct your study efforts. What we can do is to point out some of the more common of these general abilities needed in public service positions and describe some typical questions.

1) General information

Broad, general information has been found useful for predicting job success in some kinds of work. This is tested in a variety of ways, from vocabulary lists to questions about current events. Basic background in some field of work, such as sociology or economics, may be sampled in a group of questions. Often these are principles which have become familiar to most persons through exposure rather than through formal training. It is difficult to advise you how to study for these questions; being alert to the world around you is our best suggestion.

2) Verbal ability

An example of an ability needed in many positions is verbal or language ability. Verbal ability is, in brief, the ability to use and understand words. Vocabulary and grammar tests are typical measures of this ability. Reading comprehension or paragraph interpretation questions are common in many kinds of civil service tests. You are given a paragraph of written material and asked to find its central meaning.

3) Numerical ability

Number skills can be tested by the familiar arithmetic problem, by checking paired lists of numbers to see which are alike and which are different, or by interpreting charts and graphs. In the latter test, a graph may be printed in the test booklet which you are asked to use as the basis for answering questions.

4) Observation

A popular test for law-enforcement positions is the observation test. A picture is shown to you for several minutes, then taken away. Questions about the picture test your ability to observe both details and larger elements.

5) Following directions

In many positions in the public service, the employee must be able to carry out written instructions dependably and accurately. You may be given a chart with several columns, each column listing a variety of information. The questions require you to carry out directions involving the information given in the chart.

6) Skills and aptitudes

Performance tests effectively measure some manual skills and aptitudes. When the skill is one in which you are trained, such as typing or shorthand, you can practice. These tests are often very much like those given in business school or high school courses. For many of the other skills and aptitudes, however, no short-time preparation can be made. Skills and abilities natural to you or that you have developed throughout your lifetime are being tested.

Many of the general questions just described provide all the data needed to answer the questions and ask you to use your reasoning ability to find the answers. Your best preparation for these tests, as well as for tests of facts and ideas, is to be at your physical and mental best. You, no doubt, have your own methods of getting into an exam-taking mood and keeping "in shape." The next section lists some ideas on this subject.


IV. KINDS OF QUESTIONS

Only rarely is the "essay" question, which you answer in narrative form, used in civil service tests. Civil service tests are usually of the short-answer type. Full instructions for answering these questions will be given to you at the examination. But in case this is your first experience with short-answer questions and separate answer sheets, here is what you need to know:

### 1) Multiple-choice Questions

Most popular of the short-answer questions is the "multiple choice" or "best answer" question. It can be used, for example, to test for factual knowledge, ability to solve problems or judgment in meeting situations found at work.

A multiple-choice question is normally one of three types—

- It can begin with an incomplete statement followed by several possible endings. You are to find the one ending which *best* completes the statement, although some of the others may not be entirely wrong.
- It can also be a complete statement in the form of a question which is answered by choosing one of the statements listed.
- It can be in the form of a problem – again you select the best answer.

Here is an example of a multiple-choice question with a discussion which should give you some clues as to the method for choosing the right answer:

When an employee has a complaint about his assignment, the action which will *best* help him overcome his difficulty is to
    A. discuss his difficulty with his coworkers
    B. take the problem to the head of the organization
    C. take the problem to the person who gave him the assignment
    D. say nothing to anyone about his complaint

In answering this question, you should study each of the choices to find which is best. Consider choice "A" – Certainly an employee may discuss his complaint with fellow employees, but no change or improvement can result, and the complaint remains unresolved. Choice "B" is a poor choice since the head of the organization probably does not know what assignment you have been given, and taking your problem to him is known as "going over the head" of the supervisor. The supervisor, or person who made the assignment, is the person who can clarify it or correct any injustice. Choice "C" is, therefore, correct. To say nothing, as in choice "D," is unwise. Supervisors have and interest in knowing the problems employees are facing, and the employee is seeking a solution to his problem.

### 2) True/False Questions

The "true/false" or "right/wrong" form of question is sometimes used. Here a complete statement is given. Your job is to decide whether the statement is right or wrong.

SAMPLE: A person-to-person long-distance telephone call costs less than a station-to-station call to the same city.

This statement is wrong, or false, since person-to-person calls are more expensive.

This is not a complete list of all possible question forms, although most of the others are variations of these common types. You will always get complete directions for answering questions. Be sure you understand *how* to mark your answers – ask questions until you do.

## V. RECORDING YOUR ANSWERS

For an examination with very few applicants, you may be told to record your answers in the test booklet itself. Separate answer sheets are much more common. If this separate answer sheet is to be scored by machine – and this is often the case – it is highly important that you mark your answers correctly in order to get credit.

An electric scoring machine is often used in civil service offices because of the speed with which papers can be scored. Machine-scored answer sheets must be marked with a pencil, which will be given to you. This pencil has a high graphite content which responds to the electric scoring machine. As a matter of fact, stray dots may register as answers, so do not let your pencil rest on the answer sheet while you are pondering the correct answer. Also, if your pencil lead breaks or is otherwise defective, ask for another.

Since the answer sheet will be dropped in a slot in the scoring machine, be careful not to bend the corners or get the paper crumpled.

The answer sheet normally has five vertical columns of numbers, with 30 numbers to a column. These numbers correspond to the question numbers in your test booklet. After each number, going across the page are four or five pairs of dotted lines. These short dotted lines have small letters or numbers above them. The first two pairs may also have a "T" or "F" above the letters. This indicates that the first two pairs only are to be used if the questions are of the true-false type. If the questions are multiple choice, disregard the "T" and "F" and pay attention only to the small letters or numbers.

Answer your questions in the manner of the sample that follows:

32. The largest city in the United States is
    A. Washington, D.C.
    B. New York City
    C. Chicago
    D. Detroit
    E. San Francisco

1) Choose the answer you think is best. (New York City is the largest, so "B" is correct.)
2) Find the row of dotted lines numbered the same as the question you are answering. (Find row number 32)
3) Find the pair of dotted lines corresponding to the answer. (Find the pair of lines under the mark "B.")
4) Make a solid black mark between the dotted lines.

## VI. BEFORE THE TEST

Common sense will help you find procedures to follow to get ready for an examination. Too many of us, however, overlook these sensible measures. Indeed, nervousness and fatigue have been found to be the most serious reasons why applicants fail to do their best on civil service tests. Here is a list of reminders:

- Begin your preparation early – Don't wait until the last minute to go scurrying around for books and materials or to find out what the position is all about.
- Prepare continuously – An hour a night for a week is better than an all-night cram session. This has been definitely established. What is more, a night a

week for a month will return better dividends than crowding your study into a shorter period of time.
- Locate the place of the exam – You have been sent a notice telling you when and where to report for the examination. If the location is in a different town or otherwise unfamiliar to you, it would be well to inquire the best route and learn something about the building.
- Relax the night before the test – Allow your mind to rest. Do not study at all that night. Plan some mild recreation or diversion; then go to bed early and get a good night's sleep.
- Get up early enough to make a leisurely trip to the place for the test – This way unforeseen events, traffic snarls, unfamiliar buildings, etc. will not upset you.
- Dress comfortably – A written test is not a fashion show. You will be known by number and not by name, so wear something comfortable.
- Leave excess paraphernalia at home – Shopping bags and odd bundles will get in your way. You need bring only the items mentioned in the official notice you received; usually everything you need is provided. Do not bring reference books to the exam. They will only confuse those last minutes and be taken away from you when in the test room.
- Arrive somewhat ahead of time – If because of transportation schedules you must get there very early, bring a newspaper or magazine to take your mind off yourself while waiting.
- Locate the examination room – When you have found the proper room, you will be directed to the seat or part of the room where you will sit. Sometimes you are given a sheet of instructions to read while you are waiting. Do not fill out any forms until you are told to do so; just read them and be prepared.
- Relax and prepare to listen to the instructions
- If you have any physical problem that may keep you from doing your best, be sure to tell the test administrator. If you are sick or in poor health, you really cannot do your best on the exam. You can come back and take the test some other time.

VII. AT THE TEST

The day of the test is here and you have the test booklet in your hand. The temptation to get going is very strong. Caution! There is more to success than knowing the right answers. You must know how to identify your papers and understand variations in the type of short-answer question used in this particular examination. Follow these suggestions for maximum results from your efforts:

1) **Cooperate with the monitor**

The test administrator has a duty to create a situation in which you can be as much at ease as possible. He will give instructions, tell you when to begin, check to see that you are marking your answer sheet correctly, and so on. He is not there to guard you, although he will see that your competitors do not take unfair advantage. He wants to help you do your best.

2) **Listen to all instructions**

Don't jump the gun! Wait until you understand all directions. In most civil service tests you get more time than you need to answer the questions. So don't be in a hurry.

Read each word of instructions until you clearly understand the meaning. Study the examples, listen to all announcements and follow directions. Ask questions if you do not understand what to do.

### 3) Identify your papers

Civil service exams are usually identified by number only. You will be assigned a number; you must not put your name on your test papers. Be sure to copy your number correctly. Since more than one exam may be given, copy your exact examination title.

### 4) Plan your time

Unless you are told that a test is a "speed" or "rate of work" test, speed itself is usually not important. Time enough to answer all the questions will be provided, but this does not mean that you have all day. An overall time limit has been set. Divide the total time (in minutes) by the number of questions to determine the approximate time you have for each question.

### 5) Do not linger over difficult questions

If you come across a difficult question, mark it with a paper clip (useful to have along) and come back to it when you have been through the booklet. One caution if you do this – be sure to skip a number on your answer sheet as well. Check often to be sure that you have not lost your place and that you are marking in the row numbered the same as the question you are answering.

### 6) Read the questions

Be sure you know what the question asks! Many capable people are unsuccessful because they failed to *read* the questions correctly.

### 7) Answer all questions

Unless you have been instructed that a penalty will be deducted for incorrect answers, it is better to guess than to omit a question.

### 8) Speed tests

It is often better NOT to guess on speed tests. It has been found that on timed tests people are tempted to spend the last few seconds before time is called in marking answers at random – without even reading them – in the hope of picking up a few extra points. To discourage this practice, the instructions may warn you that your score will be "corrected" for guessing. That is, a penalty will be applied. The incorrect answers will be deducted from the correct ones, or some other penalty formula will be used.

### 9) Review your answers

If you finish before time is called, go back to the questions you guessed or omitted to give them further thought. Review other answers if you have time.

### 10) Return your test materials

If you are ready to leave before others have finished or time is called, take ALL your materials to the monitor and leave quietly. Never take any test material with you. The monitor can discover whose papers are not complete, and taking a test booklet may be grounds for disqualification.

## VIII. EXAMINATION TECHNIQUES

1) Read the general instructions carefully. These are usually printed on the first page of the exam booklet. As a rule, these instructions refer to the timing of the examination; the fact that you should not start work until the signal and must stop work at a signal, etc. If there are any *special* instructions, such as a choice of questions to be answered, make sure that you note this instruction carefully.

2) When you are ready to start work on the examination, that is as soon as the signal has been given, read the instructions to each question booklet, underline any key words or phrases, such as *least, best, outline, describe* and the like. In this way you will tend to answer as requested rather than discover on reviewing your paper that you *listed without describing*, that you selected the *worst* choice rather than the *best* choice, etc.

3) If the examination is of the objective or multiple-choice type – that is, each question will also give a series of possible answers: A, B, C or D, and you are called upon to select the best answer and write the letter next to that answer on your answer paper – it is advisable to start answering each question in turn. There may be anywhere from 50 to 100 such questions in the three or four hours allotted and you can see how much time would be taken if you read through all the questions before beginning to answer any. Furthermore, if you come across a question or group of questions which you know would be difficult to answer, it would undoubtedly affect your handling of all the other questions.

4) If the examination is of the essay type and contains but a few questions, it is a moot point as to whether you should read all the questions before starting to answer any one. Of course, if you are given a choice – say five out of seven and the like – then it is essential to read all the questions so you can eliminate the two that are most difficult. If, however, you are asked to answer all the questions, there may be danger in trying to answer the easiest one first because you may find that you will spend too much time on it. The best technique is to answer the first question, then proceed to the second, etc.

5) Time your answers. Before the exam begins, write down the time it started, then add the time allowed for the examination and write down the time it must be completed, then divide the time available somewhat as follows:
   - If 3-1/2 hours are allowed, that would be 210 minutes. If you have 80 objective-type questions, that would be an average of 2-1/2 minutes per question. Allow yourself no more than 2 minutes per question, or a total of 160 minutes, which will permit about 50 minutes to review.
   - If for the time allotment of 210 minutes there are 7 essay questions to answer, that would average about 30 minutes a question. Give yourself only 25 minutes per question so that you have about 35 minutes to review.

6) The most important instruction is to *read each question* and make sure you know what is wanted. The second most important instruction is to *time yourself properly* so that you answer every question. The third most

important instruction is to *answer every question*. Guess if you have to but include something for each question. Remember that you will receive no credit for a blank and will probably receive some credit if you write something in answer to an essay question. If you guess a letter – say "B" for a multiple-choice question – you may have guessed right. If you leave a blank as an answer to a multiple-choice question, the examiners may respect your feelings but it will not add a point to your score. Some exams may penalize you for wrong answers, so in such cases *only*, you may not want to guess unless you have some basis for your answer.

7) Suggestions
   a. Objective-type questions
      1. Examine the question booklet for proper sequence of pages and questions
      2. Read all instructions carefully
      3. Skip any question which seems too difficult; return to it after all other questions have been answered
      4. Apportion your time properly; do not spend too much time on any single question or group of questions
      5. Note and underline key words – *all, most, fewest, least, best, worst, same, opposite,* etc.
      6. Pay particular attention to negatives
      7. Note unusual option, e.g., unduly long, short, complex, different or similar in content to the body of the question
      8. Observe the use of "hedging" words – *probably, may, most likely,* etc.
      9. Make sure that your answer is put next to the same number as the question
      10. Do not second-guess unless you have good reason to believe the second answer is definitely more correct
      11. Cross out original answer if you decide another answer is more accurate; do not erase until you are ready to hand your paper in
      12. Answer all questions; guess unless instructed otherwise
      13. Leave time for review

   b. Essay questions
      1. Read each question carefully
      2. Determine exactly what is wanted. Underline key words or phrases.
      3. Decide on outline or paragraph answer
      4. Include many different points and elements unless asked to develop any one or two points or elements
      5. Show impartiality by giving pros and cons unless directed to select one side only
      6. Make and write down any assumptions you find necessary to answer the questions
      7. Watch your English, grammar, punctuation and choice of words
      8. Time your answers; don't crowd material

8) Answering the essay question

Most essay questions can be answered by framing the specific response around several key words or ideas. Here are a few such key words or ideas:

M's: manpower, materials, methods, money, management
P's: purpose, program, policy, plan, procedure, practice, problems, pitfalls, personnel, public relations

    a. Six basic steps in handling problems:
       1. Preliminary plan and background development
       2. Collect information, data and facts
       3. Analyze and interpret information, data and facts
       4. Analyze and develop solutions as well as make recommendations
       5. Prepare report and sell recommendations
       6. Install recommendations and follow up effectiveness

    b. Pitfalls to avoid
       1. *Taking things for granted* – A statement of the situation does not necessarily imply that each of the elements is necessarily true; for example, a complaint may be invalid and biased so that all that can be taken for granted is that a complaint has been registered
       2. *Considering only one side of a situation* – Wherever possible, indicate several alternatives and then point out the reasons you selected the best one
       3. *Failing to indicate follow up* – Whenever your answer indicates action on your part, make certain that you will take proper follow-up action to see how successful your recommendations, procedures or actions turn out to be
       4. *Taking too long in answering any single question* – Remember to time your answers properly

## IX. AFTER THE TEST

Scoring procedures differ in detail among civil service jurisdictions although the general principles are the same. Whether the papers are hand-scored or graded by machine we have described, they are nearly always graded by number. That is, the person who marks the paper knows only the number – never the name – of the applicant. Not until all the papers have been graded will they be matched with names. If other tests, such as training and experience or oral interview ratings have been given, scores will be combined. Different parts of the examination usually have different weights. For example, the written test might count 60 percent of the final grade, and a rating of training and experience 40 percent. In many jurisdictions, veterans will have a certain number of points added to their grades.

After the final grade has been determined, the names are placed in grade order and an eligible list is established. There are various methods for resolving ties between those who get the same final grade – probably the most common is to place first the name of the person whose application was received first. Job offers are made from the eligible list in the order the names appear on it. You will be notified of your grade and your rank as soon as all these computations have been made. This will be done as rapidly as possible.

People who are found to meet the requirements in the announcement are called "eligibles." Their names are put on a list of eligible candidates. An eligible's chances of getting a job depend on how high he stands on this list and how fast agencies are filling jobs from the list.

When a job is to be filled from a list of eligibles, the agency asks for the names of people on the list of eligibles for that job. When the civil service commission receives this request, it sends to the agency the names of the three people highest on this list. Or, if the job to be filled has specialized requirements, the office sends the agency the names of the top three persons who meet these requirements from the general list.

The appointing officer makes a choice from among the three people whose names were sent to him. If the selected person accepts the appointment, the names of the others are put back on the list to be considered for future openings.

That is the rule in hiring from all kinds of eligible lists, whether they are for typist, carpenter, chemist, or something else. For every vacancy, the appointing officer has his choice of any one of the top three eligibles on the list. This explains why the person whose name is on top of the list sometimes does not get an appointment when some of the persons lower on the list do. If the appointing officer chooses the second or third eligible, the No. 1 eligible does not get a job at once, but stays on the list until he is appointed or the list is terminated.

## X. HOW TO PASS THE INTERVIEW TEST

The examination for which you applied requires an oral interview test. You have already taken the written test and you are now being called for the interview test – the final part of the formal examination.

You may think that it is not possible to prepare for an interview test and that there are no procedures to follow during an interview. Our purpose is to point out some things you can do in advance that will help you and some good rules to follow and pitfalls to avoid while you are being interviewed.

*What is an interview supposed to test?*

The written examination is designed to test the technical knowledge and competence of the candidate; the oral is designed to evaluate intangible qualities, not readily measured otherwise, and to establish a list showing the relative fitness of each candidate – as measured against his competitors – for the position sought. Scoring is not on the basis of "right" and "wrong," but on a sliding scale of values ranging from "not passable" to "outstanding." As a matter of fact, it is possible to achieve a relatively low score without a single "incorrect" answer because of evident weakness in the qualities being measured.

Occasionally, an examination may consist entirely of an oral test – either an individual or a group oral. In such cases, information is sought concerning the technical knowledges and abilities of the candidate, since there has been no written examination for this purpose. More commonly, however, an oral test is used to supplement a written examination.

*Who conducts interviews?*

The composition of oral boards varies among different jurisdictions. In nearly all, a representative of the personnel department serves as chairman. One of the members of the board may be a representative of the department in which the candidate would work. In some cases, "outside experts" are used, and, frequently, a businessman or some other representative of the general public is asked to serve. Labor and management or other special groups may be represented. The aim is to secure the services of experts in the appropriate field.

However the board is composed, it is a good idea (and not at all improper or unethical) to ascertain in advance of the interview who the members are and what groups they represent. When you are introduced to them, you will have some idea of their backgrounds and interests, and at least you will not stutter and stammer over their names.

*What should be done before the interview?*

While knowledge about the board members is useful and takes some of the surprise element out of the interview, there is other preparation which is more substantive. It *is* possible to prepare for an oral interview – in several ways:

**1) Keep a copy of your application and review it carefully before the interview**

This may be the only document before the oral board, and the starting point of the interview. Know what education and experience you have listed there, and the sequence and dates of all of it. Sometimes the board will ask you to review the highlights of your experience for them; you should not have to hem and haw doing it.

**2) Study the class specification and the examination announcement**

Usually, the oral board has one or both of these to guide them. The qualities, characteristics or knowledges required by the position sought are stated in these documents. They offer valuable clues as to the nature of the oral interview. For example, if the job involves supervisory responsibilities, the announcement will usually indicate that knowledge of modern supervisory methods and the qualifications of the candidate as a supervisor will be tested. If so, you can expect such questions, frequently in the form of a hypothetical situation which you are expected to solve. NEVER go into an oral without knowledge of the duties and responsibilities of the job you seek.

**3) Think through each qualification required**

Try to visualize the kind of questions you would ask if you were a board member. How well could you answer them? Try especially to appraise your own knowledge and background in each area, *measured against the job sought*, and identify any areas in which you are weak. Be critical and realistic – do not flatter yourself.

**4) Do some general reading in areas in which you feel you may be weak**

For example, if the job involves supervision and your past experience has NOT, some general reading in supervisory methods and practices, particularly in the field of human relations, might be useful. Do NOT study agency procedures or detailed manuals. The oral board will be testing your understanding and capacity, not your memory.

**5) Get a good night's sleep and watch your general health and mental attitude**

You will want a clear head at the interview. Take care of a cold or any other minor ailment, and of course, no hangovers.

*What should be done on the day of the interview?*

Now comes the day of the interview itself. Give yourself plenty of time to get there. Plan to arrive somewhat ahead of the scheduled time, particularly if your appointment is in the fore part of the day. If a previous candidate fails to appear, the board might be ready for you a bit early. By early afternoon an oral board is almost invariably behind schedule if there are many candidates, and you may have to wait.

Take along a book or magazine to read, or your application to review, but leave any extraneous material in the waiting room when you go in for your interview. In any event, relax and compose yourself.

The matter of dress is important. The board is forming impressions about you – from your experience, your manners, your attitude, and your appearance. Give your personal appearance careful attention. Dress your best, but not your flashiest. Choose conservative, appropriate clothing, and be sure it is immaculate. This is a business interview, and your appearance should indicate that you regard it as such. Besides, being well groomed and properly dressed will help boost your confidence.

Sooner or later, someone will call your name and escort you into the interview room. *This is it.* From here on you are on your own. It is too late for any more preparation. But remember, you asked for this opportunity to prove your fitness, and you are here because your request was granted.

*What happens when you go in?*

The usual sequence of events will be as follows: The clerk (who is often the board stenographer) will introduce you to the chairman of the oral board, who will introduce you to the other members of the board. Acknowledge the introductions before you sit down. Do not be surprised if you find a microphone facing you or a stenotypist sitting by. Oral interviews are usually recorded in the event of an appeal or other review.

Usually the chairman of the board will open the interview by reviewing the highlights of your education and work experience from your application – primarily for the benefit of the other members of the board, as well as to get the material into the record. Do not interrupt or comment unless there is an error or significant misinterpretation; if that is the case, do not hesitate. But do not quibble about insignificant matters. Also, he will usually ask you some question about your education, experience or your present job – partly to get you to start talking and to establish the interviewing "rapport." He may start the actual questioning, or turn it over to one of the other members. Frequently, each member undertakes the questioning on a particular area, one in which he is perhaps most competent, so you can expect each member to participate in the examination. Because time is limited, you may also expect some rather abrupt switches in the direction the questioning takes, so do not be upset by it. Normally, a board member will not pursue a single line of questioning unless he discovers a particular strength or weakness.

After each member has participated, the chairman will usually ask whether any member has any further questions, then will ask you if you have anything you wish to add. Unless you are expecting this question, it may floor you. Worse, it may start you off on an extended, extemporaneous speech. The board is not usually seeking more information. The question is principally to offer you a last opportunity to present further qualifications or to indicate that you have nothing to add. So, if you feel that a significant qualification or characteristic has been overlooked, it is proper to point it out in a sentence or so. Do not compliment the board on the thoroughness of their examination – they have been sketchy, and you know it. If you wish, merely say, "No thank you, I have nothing further to add." This is a point where you can "talk yourself out" of a good impression or fail to present an important bit of information. Remember, *you close the interview yourself.*

The chairman will then say, "That is all, Mr. _____, thank you." Do not be startled; the interview is over, and quicker than you think. Thank him, gather your belongings and take your leave. Save your sigh of relief for the other side of the door.

*How to put your best foot forward*

Throughout this entire process, you may feel that the board individually and collectively is trying to pierce your defenses, seek out your hidden weaknesses and embarrass and confuse you. Actually, this is not true. They are obliged to make an appraisal of your qualifications for the job you are seeking, and they want to see you in your best light. Remember, they must interview all candidates and a non-cooperative candidate may become a failure in spite of their best efforts to bring out his qualifications. Here are 15 suggestions that will help you:

**1) Be natural – Keep your attitude confident, not cocky**

If you are not confident that you can do the job, do not expect the board to be. Do not apologize for your weaknesses, try to bring out your strong points. The board is interested in a positive, not negative, presentation. Cockiness will antagonize any board member and make him wonder if you are covering up a weakness by a false show of strength.

**2) Get comfortable, but don't lounge or sprawl**

Sit erectly but not stiffly. A careless posture may lead the board to conclude that you are careless in other things, or at least that you are not impressed by the importance of the occasion. Either conclusion is natural, even if incorrect. Do not fuss with your clothing, a pencil or an ashtray. Your hands may occasionally be useful to emphasize a point; do not let them become a point of distraction.

**3) Do not wisecrack or make small talk**

This is a serious situation, and your attitude should show that you consider it as such. Further, the time of the board is limited – they do not want to waste it, and neither should you.

**4) Do not exaggerate your experience or abilities**

In the first place, from information in the application or other interviews and sources, the board may know more about you than you think. Secondly, you probably will not get away with it. An experienced board is rather adept at spotting such a situation, so do not take the chance.

**5) If you know a board member, do not make a point of it, yet do not hide it**

Certainly you are not fooling him, and probably not the other members of the board. Do not try to take advantage of your acquaintanceship – it will probably do you little good.

**6) Do not dominate the interview**

Let the board do that. They will give you the clues – do not assume that you have to do all the talking. Realize that the board has a number of questions to ask you, and do not try to take up all the interview time by showing off your extensive knowledge of the answer to the first one.

**7) Be attentive**

You only have 20 minutes or so, and you should keep your attention at its sharpest throughout. When a member is addressing a problem or question to you, give him your undivided attention. Address your reply principally to him, but do not exclude the other board members.

### 8) Do not interrupt
A board member may be stating a problem for you to analyze. He will ask you a question when the time comes. Let him state the problem, and wait for the question.

### 9) Make sure you understand the question
Do not try to answer until you are sure what the question is. If it is not clear, restate it in your own words or ask the board member to clarify it for you. However, do not haggle about minor elements.

### 10) Reply promptly but not hastily
A common entry on oral board rating sheets is "candidate responded readily," or "candidate hesitated in replies." Respond as promptly and quickly as you can, but do not jump to a hasty, ill-considered answer.

### 11) Do not be peremptory in your answers
A brief answer is proper – but do not fire your answer back. That is a losing game from your point of view. The board member can probably ask questions much faster than you can answer them.

### 12) Do not try to create the answer you think the board member wants
He is interested in what kind of mind you have and how it works – not in playing games. Furthermore, he can usually spot this practice and will actually grade you down on it.

### 13) Do not switch sides in your reply merely to agree with a board member
Frequently, a member will take a contrary position merely to draw you out and to see if you are willing and able to defend your point of view. Do not start a debate, yet do not surrender a good position. If a position is worth taking, it is worth defending.

### 14) Do not be afraid to admit an error in judgment if you are shown to be wrong
The board knows that you are forced to reply without any opportunity for careful consideration. Your answer may be demonstrably wrong. If so, admit it and get on with the interview.

### 15) Do not dwell at length on your present job
The opening question may relate to your present assignment. Answer the question but do not go into an extended discussion. You are being examined for a *new* job, not your present one. As a matter of fact, try to phrase ALL your answers in terms of the job for which you are being examined.

*Basis of Rating*

Probably you will forget most of these "do's" and "don'ts" when you walk into the oral interview room. Even remembering them all will not ensure you a passing grade. Perhaps you did not have the qualifications in the first place. But remembering them will help you to put your best foot forward, without treading on the toes of the board members.

Rumor and popular opinion to the contrary notwithstanding, an oral board wants you to make the best appearance possible. They know you are under pressure – but they also want to see how you respond to it as a guide to what your reaction would be under the pressures of the job you seek. They will be influenced by the degree of poise you display, the personal traits you show and the manner in which you respond.

# EXAMINATION SECTION

# EXAMINATION SECTION

## TEST 1

DIRECTIONS: Each question or incomplete statement is followed by several suggested answers or completions. Select the one that BEST answers the question or completes the statement. *PRINT THE LETTER OF THE CORRECT ANSWER IN THE SPACE AT THE RIGHT.*

1. Which of the following is MOST advisable in the removal and transportation of objects bearing fingerprints?
   A. Cellophane sheets should never be used for protecting papers.
   B. After removal from the scene, the latent print should be photographed so that the image is the size of the print.
   C. Objects should never be wrapped in a handkerchief or a towel.
   D. Small objects should be placed in a paper bag.

1.___

2. Which of the following practices concerning attitude and demeanor is LEAST appropriate during the interrogation of a suspect?
   A. The interrogator should occasionally convey a sense of inattentiveness in order to make the suspect feel more relaxed.
   B. The language of the interrogator should be adapted to the suspect's cultural level.
   C. The interrogator should explain the purpose of the investigation to the suspect in general terms.
   D. Slang may be used when it promotes ease of speech or fluency for the suspect.

2.___

3. In its consideration of the penalties to be imposed for drug offenses, the President's Commission on Law Enforcement and Administration of Justice has recommended that
   A. suspended sentences, probation, and parole be prohibited for all but the first offense of unlawful possession
   B. the policy of mandatory minimum terms of imprisonment be maintained
   C. maximum sentences for possession with intent to sell be made more severe
   D. courts and correctional authorities be given enough discretion to deal flexibly with violators

3.___

4. In a field study, two police forces were compared in their handling of juvenile delinquents. The first force put particular emphasis on education, training, merit promotions, and centralized control. The second force relied more on organization by precinct, seniority, and on-the-job experience.

4.___

In regard to the rates of processing (police contacts short of arrest but requiring an official record) and arrest (formal police action against the juvenile), it was found that
   A. the processing rate for the first force was higher, but the arrest rate was lower
   B. the arrest rate for the first force was higher, but the processing rate was lower
   C. both the processing rate and the arrest rate were significantly higher for the first force
   D. both the processing rate and the arrest rate were significantly lower for the first force

5. The President's Commission on Law Enforcement and Administration of Justice has recommended that undergraduate programs for potential and existing law enforcement personnel emphasize
   A. vocational subjects      B. liberal arts
   C. management principles    D. technical courses

6. In its survey on the capability of selected police departments to control civil disorders, the National Advisory Commission on Civil Disorders found that the MOST critical deficiency of all was inadequacy of
   A. training programs        B. mobilization planning
   C. logistical support       D. intelligence gathering

7. In a report, the National Commission on Marijuana and Drug Abuse has recommended all of the following EXCEPT that
   A. private possession of marijuana for personal use should no longer be an offense
   B. an ounce or less of marijuana possessed in public would be contraband subject to summary seizure and forfeiture
   C. a plea of marijuana intoxication shall be a defense to certain criminal acts committed under the influence
   D. casual distribution of small amounts of marijuana not involving a profit should no longer be an offense

8. The Governor of the State has made all of the following proposals in the area of crime and the courts EXCEPT to
   A. free judges and courts from much of the burden of thousands of housing violations cases
   B. reduce from 12 to 6 the number of jurors required in certain civil cases
   C. authorize presiding judges, rather than attorneys, to initiate questioning of prospective jurors in criminal cases
   D. require the prosecution to bring to trial all defendants in criminal cases within six months of their arrest

9. The Governor of the State has made all of the following proposals concerning prison reform EXCEPT
   A. establishment of half-way houses close to the homes of inmates nearing parole
   B. intensified recruitment among members of minority groups for correction officer positions
   C. temporary release programs, including occasional furloughs for family visits
   D. creation of citizen observer panels whose members would be appointed jointly by correction officials and inmates

10. According to Uniform Crime Reports, the number of murders committed in the preceding year increased by the GREATEST percentage in
   A. rural areas        B. large cities
   C. suburban areas     D. metropolitan areas

11. According to Uniform Crime Reports, which of the following statements concerning arrest trends for juveniles during the preceding year is INCORRECT?
   A. The increase in arrests of females under 18 years of age was more than twice the increase in arrests for males under 18.
   B. A relatively small percentage of the total youth population become involved in criminal acts.
   C. The increase in juvenile arrests for property crimes was significantly higher than the increase in juvenile arrests for violent crimes.
   D. The involvement of young persons in criminal activity as measured by police arrests has greatly exceeded their percentage increase in the national population.

12. Following are four statements concerning the rights of defendants in criminal proceedings:
   I. Before the police begin to question a suspect, he must be informed of his rights to remain silent and to be represented by a lawyer.
   II. The right to counsel and the guarantee against self-incrimination have been extended to defendants appearing in state criminal courts.
   III. Questioning of a suspect in custody is prohibited unless counsel is present.
   IV. When an investigation shifts to the accusatory stage, a defendant is entitled to counsel, even during interrogation before indictment.

   Which of the following choices lists ALL of the above statements that are TRUE?
   A. I, II, III, IV      B. I, II, IV
   C. II, III, IV         D. II, IV

13. One method of identifying unknown criminals when eyewitnesses are available is to have an artist draw a composite of the features as described by these eyewitnesses.
    Which of the following steps is LEAST appropriate for the preparation of such a composite drawing?
    A. The witnesses should compare their impressions of the criminal and exchange opinions concerning the dominant characteristics.
    B. After obtaining an oral account, the investigator should have each witness reduce his description to writing.
    C. The artist should make up several preliminary sketches which are variants of the common impression.
    D. The witnesses should separately examine each preliminary sketch, select the closest approximation, and make suggestions for improvement.

14. As a general rule, a witness must testify to facts rather than opinions, inferences, or conclusions. Exceptions to this rule include common experiences that can be described only in the form of conclusions, matters of common knowledge, and opinions based on familiar experiences.
    An ordinary witness may testify to all of the following EXCEPT whether
    A. a hole appeared to be of a certain depth even though exact measurements had not been taken
    B. the actions of a person whose sanity is in question seemed to be rational or irrational
    C. a person looked as if he wanted to get away from a certain neighborhood
    D. a vehicle was moving rapidly or slowly

15. Assume that an officer who is investigating a burglary discovers a tool impression at the door of a building which has been broken into. When a jimmy is found nearby, the officer places the tool against the door to determine whether the blade of the tool fits the impression.
    This action by the officer is BASICALLY
    A. *advisable*, chiefly because the officer can tell immediately whether the jimmy might have been used in the commission of the crime
    B. *inadvisable*, chiefly because evidence samples should not come into contact with other samples or with contaminating matter
    C. *advisable*, chiefly because any paint traces on the blade of the tool can then be compared with the material where the door was damaged
    D. *inadvisable*, chiefly because comparison of samples should not be made until the evidence has been removed to the laboratory

16. Of the following, an officer who has just arrived at the scene of a crime and is ready to begin his investigation should FIRST
    A. determine which kinds of evidence are most important for solving the particular crime

B. stand to one side and make an estimate of the entire situation
C. select the method of search that will most efficiently cover all the ground
D. form preliminary opinion of what has happened and attempt to verify it by examining various articles

17. In programs designed to treat drug abusers, the one of the following which was found to be MOST important in achieving success is
    A. the desire of the user to stop using drugs
    B. acceptance by the patient of non-drug alternatives
    C. involvement of the patient in group therapy
    D. the employment of ex-abusers as counselors in the treatment program

18. The one of the following terms which BEST describes the psychological desire to repeat the use of a drug intermittently or continuously because of emotional needs is
    A. addiction           B. euphoria
    C. tolerance           D. habituation

19. It is generally accepted that the effect of repeated use of marijuana in heavy dose is that users will
    A. develop a tolerance and will suffer physical withdrawal symptoms if they stop suddenly
    B. develop a tolerance but will not suffer physical withdrawal symptoms if they stop suddenly
    C. not develop a tolerance but will suffer physical withdrawal symptoms if they stop suddenly
    D. not develop a tolerance and will not suffer physical withdrawal symptoms if they stop suddenly

20. In the context of civil disorder, appearances and reality are of almost equal importance in the handling of citizen complaints against the police.
    The one of the following which is MOST consistent with the viewpoint of the foregoing statement is that
    A. the police should not be the only municipal agency subject to outside scrutiny and review
    B. the benefits and liabilities of civilian review boards have both been exaggerated
    C. the police department itself should receive and act on complaints in order to protect police against unfounded charges
    D. in addition to adequate machinery for handling complaints, there must be belief among citizens that the procedures are adequate

21. In most police departments, the patrol operations of juvenile divisions are supplementary to those of the uniform patrol division.
    When complaints regarding the commission of offenses are received, they should GENERALLY be answered by
    A. beat officers unless it is certain that a juvenile offender is involved

B. juvenile division officers if it is the type of case in which juveniles are usually involved
C. beat officers regardless of whether juveniles are involved
D. juvenile division officers if a juvenile offender is suspected of being involved

22. Which of the following statements regarding the investigation of arson cases is INCORRECT?
    A. It is essential that a human being actually be present for a building to be considered inhabited.
    B. Direct evidence connecting the offender with the crime is ordinarily lacking.
    C. Every fire is presumed to be of accidental origin until it is proved otherwise.
    D. Qualified experts may testify to the absence of defects and deficiencies which could cause fire.

23. Funds that are made available to state and local governments as a result of passage of the Safe Streets Act in 1968 are allocated on the basis of
    A. crime rates
    B. size of population
    C. state planning agency recommendations
    D. requests from local governments

24. In response to an increase in the amount of crime that is committed in apartment buildings, several local police precincts have started programs to combat indoor crime. Under these programs,
    A. bi-weekly meetings are held with tenants to recommend improved security procedures
    B. police in patrol cars park and make periodic vertical patrols of apartment buildings
    C. building superintendents are required to fill out checklists of security deficiencies in their buildings
    D. the number of foot patrolmen is doubled in order to increase police visibility

25. Suppose that, at a police training lecture, you are told that many of the men in our penal institutions today are second and third offenders.
    Of the following, the MOST valid inference you can make SOLELY on the basis of this statement is that
    A. second offenders are not easily apprehended
    B. patterns of human behavior are not easily changed
    C. modern laws are not sufficiently flexible
    D. laws do not breed crimes

## KEY (CORRECT ANSWERS)

| | | | | |
|---|---|---|---|---|
| 1. C | 6. A | 11. C | 16. B | 21. C |
| 2. A | 7. C | 12. B | 17. A | 22. A |
| 3. D | 8. D | 13. A | 18. D | 23. B |
| 4. C | 9. D | 14. C | 19. D | 24. B |
| 5. B | 10. A | 15. B | 20. D | 25. B |

# TEST 2

DIRECTIONS: Each question or incomplete statement is followed by several suggested answers or completions. Select the one that BEST answers the question or completes the statement. *PRINT THE LETTER OF THE CORRECT ANSWER IN THE SPACE AT THE RIGHT.*

Questions 1-3.

DIRECTIONS: Questions 1 through 3 are based on the following example of a police report. The report consists of nine numbered sentences, some of which are not consistent with the principles of good police report writing.

1. At 10:30 P.M., May 23, I received a radio message from Sergeant William Smith, who directed me to report to the Tremont Motel, 10 Wilson Avenue, to investigate an attempted burglary. 2. When I arrived at the motel at 10:45 P.M., John Jones told me that he had seen a blue sedan park across the street earlier in the evening. 3. A few minutes later, Jones heard a noise at the far end of the motel. 4. Noticing that the door to one of the motel units was open, Jones walked in and saw a man about six feet tall and 25-30 years old. 5. When he saw Jones, the man ran into the next room and escaped through a window. 6. While returning to the motel office, Jones passed several cars parked in front of other units. 7. He then saw the man run across the street and get into the blue sedan, which immediately sped away. 8. No evidence was obtained at the scene of the attempted burglary. 9. Jones could not remember the license number of the car, but he thought that it was an out-of-state license plate.

1. A good police report should be arranged in logical order. Which of the following sentences from the report does NOT appear in its proper sequence in the report?
   Sentence
   A. 3   B. 5   C. 7   D. 9

2. Only material that is relevant to the main thought of a report should be included.
   Which of the following sentences from the report contains material which is LEAST relevant to this report?
   Sentence
   A. 2   B. 3   C. 6   D. 8

3. Police reports should include all essential information. Which of the following sentences from the report is LEAST complete in terms of providing necessary information?
   Sentence
   A. 2   B. 4   C. 5   D. 9

Questions 4-10.

DIRECTIONS: Questions 4 through 10 are to be answered on the basis of the information contained in the following tables and chart.

### TABLE 1
Number of Murders by Region, United States: 1989 and 1990

| Region | Year 1989 | Year 1990 |
|---|---|---|
| Northeastern States | 2,521 | 2,849 |
| North Central States | 3,427 | 3,697 |
| Southern States | 6,577 | 7,055 |
| Western States | 2,062 | 2,211 |

Number in each case for given year and region represents total number (100%) of murders in that region for that year.

### TABLE 2
Murder by Circumstance, U.S. - 1990
(Percent distribution by category)

| Region | Total | Spouse killing spouse | Parent killing child | Other family killings | Romantic triangle and lovers' quarrels | Other arguments | Known felony type | Suspected felony type |
|---|---|---|---|---|---|---|---|---|
| Northeastern States | 100.0 | 9.6 | 3.7 | 6.1 | 7.9 | 38.4 | 25.4 | 8.9 |
| North Central States | 100.0 | 11.3 | 3.0 | 8.9 | 5.0 | 39.5 | 22.4 | 9.9 |
| Southern States | 100.0 | 13.8 | 2.2 | 8.8 | 8.4 | 46.0 | 13.9 | 6.9 |
| Western States | 100.0 | 12.5 | 4.9 | 7.0 | 6.4 | 32.2 | 28.0 | 9.0 |

## CHART 1
### Murder by Type of Weapon Used, U.S. - 1990
### (Percent Distribution)

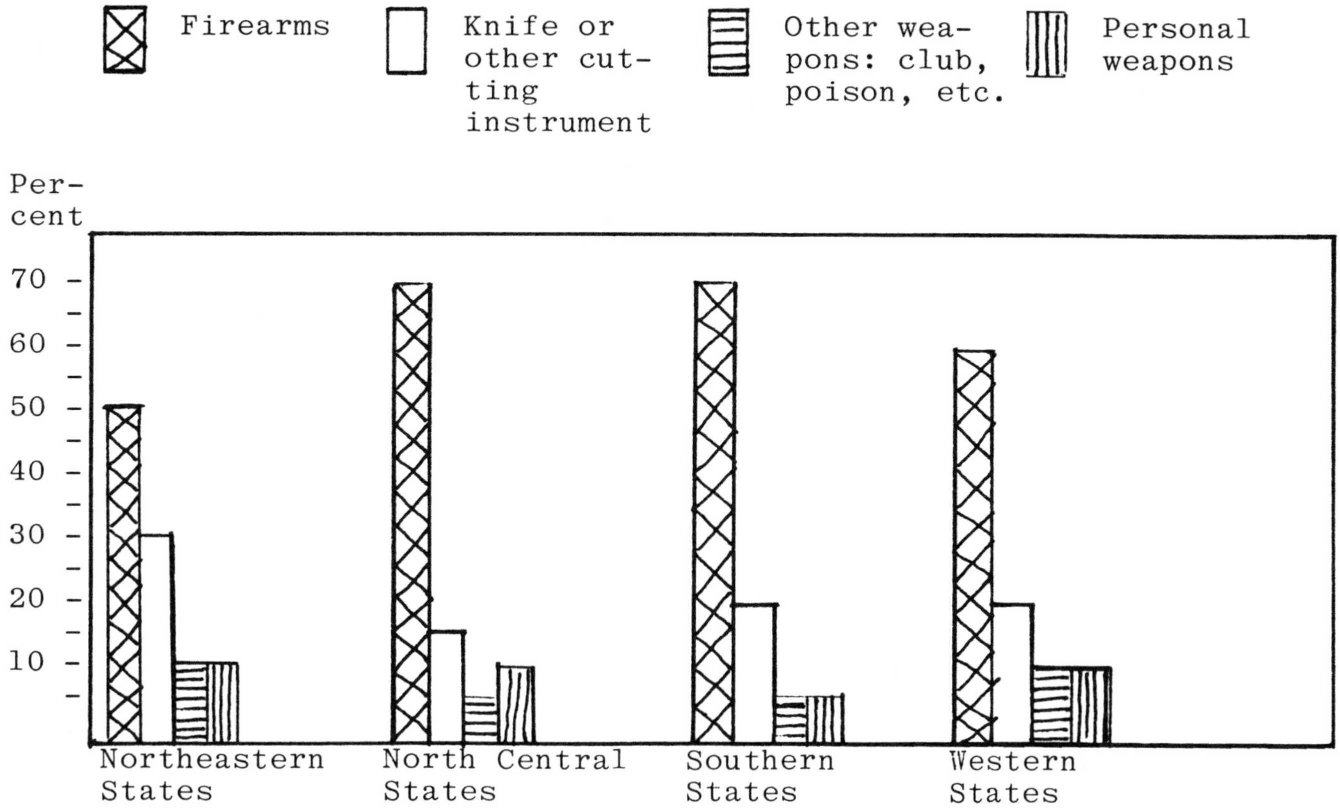

⊠ Firearms   ☐ Knife or other cutting instrument   ≡ Other weapons: club, poison, etc.   ‖‖‖ Personal weapons

4. The number of persons murdered by firearms in the Western States in 1990 was MOST NEARLY
    A. 220   B. 445   C. 1235   D. 1325

5. In 1990, the number of murders in the category *Parent killing child* was GREATEST in the _____ States.
    A. Northeastern   B. North Central
    C. Southern   D. Western

6. The difference between the number of persons murdered with firearms and the number of persons murdered with other weapons (club, poison, etc.) in the North Central States in 1990 is MOST NEARLY
    A. 2200   B. 2400   C. 2600   D. 2800

7. In 1990, the ratio of the number of murders in the Western States to the total number of murders in the U.S. was MOST NEARLY
    A. 1 to 4   B. 1 to 5   C. 1 to 7   D. 1 to 9

8. The total number of murders in the U.S. in the category    8.____
   of romantic triangles and lovers' quarrels in 1990 was
   MOST NEARLY
      A. 850         B. 950         C. 1050        D. 1150

9. Which of the following represents the GREATEST number of    9.____
   murders in 1990?
   Persons murdered by _____ States.
      A. firearms in the Western
      B. knives or other cutting instruments in the Southern
      C. knives or other cutting instruments and persons
         murdered by other weapons (club, poison, etc.) in
         the Northeastern
      D. knives or other cutting instruments, persons murdered
         by other weapons (club, poison, etc.) and persons
         murdered by personal weapons in the North Central

10. From 1989 to 1990, the total number of murders increased   10.____
    by the GREATEST percentage in the _____ States.
       A. Northeastern           B. North Central
       C. Southern               D. Western

Questions 11-13.

DIRECTIONS: Questions 11 through 13 are to be answered SOLELY on
            the basis of the following passage.

   The criminal justice system is generally regarded as having the
basic objective of reducing crime. However, one must also consider
its larger objective of minimizing the total social costs associated
with crime and crime control. Both of these components are complex
and difficult to measure completely. The social costs associated
with crime come from the long- and short-term physical damage, psychological harm, and property losses to victims as a result of crimes
committed. Crime also creates serious indirect effects. It can
induce a feeling of insecurity that is only partially reflected in
business losses and economic disruption due to anxiety about venturing
into high crime rate areas.

   Balanced against these costs associated with crime must be the
consequences of actions taken to reduce them. Money spent on developing, maintaining, and operating criminal justice agencies is part of
the cost of the crime control system. But there are also indirect
costs, such as welfare payments to prisoners' families, income lost by
offenders who are denied good jobs, legal fees, and wages lost by
witnesses. In addition, there are penalties suffered by suspects
erroneously arrested or sentenced, the limitation on personal liberty
resulting from police surveillance, and the invasion of privacy in
maintaining criminal records.

11. Of the following, the MOST appropriate title for this      11.____
    passage would be
       A. THE EFFECTIVENESS OF CRIME CONTROL EFFORTS
       B. PROTECTING CITIZENS' RIGHTS
       C. THE COSTS OF CRIME
       D. IMPROVING THE CRIMINAL JUSTICE SYSTEM

12. According to this passage, all of the following are indirect costs of the crime control system EXCEPT
    A. wages lost by witnesses
    B. money spent for legal services
    C. payments made to the families of prisoners
    D. money spent on operating criminal justice agencies

13. According to this passage, actions taken to reduce crime
    A. will reduce the indirect costs of the crime control system
    B. may result in a decrease of personal liberty
    C. may cause psychological harm to victims of crime
    D. should immediately start improving the criminal justice system

Questions 14-16.

DIRECTIONS: Questions 14 through 16 are to be answered SOLELY on the basis of the following passage.

Probably the most important single mechanism for bringing the resources of science and technology to bear on the problems of crime would be the establishment of a major prestigious science and technology research program within a research institute. The program would create interdisciplinary teams of mathematicians, computer scientists, electronics engineers, physicists, biologists, and other natural scientists, psychologists, sociologists, economists, and lawyers. The institute and the program must be significant enough to attract the best scientists available, and, to this end, the director of this institute must himself have a background in science and technology and have the respect of scientists. Because it would be difficult to attract such a staff into the Federal Government, the institute should be established by a university, a group of universities, or an independent non-profit organization, and should be within a major metropolitan area. The institute would have to establish close ties with neighboring criminal justice agencies that would receive the benefit of serving as experimental laboratories for such an institute. In fact, the proposal for the institute might be jointly submitted with the criminal justice agencies. The research program would require in order to bring together the necessary *critical mass* of competent staff, an annual budget which might reach 5 million dollars, funded with at least three years of lead time to assure continuity. Such a major scientific and technological research institute should be supported by the Federal Government.

14. Of the following, the MOST appropriate title for the above passage is
    A. RESEARCH - AN INTERDISCIPLINARY APPROACH TO FIGHTING CRIME
    B. A CURRICULUM FOR FIGHTING CRIME
    C. THE ROLE OF THE UNIVERSITY IN THE FIGHT AGAINST CRIME
    D. GOVERNMENTAL SUPPORT OF CRIMINAL RESEARCH PROGRAMS

15. According to the above passage, in order to attract the best scientists available, the research institute should
    A. provide psychologists and sociologists to counsel individual members of interdisciplinary teams
    B. encourage close ties with neighboring criminal justice agencies
    C. be led by a person who is respected in the scientific community
    D. be directly operated and funded by the Federal Government

16. The term *critical mass*, as used in the above passage, refers MAINLY to
    A. a staff which would remain for three years of continuous service to the institute
    B. staff members necessary to carry out the research program of the institute successfully
    C. the staff necessary to establish relations with criminal justice agencies which will serve as experimental laboratories for the institute
    D. a staff which would be able to assist the institute in raising adequate funds

Questions 17-19.

DIRECTIONS: Questions 17 through 19 are to be answered SOLELY on the basis of the following passage.

An assassination is an act that consists of a plotted, attempted or actual murder of a prominent political figure by an individual who performs this act in other than a governmental role. This definition draws a distinction between political execution and assassination. An execution may be regarded as a political killing, but it is initiated by the organs of the state, while an assassination can always be characterized as an illegal act. A prominent figure must be the target of the killing, since the killing of lesser members of the political community is included within a wider category of internal political turmoil, namely, terrorism. Assassination is also to be distinguished from homicide. The target of the aggressive act must be a political figure rather than a private person. The killing of a prime minister by a member of an insurrectionist or underground group clearly qualifies as an assassination. So does an act by a deranged individual who tries to kill not just any individual, but the individual in his political role - as President, for example.

17. Of the following, the MOST appropriate title for the above passage would be
    A. ASSASSINATION - LEGAL ASPECTS
    B. POLITICAL CAUSES OF ASSASSINATION
    C. ASSASSINATION - A DEFINITION
    D. CATEGORIES OF ASSASSINATION

18. Assume that a nationally prominent political figure is charged with treason by the state, tried in a court of law, found guilty and hanged by the state.
    According to the above passage, it would be MOST appropriate to regard his death as a(n)
    A. assassination
    B. execution
    C. aggressive act
    D. homicide

19. According to the above passage, which of the following statements is CORRECT?
    A. The assassination of a political figure is an illegal act.
    B. A private person may be the target of an assassination attempt.
    C. The killing of an obscure member of a political community is considered an assassination event.
    D. An execution may not be regarded as a political killing.

Questions 20-27.

DIRECTIONS: Questions 20 through 27 consist of sentences concerning police operations. Some are correct according to ordinary formal English usage. Others are incorrect because they contain errors in English usage, spelling, or punctuation. Consider a sentence correct if it contains no errors in English usage, spelling, or punctuation, even if there may be other ways of writing the sentence correctly.
Mark your answer:
  A. If only Sentence I is correct;
  B. If only Sentence II is correct;
  C. If Sentences I and II are correct;
  D. If neither Sentence I nor II is correct.

20. I. The influence of recruitment efficiency upon administrative standards is readily apparant.
    II. Rapid and accurate thinking are an essential quality of the police officer.

21. I. The administrator of a police department is constantly confronted by the demands of subordinates for increased personnel in their respective units.
    II. Since a chief executive must work within well-defined fiscal limits, he must weigh the relative importance of various requests.

22. I. The two men whom the police arrested for a parking violation were wanted for robbery in three states.
    II. Strong executive control from the top to the bottom of the enterprise is one of the basic principals of police administration.

23. I. When he gave testimony unfavorable to the defendant loyalty seemed to mean very little.      23.___
    II. Having run off the road while passing a car, the patrolman gave the driver a traffic ticket.

24. I. The judge ruled that the defendant's conversation with his doctor was a priviliged communication.      24.___
    II. The importance of our training program is widely recognized; however, fiscal difficulties limit the program's effectiveness.

25. I. Despite an increase in patrol coverage, there were less arrests for crimes against property this year.      25.___
    II. The investigators could hardly have expected greater cooperation from the public.

26. I. Neither the patrolman nor the witness could identify the defendant as the driver of the car.      26.___
    II. Each of the officers in the class received their certificates at the completion of the course.

27. I. The new commander made it clear that those kind of procedures would no longer be permitted.      27.___
    II. Giving some weight to performance records is more advisable than making promotions solely on the basis of test scores.

---

# KEY (CORRECT ANSWERS)

| | | |
|---|---|---|
| 1. D | 10. A | 19. A |
| 2. C | 11. C | 20. D |
| 3. A | 12. D | 21. C |
| 4. D | 13. B | 22. A |
| 5. C | 14. A | 23. D |
| 6. B | 15. C | 24. B |
| 7. C | 16. B | 25. B |
| 8. D | 17. C | 26. A |
| 9. B | 18. B | 27. D |

# Notes

# Notes

# EXAMINATION SECTION
## TEST 1

DIRECTIONS: Each question or incomplete statement is followed by several suggested answers or completions. Select the one that BEST answers the question or completes the statement. *PRINT THE LETTER OF THE CORRECT ANSWER IN THE SPACE AT THE RIGHT.*

1. A police team consisting of a supervisor, S, and three men is on patrol in a riot area. A sniper in a building opens fire on the team, and one police officer is wounded. He is unable to get out of the open area and behind cover. Which of the following is the MOST important action for his two fellow officers to take?

    A. Immediately to carry the wounded officer to cover
    B. Immediately to commence cover fire directed at the building in which the sniper is located
    C. First to wait for the sniper to fire again before taking any action
    D. First to wait for a command from supervisor S before taking any action
    E. First to ascertain whether or not the officer is alive before taking any action

    1. A

2. A police officer is testifying at the jury trial of a suspect he arrested.
Which one of the following actions, taken by the officer while on the witness stand, is MOST likely to favorably affect the acceptance of his testimony? The officer

    A. refers to his memo book before he answers every question
    B. directs his testimony to the jury, not to the judge or counsel
    C. responds to obviously silly questions with equally silly answers
    D. carefully presents both the facts asked for and also the conclusions he is able to draw from them
    E. adds explanations and support to his answers, rather than merely replying to a question with a direct answer

    2. B

3. A certain police supervisor has been unexpectedly asked to interview a potential witness to a robbery. When he was introduced to the witness, the supervisor did not know the witness and did not know any details about the robbery.
Which one of the following is the BEST course of action for the supervisor to take *immediately after* he has been introduced to the witness?
To

    A. ask the witness to start to tell his story
    B. establish rapport with the witness by discussing some neutral topic of conversation
    C. admit that he does not know the facts of the case and ask the witness to brief him on the case
    D. admit that he does not know the facts of the case and ask the witness to tell a little about himself
    E. excuse himself for a few minutes and to review the facts about the case and the background of the witness

    3. E

4. Which one of the following drug users faces the MOST serious risk of death from withdrawal after the arrest and lockup of the user?
A user of

   A. LSD
   B. heroin
   C. cocaine
   D. morphine
   E. barbiturates

5. A patrol sergeant is called to a large warehouse where a strike is in progress. There are a large number of pickets outside the fenced-in warehouse and parking lot area. The pickets are angry, but show no signs of violence at this point.
Which one of the following would be the MOST appropriate action for the sergeant to take?
To

   A. direct pedestrians away from sidewalk areas being used by the pickets
   B. direct officers at the scene to arrest any person who creates any disturbance no matter how minor
   C. obtain written permission from company officials for patrol cars to be parked on the company parking lot while officers guard the property
   D. individually seek out official representatives of the company and the union and advise them that no force or violence will be allowed
   E. immediately decide how many pickets will be permitted at the scene, and inform the union representative that this decision may be appealed to the precinct commander

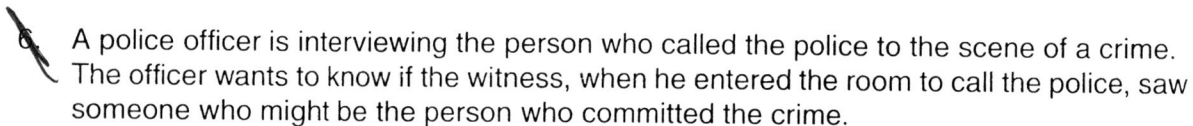

6. A police officer is interviewing the person who called the police to the scene of a crime. The officer wants to know if the witness, when he entered the room to call the police, saw someone who might be the person who committed the crime.
Which one of the following is the BEST way for the officer to phrase his question to the witness?

   A. What did you observe when you entered the room?
   B. Didn't you see anyone when you entered the room?
   C. Was the person who committed the crime still in the room when you entered?
   D. Was someone who could have committed the crime in the room when you entered?
   E. Didn't you see someone who could have committed the crime when you entered the room?

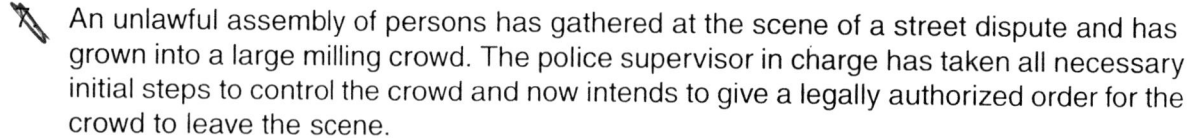

7. An unlawful assembly of persons has gathered at the scene of a street dispute and has grown into a large milling crowd. The police supervisor in charge has taken all necessary initial steps to control the crowd and now intends to give a legally authorized order for the crowd to leave the scene.
Which one of the following is the MOST accurate statement of how, if at all, time limits should be used in this order?
Announce a(n)

   A. unrealistically short time limit to hasten leaving the scene
   B. time limit for leaving the scene and also give frequent *countdowns* of the time remaining
   C. time limit for leaving the scene and when it is up, extend the limit, and do this several times, to give the crowd every opportunity to disperse

D. time limit for leaving the scene but allow a very *long count* if, when the time limit is up, people are attempting to leave the scene but are slowed by traffic, etc.
E. none of the above, since a time limit should not be used as it serves only to bait the crowd

8. Two independent witnesses to a robbery have been brought in to the precinct house to identify a suspect in a lineup.
Following are three guidelines for conducting the line-up that might possibly be appropriate:

   I. The suspect should be *lined up* with a group of people similar in dress and appearance
   II. The line-up should be conducted by the officers who were responsible for catching the suspect
   III. The two witnesses should be prohibited from talking with each other before viewing the line-up

   Which one of the following choices MOST accurately classifies the above guidelines into those which are appropriate and those which are not?

   A. I and II are appropriate, but III is not.
   B. I and III are appropriate, but II is not.
   C. II and III are appropriate, but I is not.
   D. III is appropriate, but I and II are not.
   E. All are appropriate.

8. B

9. A police supervisor has just arrived at the scene of sniper fire. Three other patrol cars are already on the scene, and the six patrol officers have taken cover behind one of the cars. The patrol officers have seen muzzle flashes in a darkened window in one of the nearby buildings and, from the sound of the shots, have concluded that the weapon being used is a high-powered rifle.
Which one of the following orders is it MOST important for the supervisor to give *before* he gives any of the other orders?
To order

   A. the patrol officers to spread out and seek better cover
   B. the patrol officers to return the sniper's fire each time they see his muzzle fire
   C. one two-man patrol team to enter the building where the sniper is suspected to be and go directly to the roof
   D. the patrol officers not to return the fire until the location of the sniper can be more accurately pinpointed
   E. two of the two-man patrol teams to the roof of a building next to the one where the muzzle flashes have been seen

9. D

10. Two patrol officers responding to a *dispute* call find the complainant is a woman who says her neighbor is beating his child. They knock on his door and interview the man. He is drunk and alone with his 8-year-old son. The boy is badly beaten, and the father is still in a rage and yells at the officers to get out.
Which one of the following, if any, MOST accurately states the person or agency that is both in the best position to promptly remove the child against the father's will in this situation and that also has the authority to do so?

    A. A patrol supervisor
    B. The patrol officers on the scene

10. D

C. A youth aid division officer
D. The Family Court, through issuance of a warrant authorizing the police to remove the child
E. None of the above has authority to remove the child against the father's will

11. A police officer has responded to a gas station robbery and is interviewing the victim. Among other things, he asks if the victim can remember the exact words of the suspect and his manner of speech.
Which one of the following BEST states both whether or not this is an important area of investigation and also the BEST reason therefor?
It is

   A. *not important,* because it could not be admissible as evidence in court
   B. *important,* because it is necessary to prove the element of intent in robbery
   C. *not important,* because most robbers don't say enough to determine any identifying characteristic
   D. *not important,* because a robbery victim will be too upset to be very accurate on this matter
   E. *important,* because the robber's choice of phrases is often highly characteristic and, therefore, helpful in identification

12. If the primary purpose of traffic law enforcement is the prevention of accidents, then which one of the following is the MOST appropriate attitude for the police to have regarding enforcing traffic laws?

   A. Police officers should attempt to issue as many citations as time permits.
   B. Police officers should avoid using warnings because warnings have very little prevention value.
   C. Motorists should be encouraged to comply voluntarily with traffic laws and educated regarding such laws, whenever possible.
   D. To the extent possible, all traffic laws should be enforced equally, without regard to time, place, or type of violation.
   E. Enforcement of traffic laws should be the sole responsibility of specialists who devote full time to accident prevention.

13. A foot patrol officer in a business district observes a man walking in front of him whom he recognizes as a wanted felon. They are at an intersection crowded with people. The suspect is not aware of the patrol officer's presence and continues across the intersection.
Which one of the following is the BEST place at which to make the arrest?

   A. In a restaurant or store, if the suspect should enter
   B. Immediately at the intersection where he has observed the suspect
   C. At the first intersection which has little or no pedestrian movement
   D. In the middle of the first block which has little or no pedestrian traffic
   E. In the middle of the next block, but only if this block is still congested with pedestrians

14. Which one of the following cars is MOST likely to appear to a witness to be traveling faster than its true speed?
A

   A. large car     B. noisy car     C. quiet car
   D. car painted a solid color   E. car painted two or more colors

15. A police officer has arrested five different persons for committing the five different violations of a loitering statute which are described in the choices below.
For which one of the following arrests is the police officer MOST likely to be required to cause the arrestee to be fingerprinted?
The person was arrested for loitering in a

15. **C**

   A. public place for the purpose of begging
   B. transportation facility and was unable to give a satisfactory explanation for his presence
   C. public place for the purpose of soliciting another person to engage in deviant sexual intercourse
   D. transportation facility for the purpose of selling merchandise without being specifically authorized to do so
   E. place without apparent reason under circumstances which justified suspicion that he may have been about to engage in a crime and, upon inquiry, refused to identify himself and refused to give a credible account of his conduct or purpose

16. A police officer, if within the geographical area of his employment, may stop a person in a public place when he reasonably suspects that such person is, has, or is about to commit certain offenses and may demand of this person his name, address, and an explanation of his conduct. Which one of the following choices BEST states the offenses for which a police officer is authorized to conduct this temporary questioning?
For

16. **D**

   A. all crimes
   B. any offense
   C. felonies only
   D. felonies and all misdemeanors only
   E. felonies and Class A misdemeanors only

17. Under which one of the following conditions is a police officer, who is executing a legal search warrant of a premise, authorized to enter without first giving, or reasonably attempting to give, notice of his authority and purpose? (Assume that the search warrant does not expressly authorize entry without notice.)
If

17. **E**

   A. the officer reasonably believes that the premise is unoccupied
   B. the officer reasonably believes that he will encounter physical force in executing the search warrant
   C. the officer reasonably believes that he will encounter deadly physical force in executing the search warrant
   D. the officer reasonably believes that the premise is occupied by a person in possession of a deadly weapon
   E. he also has in his possession an arrest warrant for a person who he reasonably believes to be within the premise and that arrest warrant is for a felony

18. Which one of the following amounts is the MAXIMUM amount of pre-arraignment bail which might properly be fixed by a desk officer when the arrest was for a class B misdemeanor or an unclassified misdemeanor?

   A. $100.00
   B. $250.00
   C. $400.00
   D. $500.00
   E. $1,000.00

Questions 19-23.

DIRECTIONS: Questions 19 through 23 contain a negative expression in that they call for consideration of an attribute such as *LEAST* likely or most serious *ERROR*. To emphasize this format, the words *LEAST* and *ERROR* have been italicized.

19. Two officers have arrested three suspects in a stolen car. The suspects have been positioned against a wall for searching. One officer covers the group with his gun drawn. The other officer then thoroughly searches the first suspect on the right and then proceeds to thoroughly search each other suspect in order, moving down the wall from right to left. Which one of the following states the MOST serious *ERROR*, if any, made by the officers in this situation?

   A. The officer assigned to covering and observing the group while they were being searched should not have removed his gun from its holster.
   B. The searching officer should have first gone down the line and *patted down* each suspect before starting the thorough searches.
   C. The searching officer should have started with the suspect to the left of the line and then searched each suspect in turn, moving from left to right.
   D. When the officer finished the search of the first suspect, he should have ordered him to move to the other end of the line before searching the next suspect.
   E. None of the above, since the officers made no error in handling the situation.

20. A police supervisor is conducting a refresher training session on riot control. Which one of the following points, if made in his lecture, would be MOST *OPPOSED* to present-day theory on riot control?
   The importance, in riot control work,

   A. of police officers being able to work independently and without direct supervision
   B. of police officers being trained to function as a highly disciplined military unit
   C. of the police being able to use tear gas effectively as a weapon to control violent mobs
   D. for police officers to always resist the desire to react to intense verbal abuse, no matter how severe
   E. of police officers being able to effectively utilize the police baton as a weapon for low level force in crowd control

21. A certain police administrator finds that he has so many division heads reporting directly to him as his immediate subordinates that he cannot find time for other more important tasks.
   Which one of the following methods of correcting this situation is *LEAST* desirable?
   To

   A. consolidate functions so fewer division heads report directly to him
   B. create the position of executive officer, in the line of command between himself and the division heads

C. narrow his span of control by creating several intermediaries between himself and the division heads
D. create the position of executive assistant, not in the line of command between himself and his division heads
E. retain his present span of control and obtain assistance by creating an aide to him who is not in the line of command

22. The way a supervisor gives an order can affect the way in which it is carried out, since different people require different supervisory methods.
Which one of the following is LEAST likely to be an example of a good order-giving procedure?
To give the order as a(n)

22. __E__

A. request, to a reliable officer who has been employed for a long time
B. direct command, to a careless, lazy officer
C. request, to a sensitive or easily offended officer
D. direct command, to all officers in emergency conditions
E. implied directive, to a new, inexperienced officer

23. A certain Neighborhood Police Team (N.P.T.) regional commander is informed by several businessmen on a certain block that large groups of juveniles are congregating in front of their stores. The lieutenant delegates responsibility to the N.P.T. sergeant in whose section this problem is occurring and tells him that he wants it corrected. The sergeant has handled this problem in other areas several times.
Which one of the following statements, if made to the sergeant by the lieutenant, most clearly VIOLATES one of the accepted principles of delegating responsibility? The lieutenant told the sergeant

23. __A__

A. how the problem was to be corrected
B. that he (the sergeant) was responsible only to the lieutenant for the desired result
C. that he (the sergeant) alone will be held responsible by the lieutenant for the results
D. that he (the lieutenant) was not giving up his own final responsibility for the desired result
E. that he (the lieutenant) was delegating all necessary authority to the sergeant to carry out the task

24. A certain police supervisor is primarily interested in fixing blame and disciplining the person responsible when something goes wrong.
Which one of the following is the MOST likely result of his approach in handling situations in which something goes wrong?

24. __B__

A. Subordinates will seldom make the same mistake twice.
B. Subordinates will spend time covering up mistakes and trying to avoid looking wrong.
C. Morale will improve because good subordinates will know bad performance is not tolerated.
D. The approach discourages the *stool pigeon* and tends to increase the likelihood of a harmonious work group.
E. The approach interferes with downward communications and makes it more difficult to higher management to communicate its desires to the supervisor.

25. Which one of the following BEST states the most appropriate attitude for a police supervisor to take with regard to the individual personal goals of his subordinates?
The supervisor should
    A. not be concerned with the individual personal goals of his subordinates under any circumstances
    B. support only those individual personal goals of his subordinates which are job-related in nature
    C. support all individual personal goals of his subordinates even when they temporarily interfere with the overall objectives of the police department
    D. support individual personal goals of his subordinates as long as they do not interfere with the overall objectives of the police department
    E. not be concerned with the individual personal goals of his subordinates unless they clearly conflict with the overall objectives of the police department

## KEY (CORRECT ANSWERS)

| | | | | |
|---|---|---|---|---|
| 1. | D | | 11. | E |
| 2. | B | | 12. | C |
| 3. | E | | 13. | D |
| 4. | E | | 14. | B |
| 5. | D | | 15. | C |
| 6. | A | | 16. | E |
| 7. | D | | 17. | A |
| 8. | B | | 18. | B |
| 9. | A | | 19. | D |
| 10. | A | | 20. | A |

21. B
22. E
23. A
24. B
25. D

# TEST 2

DIRECTIONS: Each question or incomplete statement is followed by several suggested answers or completions. Select the one that BEST answers the question or completes the statement. *PRINT THE LETTER OF THE CORRECT ANSWER IN THE SPACE AT THE RIGHT.*

1. *Filtering of information* occurs when information is changed as one individual communicates it to another. Filtering often occurs when a subordinate passes on information to his superior. This generally occurs because the subordinate desires to please his boss. Which one of the following states both whether or not filtering is an advantage or disadvantage and also the BEST reason therefor?
It is a(n)

   A. *advantage*, because it keeps a superior from bogging down with too much information
   B. *advantage*, because it helps the superior to judge his subordinate's powers of discrimination
   C. *advantage*, because it helps police officers become skillful in communicating in an economical manner
   D. *disadvantage*, because an officer may inadvertently filter out information that is important for his superior to have
   E. *disadvantage*, because it places too much responsibility on a subordinate to be aware of what pleases his superior

2. Visual aids can be of great benefit to a police supervisor who is responsible for training his subordinates. Magnetic boards are a type of visual aid.
For which one of the following lessons would a police supervisor find a magnetic board MOST useful?
The supervisor is

   A. explaining how juvenile gangs are organized
   B. making his men aware of sensitive locations in the precinct
   C. demonstrating how a new form issued by the department should be filled out
   D. reviewing the photographs and descriptions of fugitives wanted by the department
   E. showing how personnel and equipment should be deployed at the scene of a civil disorder

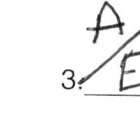

3. Which one of the following abilities MOST differentiates a supervisor who is an effective leader from one who is not an effective leader?
The ability to

   A. exercise his authority fairly
   B. eliminate personality conflicts among his subordinates
   C. establish strong personal relationships with subordinates
   D. consider the job related problems of his men as his most important problem
   E. fulfill the individual needs of his subordinates in addition to fulfilling the department's goals

4. Which one of the following statements, on the use of praise as a tool of police supervision, is MOST accurate?

   A. The use of praise should be limited to cases of exceptional merit.
   B. Supervisors should use praise every time they reprimand a subordinate.
   C. Supervisors should recognize that there is no such thing as too much praise.
   D. Supervisors should praise officers only through official written commendations.
   E. Supervisors should try to praise subordinates in front of their fellow officers.

5. A certain large metropolitan area experimented with assigning a conspicuously marked patrol vehicle to a single police officer on a 24-hour basis. The officer was allowed to use the vehicle for personal business during his off-duty time in and around the city, but could not use it for trips of any significant length outside the city.
   In which one of the following areas, important to the administration of a police department, is the experiment MOST likely to have negative results?
   In

   A. the adequate supervision of patrol officers
   B. the adequate prevention of traffic offenses
   C. the adequate prevention of criminal activity
   D. the maintenance of adequate patrol car coverage
   E. obtaining fast response time to emergency calls

6. A rookie police officer, who has just graduated from the police academy, reports to his supervisor for his first precinct assignment. The supervisor sets aside some time to have an initial interview with the man.
   Which one of the following is the MOST important objective for the supervisor to accomplish in this initial interview?
   To

   A. size up the new officer and form an opinion as to his ability
   B. tell him what will happen if he fails to live up to what is expected of him in the precinct
   C. create in the rookie a good attitude toward the supervisor, the unit, and the police service
   D. convince the rookie of the leadership qualities of the supervisor and other precinct superior officers
   E. make it clear to the rookie that police work in the field is not always done in the way he was taught in the academy

7. Which one of the following is the BEST indication that a police supervisor, who is conducting a conference on a specific problem, is doing a good job?

   A. The supervisor's solutions are eventually accepted.
   B. His subordinates are apparently leading and directing the discussion.
   C. The subordinates and supervisor in the end agree on a single conclusion.
   D. The discussion is never allowed to branch off from a predetermined outline.
   E. The supervisor dominates the conference through his mastery of the subject matter.

8. A certain Neighborhood Police Team supervisor believes very strongly in participatory supervision. He works hard at permitting subordinates to influence the decision making process of the team because he feels that participation builds high team motivation and allows the team to exert pressures on its own members for higher level performance.
Which one of the following BEST states both whether or not the supervisor's technique is appropriate and also the BEST reason therefor?
The technique is

   A. *not appropriate,* because it will weaken and possibly ruin the supervisor's authority for making the final decision
   B. *appropriate,* because group pressures, by their very nature, must work to improve the achievement of individual members
   C. *not appropriate,* because it is possible for group pressures to act to prevent achievement by individual group members
   D. *appropriate,* because the basic purpose of team policing is to remove decision making responsibility from supervisory officers
   E. *appropriate,* because permitting police officers to influence the direction of the team will pay off in increased output and improve job satisfaction

8. A

9. A written communication has reached L, a lieutenant. L must see to it that each sergeant under his command receives a detailed written statement on the same subject. In addition, two subordinate patrol officers are also affected by the communication, but the remaining patrol officers are only indirectly affected.
Which one of the following would be both the BEST action for L to take in relaying information and also the BEST reason therefor?
To give a detailed written communication

   A. to all of the men under him, because subordinates usually have a strong desire to be well informed
   B. to all of the men under him, because it is improper to give information to some men at the same rank but not others
   C. only to the men who are directly affected, because confusion arises from information being given to persons to whom it does not apply
   D. only to the men who are directly affected, because too much unnecessary information dilutes the effectiveness of important communications
   E. only to those sergeants who are directly affected, because the patrol officers will eventually learn for themselves through internal communications

9. A

10. A certain sergeant has received complaints from his subordinates that their captain made an obviously bad decision which adversely affected all of them, including the sergeant. Although the sergeant also recognizes the decision as bad, he understands the circumstances which led the captain to make the decision.
Which one of the following is the BEST course of action for the sergeant to take in this situation?
To

   A. offer his subordinates a helpful explanation for the captain's bad decision
   B. sympathize with the subordinates by agreeing that it was an obviously bad decision
   C. offer to his subordinates some indication that the captain's decision was a good decision

10. E

D. tell the subordinates they are justified in taking their complaint to the commanding officer of the captain
E. tell his subordinates that it is neither his nor their responsibility to question decisions of higher ranking personnel

11. When police provide patrol services on the basis of workload, a high concentration of patrol officers in minority group neighborhoods often results. The police then are subject to criticism both from minority residents who feel persecuted by the police and from residents of other neighborhoods who feel they are not receiving the same level of police protection.
Which one of the following BEST states both whether or not, under these conditions, patrol distribution should be changed and also the BEST reason therefor? It should

A. *not be changed*, because community pressure should not be allowed to influence police decisions
B. *be changed*, because all neighborhoods in the community are entitled to the same level of police protection
C. *be changed*, because it is necessary for the police to respond to community pressures in order to improve community relations
D. *not be changed*, because having police concentration in minority neighborhoods protects the remainder of the community from riot situations
E. *not be changed*, because to do so would deprive law-abiding minority neighborhood residents of police protection in proportion to their need

12. A certain boy is raised by parents who are concerned with status, social position, the *right* occupation, the *right* friends, the *right* neighborhood, etc. Social behavior plays a vital role in their lives and their outlook with regard to rearing children can best be summed up by *children should be seen and not heard.*
Following are four descriptive terms their son might possibly be likely to use if he were asked to describe the *perfect boy:*
 I. Being polite
 II. Being a good companion
 III. Being clean
 IV. Being fun
Which one of the following choices MOST accurately classifies the above statements into those the boy is most likely to use when describing the *perfect boy* and those which he is LEAST likely to use? He is

A. most likely to use I and II and least likely to use III and IV
B. most likely to use I and III and least likely to use II and IV
C. most likely to use I, II, and III and least likely to use IV
D. most likely to use II and IV and least likely to use I and III
E. equally likely to use any of I, II, III, and IV

13. People adjust to frustrations or conflicts in many different ways. One of these ways of adjustment is known as projection.
Which one of the following behaviors is the BEST example of projection?
A person

A. who is properly arrested for inciting a riot protests against police brutality and violence

B. stopped for going through a red light claims that he couldn't help it because his brakes wouldn't hold
C. who is arrested for a crime persistently claims to have forgotten the whole incident that led to his arrest
D. who is arrested for a crime cries, screams, and stamps his feet on the floor like a child having a temper tantrum
E. who is stopped for a traffic violation claims that he is a close friend of the mayor, in order to escape blame for the violation

14. A certain police officer was patrolling a playground area where adolescent gangs had been causing trouble and holding drinking parties. He approached a teenage boy who was alone and drinking from a large paper cup. He asked the boy what he was drinking and the boy replied *Coke*. The officer asked the boy for the cup, and the boy refused to give it to him. The officer then explained that he wanted to check the contents, and the boy still refused
to give it to him. The officer then demanded the cup, and the boy reluctantly gave it to him. The officer smelled the contents of the cup and determined that it was, in fact, Coke. He then told the boy to move along, and emptied the Coke on the ground.
Which one of the following is the MOST serious error, if any, made by the officer in handling this situation?

   A. The officer should not have made any effort to determine what was in the cup.
   B. The officer should not have explained to the boy why he wanted to have the cup.
   C. The officer should have returned the Coke to the boy and allowed the boy to stay where he was.
   D. The officer should have first placed the boy under arrest before taking the cup from him.
   E. None of the above, since the officer made no error in handling the situation.

15. Because of the effect that certain physical conditions have on human perception, testimony of well-intentioned witnesses is sometimes unreliable.
Which one of the following claims by a witness (all of which are affected by physical conditions) is MOST likely to be reliable?
A witness

   A. claims that a taxicab, parked at night under a sodium vapor street lamp, was yellow and not white
   B. who is farsighted, claims that he saw clearly a robbery suspect, 25 feet away, even though he was not wearing glasses at the time
   C. who had just entered a dark house from a brightly lighted street claims that he can identify the prowler he saw escaping through the window of the house at that moment
   D. who was in a very dimly lighted area claims to have seen a certain man wearing blue pants and a jacket of a color he could not identify
   E. who had been sitting in a movie theater for about an hour claims that he did not see a blue flashing light, but did see a red *exit* light; the lights were later found to be of equal brightness

16. A certain police administrator wants to establish a police community relations program aimed at juvenile gangs in his precinct.
Which one of the following BEST states when, if at all, the police administrator should FIRST consult members of the juvenile gangs in his precinct with regard to the program?

   A. During the planning for the program
   B. After the plan for the program has been prepared, as an orientation to the program
   C. As soon as the administrator is reasonably sure that the program will produce good results
   D. Only after an evaluation of a pilot program has been completed and results have been compiled
   E. None of the above, since a police administrator should not consult with juvenile gang members about such a program

17. A motorist complains to two police officers that a truck was double-parked in front of his house. While the truck was unloading, the man was unable to move his car for several hours. Since the truck has been moved, it is clear to the officers that they can do nothing about the situation at this time.
Which one of the following is the BEST course of action for the officers to pursue as the man continues with his complaint?
They should

   A. politely interrupt the man and tell him that they will check into the matter
   B. politely interrupt the man and inform him he does not have a valid police complaint
   C. listen attentively until the man is finished, then tell him that they will check into the matter
   D. politely interrupt the man and tell him that there is nothing they can do since the truck has been moved
   E. listen attentively until the man is finished, then tell him that there is nothing they can do since the truck has been moved

18. In a certain community, a railroad tank car containing propane gas has sprung a leak, and a cloud of the gas is spreading over the community. The local police commander is concerned as much about panic as he is about the actual danger.
Following are three actions that it might be appropriate for the police commander to take in this situation to reduce the likelihood of panic:
   I. To halt all traffic into the community
   II. To evacuate residents who live in low-lying parts of the community
   III. To withhold from residents information about the seriousness of the situation

Which one of the following choices MOST accurately classifies the above actions into those which are appropriate and those which are not?

   A. I is appropriate, but II and III are not.
   B. I and II are appropriate, but III is not.
   C. I and III are appropriate, but II is not.
   D. All of I, II, and III are appropriate.
   E. III is appropriate, but I and II are not.

19. Sociological studies have revealed a great deal of information about the behavior and characteristics of homosexuals.
Which one of the following statements about male homosexuals is MOST accurate?

    A. Male homosexual activity is engaged in by less than 10% of the population.
    B. Most male homosexuals would like to be cured if it were possible.
    C. Male homosexuals are more likely than other sex deviants to commit assaults on female children.
    D. Most male homosexuals pose a threat to the morals and safety of a community, and should be removed from the streets.
    E. Most male homosexuals pose no threat to a community and are content to restrict their activities to people of similar tastes.

19. E

20. Which one of the following is the MOST important factor for the police department to consider in building a good public image?

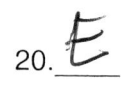

    A. A good working relationship with the news media
    B. An efficient police-community relations program
    C. An efficient system for handling citizen complaints
    D. The proper maintenance of police facilities and equipment
    E. The behavior of individual officers in their contacts with the public

20. E

21. Following are four aspects of Black culture which sociologists and psychologists might possibly consider as health aspects:
    I. Use of hair straighteners
    II. Use of skin bleaches
    III. Use of natural Afro hair styles
    IV. Use of African style of dress

Which one of the following MOST accurately classifies the above into those that sociologists and psychologists do consider healthy and those that they do not?

    A. I and III are considered healthy, but II and IV are not.
    B. I, III, and IV are considered healthy, but II is not.
    C. None of I, II, III, and IV are considered healthy.
    D. III is considered healthy, but I, II, and IV are not.
    E. III and IV are considered healthy, but I and II are not.

21. B (E circled)

22. Which one of the following situations is MOST responsible for making police community relations more difficult in a densely populated, low income precinct?

    A. The majority of residents in such precincts do not want police on patrol in their communities.
    B. Radio patrol car sectors in such precincts are too small to give patrol officers an understanding of community problems.
    C. The higher ratio of arrests per capita in such precincts leads law-abiding residents in such a precinct to feel oppressed by police.
    D. Such precincts tend to have little or no communication among residents, so efforts to improve police-community relations must be on an individual level.
    E. This type of precinct has a higher rate of crime and, therefore, law-abiding residents are often bitter because they feel the police give them inferior protection.

22. D

23. Research studies, based on having children draw pictures of police officers at work, have shown that children of low-income minority group parents are more likely to see police as aggressive than children of upper middle class White parents. One police department had a group of low-income children participate in a 20-minute discussion with a police officer, and then allowed the youngsters a chance to sit in a police car, blow the siren, etc. Which one of the following BEST states what effect, if any, this approach MOST likely had on the pictures drawn by the children when they were retested two days later?

    A. The children showed almost no hostility toward police.
    B. The children showed significantly less hostility toward police.
    C. The children showed significantly more hostility toward police.
    D. There was essentially no change in the attitudes of the children.
    E. The children showed a loss of respect for the police, seeing them as weak and permissive.

24. Officers M and F are observing the actions of T, a teenager. M believes strongly that most teenagers are inclined to get in trouble. F believes that only very few teenagers are bad, and they give all teenagers a bad name. Both M and F observe T look their way, turn around, and walk around the corner behind a building. Which one of the following is the MOST accurate statement of how M and F are likely to view this action?

    A. F is more likely than M to view T's actions as suspicious.
    B. Both M and F are equally likely to view T's actions as harmless.
    C. Both M and F are equally likely to view T's actions as suspicious.
    D. M is more likely than F to view T's actions as suspicious.
    E. Both M and F are equally likely to form no opinion of T's actions until they investigate further.

25. Following are three possible complaints against police which might be made frequently by Blacks living in cities where riots have taken place:
    I. Lack of adequate channels for complaints against police officers
    II. Failure of police departments to provide adequate protection for Blacks
    III. Discriminatory police employment or promotional practices with regard to Black officers

    Which one of the following choices MOST accurately classifies the above into those which have been frequent complaints and those which have not?

    A. I is a frequent complaint, but II and III are not.
    B. I and II are frequent complaints, but III is not.
    C. I and III are frequent complaints, but II is not.
    D. All of I, II, and III are frequent complaints.
    E. None of I, II, or III are frequent complaints.

## KEY (CORRECT ANSWERS)

| | | | | |
|---|---|---|---|---|
| 1. | D | | 11. | E |
| 2. | E | | 12. | B |
| 3. | E | | 13. | A |
| 4. | E | | 14. | C |
| 5. | A | | 15. | B |
| 6. | C | | 16. | A |
| 7. | B | | 17. | E |
| 8. | E | | 18. | B |
| 9. | A | | 19. | E |
| 10. | A | | 20. | E |

21. E
22. E
23. B
24. D
25. D

———

# EXAMINATION SECTION
## TEST 1

DIRECTIONS: Each question or incomplete statement is followed by several suggested answers or completions. Select the one that BEST answers the question or completes the statement. *PRINT THE LETTER OF THE CORRECT ANSWER IN THE SPACE AT THE RIGHT.*

1. A *career criminal* is one who actively engaged in crime as his lifework. Which one of the following statements about career criminals is MOST accurate? A career criminal    1. A

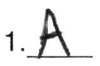

    A. understands that prison is a normal occupational hazard
    B. is very likely to suffer from deep emotional and psychological problems
    C. has a lower average intelligence than the average for the general public
    D. is just as likely to engage in violence during a crime as any other criminal
    E. is less likely to have begun his crime career as a juvenile when compared to other criminals

2. Which one of the following choices BEST describes the tactic of non-violent resistance as used by civil rights groups? The    2. E

    A. willingness of persons to accept unlawful arrest without resistance
    B. avoiding of prosecution for violations of law by refusing to appear in court when required
    C. teasing and verbal harassment of police officers in order to cause unlawful arrests
    D. intentional violation of a particular law by persons unwilling to accept the penalty for violating that law
    E. intentional violation of a particular law by persons willing to accept the penalty for violating that law

3. Which one of the following is the MOST accurate statement about the civil disorders that occurred in the United States in the first nine months of 1967?    3. D

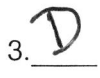

    A. Damage caused by riots was much greater than initial estimates indicated.
    B. They tended to be unplanned outbursts, not events planned by militants or agitators.
    C. The principal targets of attack were homes, schools, and businesses owned by Black merchants.
    D. There were very few minor riots; either there were major riots or there were no riots at all.
    E. The majority of persons killed or injured in the disorders were police officers or White civilians.

Questions 4-10.

DIRECTIONS: Questions 4 through 10 contain a negative expression in that they call for consideration of an attribute such as *LEAST* likely or most serious *ERROR*. To emphasize this format, the words *LEAST* and *ERROR* have been italicized.

4. A police officer is addressing a community group. The officer adjusts the language level of his talk to the level and experience of the people he is talking to. He stresses areas in which the people and police are in agreement, keeping the attention of the group away from minor points of difference. When confronted by hostile members of the group, he avoids giving the impression that his opinion is the only correct opinion and indicates those points brought up by the hostile members that have merit. He works towards a pre-determined conclusion, but uses the group's questions and responses to determine how he arrives at his conclusion.
Which one of the following procedures, if any, in the officer's presentation is MOST improper?

   A. Predetermining the conclusion of his presentation
   B. Adjusting his language level to the level of the audience
   C. Allowing group questions to influence how he concludes his presentation
   D. Giving hostile members of the group credibility by indicating merit in some of their ideas
   E. None of the above, since all of his procedures were proper

5. A man enters a precinct station house, approaches the station house officer, and tells the officer that he has a complaint against a precinct patrol officer. The man is obviously intoxicated. The lieutenant assigned to investigate citizen complaints in this precinct is on duty and the matter is turned over to him. The lieutenant takes the complainant's name and address. Without questioning him further, he suggests that the complainant go home and that he will be contacted later. After the complainant leaves, the lieutenant checks the complainant's record and finds that he has made three similar complaints against police officers. The next day, the lieutenant contacts the complainant and arranges for an interview at his home. During the interview, the lieutenant asks the complainant to describe the incident in his own words. He then tactfully has the complainant repeat the story several times.
Which one of the following, if any, is either the most serious ERROR or OMISSION made by the lieutenant in handling the situation up to this point?

   A. He should have called the complainant back to the station house after he was sober, instead of going to his home.
   B. He should not have checked the complainant's background since that might possibly have affected his objectivity.
   C. He should have interviewed the complainant at the time the complaint was made, as well as interviewing him at a later date.
   D. He should not have asked the complainant to repeat his story several times since it gives the impression the lieutenant did not believe the story.
   E. None of the above, since no serious error or serious omission was committed in this situation.

6. A certain police authority has stated that a police record system is not a question of bookkeeping but rather it is a form of accounting for the police business. On the basis of the reasoning behind this statement, which one of the following uses of a police record system is the LEAST important?
Use as a basis for

   A. planning the police operations
   B. eliminating wasteful operations
   C. control over the police business

D. making a record of what has happened
E. determining the size and distribution of the force

7. Which one of the following statistics is LEAST important to the planning of a program of selective enforcement of traffic laws?   7. A

   A. Seasonal variations in traffic volume
   B. Daily variations in number of accidents
   C. Hourly variations in number of accidents
   D. Frequency of accidents at different locations
   E. Frequency of different types of violations contributing to accidents

8. Some managers try to achieve goals by manipulating or deceiving subordinates into doing what the managers want. Such a manager normally is motivated by a desire to control people or by a desire to hide his own inadequacies. Such a manager also wants to hidethe reasons for his actions from those he manages. This type of manager is often referred to as a *facade builder.*   8. D
   Which one of the following types of behavior is LEAST characteristic of this type of manager?
   He

   A. shows concern for other people
   B. avoids criticizing other people
   C. gives praise and approval easily
   D. delegates responsibility for administering punishment
   E. avoids getting involved in internal conflicts within the organization

9. The patrol sector boundaries in a certain precinct of a typical large, fully built-up city have not changed since 1980. In this time, there have been population changes and changes in business and social organizations within the precinct.   9. B
   On the basis of these facts, which one of the following conclusions is LEAST likely to be accurate?

   A. The men assigned to patrol sectors are contented and efficient.
   B. The men assigned to some sectors are overworked and inefficient.
   C. Criminals plan their crimes on the basis of the weaknesses of the sector assignment.
   D. Complaints arise among the men that the distribution of the patrol force involves discrimination.
   E. The men assigned to some sectors become lazy because they do not have enough to do.

10. Calculating the required number of patrol sectors for a certain precinct requires consideration of a number of factors.   10. C
    Which one of the following is LEAST likely to be an important factor when estimating the required number of patrol sectors?

    A. Amount of time desired for preventive patrol
    B. The average time required by a patrol officer to make a preliminary investigation of a case
    C. Differences in the distances between intersections in certain areas of the precinct

D. Differences in workload for the two night shifts between weekend nights and non-weekend nights
E. Small, distinctive, and highly concentrated areas of the precinct with unusually high workloads

11. In a certain police department, all operations dealing with traffic control and regulation have been assigned to a traffic division headed by a chief inspector. In this department, the patrol division is also headed by a chief inspector. Both chief inspectors report directly to a deputy commissioner. The chief inspector in command of patrol operates a tightly controlled organization and the chief inspector in charge of traffic does not. In this department, the police officers in the patrol division have come to ignore even the most serious traffic violations.
Which one of the following is the MOST probable reason why the patrol officers ignore traffic violations?

    A. Less competent police officers are assigned to the traffic division.
    B. The traffic division has largely eliminated serious traffic violations.
    C. The patrol division is closely supervised and the traffic division is not.
    D. The other responsibilities of patrol officers are much more important than even serious traffic violations.
    E. As a result of the organizational structure, the patrol officers have developed the belief that traffic violations are the exclusive concern of the traffic division.

12. Lieutenant X is preparing a report to submit to his commanding officer in order to get approval of a plan of operation he has developed. The report starts off with the statement of the problem and continues with the details of the problem. It contains factual information gathered with the help of field and operational personnel. It contains a final conclusion and recommendation for action. The recommendation is supplemented by comments from other precinct staff members on how the recommendations will affect their areas of responsibility. The report also includes directives and general orders ready for the commanding officer's signature. In addition, it has two statements of objections presented by two precinct staff members.
Which one of the following, if any, is either an item that Lieutenant X should have included in his report and which is not mentioned above, or is an item which Lieutenant X improperly did include in his report?

    A. Considerations of alternative courses of action and their consequences should have been covered in the report.
    B. The additions containing documented objections to the recommended course of action should not have been included as part of the report.
    C. A statement on the qualifications of Lieutenant X, which would support his experiences in the field under consideration, should have been included in the report.
    D. The directives and general orders should not have been prepared and included in the report until the commanding officer had approved the recommendations.
    E. None of the above, since Lieutenant X's report was both proper and complete.

5 (#1)

13. In a certain police organization, lieutenants are in command of the patrol forces, of the records section, of the juvenile aid unit, and of the detective unit. All these lieutenants report to a captain. In this organization, patrol sergeants and their men take orders only from the patrol lieutenant on duty. As a result, the quality of the work of the patrol force is poor in the areas of records, juveniles, and investigations. The captain in charge decides to try to improve work performance by requiring each patrol sergeant to take orders not only from his patrol lieutenant but also from the lieutenants on duty in charge of the records, juvenile, and detective units in matters within the jurisdiction of each.
Which one of the following is the MOST likely result of this change?

13. A

    A. Patrol sergeants will become confused and inefficient, and the quality of work will become poorer.
    B. Each lieutenant will better be able to supervise work in his area, and the quality of the work will become better.
    C. Functional supervision will replace indirect supervision, and the quality of the work will improve.
    D. Differences will occur in the level of efficiency of the various lieutenants, and the quality of work will become worse overall.
    E. No significant change for better or worse will occur.

14. A well-regarded national police organization made some specific recommendations about determining the proper beat size for a single patrol unit. Generally speaking, beat size is initially determined by establishing the boundaries of the beat so that a work load is obtained that requires one-third of the unit's time being spent on calls for services. This then allows two-thirds of the unit's time for preventive patrol, special services, etc.
Which one of the following BEST states why the one-third/ two-thirds ratio was recommended?

14. B

    A. Because studies have shown that a one-third/two-thirds ratio is best for preventing crime
    B. To set a reasonable ratio as a starting place for determining what the best ratio might be
    C. To standardize beat sizes so that meaningful studies can be made on the effect the beat size has on a patrol officer's performance
    D. Because studies have shown that patrol officer fatigue is at a minimum when the patrol officer spends two-thirds of his time in non-called for service
    E. To assure that the number of police patrol officers a municipality must hire is proportional to the work load generated in that municipality

15. In a certain police department, detectives are charged with the total investigative responsibility. The patrol officer merely answers the radio call, makes an arrest, if by chance he can, and protects the scene until the detective arrives.
According to modern police thinking, which one of the following is the BEST evaluation of this policy? It is a

15. D

    A. *good* policy, because it frees the patrol forces to perform other duties
    B. *good* policy, because it fully utilizes the specialized skills of highly trained investigators
    C. *bad* policy, because it brings follow-up pressures from headquarters on the individual patrol officer

D. *good* policy, because it provides a clear-cut distinction between the duties of a patrol officer and the duties of a detective
E. *bad* policy, because the detective division usually finds itself overloaded with uncleared cases in every category

16. A certain Lieutenant L might be assigned to any of the five supervisory tasks described in the choices below.
In which of the following assignments would Lieutenant L's span of control require the GREATEST abilities? In an assignment

   A. in which he supervises six sergeants, all of whom are on the same shift
   B. in which he supervises six radio car patrol officers, all of whom are on the same shift
   C. in which he supervises six sergeants, two of whom are on each of three different shifts
   D. in which he supervises three patrol sergeants on different shifts, two detective sergeants on different shifts, and a juvenile sergeant
   E. involving command of the communications operation in which he supervises six radio communication dispatchers, all of whom are on the same shift

17. Following are three statements that might possibly be accurate regarding the distribution of police manpower in proportion to need:
   I. No absolute measure of the time needed to accomplish satisfactory routine preventive patrol has been developed
   II. No standard of optimum patrol strength has been established
   III. Sufficient data on the time and location of police hazards, which is necessary for an absolute measure of required patrol time, is readily available in most police departments

   Which one of the following choices MOST accurately classifies the above statements into those that are accurate and those that are not?

   A. I is accurate, but II and III are not.
   B. I and II are accurate, but III is not.
   C. I and III are accurate, but II is not.
   D. II and III are accurate, but I is not.
   E. All of I, II, and III are accurate.

18. In a certain police department, the major divisions and all of the sections and units have been organized on the basis of the management principle known as *organization by major process*. Assume that the reorganization is skillfully planned in accordance with that principle. Which one of the following, if any, is MOST likely to result after every one of the units has become familiar with the new organizational structure?

   A. More efficient utilization of persons with specialized skills
   B. Decentralization of authority will result in increased efficiency
   C. Decentralization of authority will result in decreased efficiency
   D. A decrease in the efficient utilization of persons with specialized skills
   E. No real difference in efficiency will result

19. A certain new traffic regulation was adopted about a year ago by the appropriate legislative body. Experience since its adoption has disclosed that a high degree of compliance is essential if the regulation is to accomplish its purpose. Compliance failure results in a greater hazard than existed before the regulation was adopted. Enforcement requires that police exert an effort out of proportion to the value of the regulation. Driver-disregard for this regulation is increasing disrespect for other traffic regulations.
On the basis of this information, which one of the following is the MOST proper conclusion to be drawn?
That

   A. few drivers are law-abiding by nature
   B. the regulation should not have been enacted
   C. drivers generally do not resent overenforcement
   D. police officers generally are not doing their jobs properly
   E. police management is not properly requiring enforcement of the regulation

20. A well-known police authority has stated that the total number of personnel engaged in investigative work, not including officers assigned to vice control and youth sections, should not exceed 10% of the sworn personnel of the force. In a certain police department, 20% of the sworn personnel are engaged in investigative work, not including vice control and youth work. Each investigator is carrying a very large case load. For many cases, the investigation is largely routine. The clearance rate is very low.
Which one of the following procedural changes is MOST likely to be necessary in this situation, in view of this authority?

   A. More investigators should be assigned to the detective division.
   B. The length of time a case is kept in active status should be restricted.
   C. The patrol division should be given much greater responsibility for preliminary investigations.
   D. Responsibility for preliminary investigations should be reassigned from the patrol forces to the detective division.
   E. No follow-up investigation should be made on any case in which the evidence produced by initial investigation is so little that successful solution is improbable.

21. Following are three principles which might possibly be appropriately applied to the distribution of manpower between field patrol and other functions:
   I. Whenever another unit of the department is temporarily shorthanded, trained men should be temporarily assigned from the field patrol force to bring the other unit up to strength
   II. When absences and vacancies reduce the patrol division manpower below strength, it is better to have the field assignments shorthanded rather than the station house assignments
   III. The greater the number of men assigned to field patrol, if they are performing effectively, the less the need for men assigned to specialized functions
Which one of the following choices BEST classifies all of the above into principles that are generally accepted as good and those which are not?

   A. I and II are generally accepted principles, but III is not.
   B. I and III are generally accepted principles, but II is not.
   C. II is a generally accepted principle, but I and III are not.
   D. II and III are generally accepted principles, but I is not.
   E. III is a generally accepted principle, but I and II are not.

8 (#1)

22. A relatively new method of deployment of the patrol force is called the *fluid patrol system*. Which one of the following is MOST similar in concept to the fluid patrol system?

    A. Fixed beat system
    B. Ride-along program
    C. Tactical unit system
    D. Dismounted motor patrol system
    E. One-man or two-man car system

23. One approach to the assignment of manpower is to measure patrol work load by giving different weight to certain types of incidents. Authorities recommend that this weighting be based partly on the time required to handle the event and partly on the seriousness of the event. Which one of the following classes of incidents should receive the HIGHEST weight in this weighting system?

    A. Part I crimes
    B. Part I arrests
    C. Traffic accidents
    D. Arrests for drunkenness
    E. Offenses other than Part I crimes

24. Which one of the following choices states both the MOST probable effect on crime rate statistics of increased public confidence in police and also the MOST important reason for this effect?

    A. The overall statistical crime rate would decrease because people would be less likely to commit crimes.
    B. The overall statistical crime rate would increase because people would be more likely to report crimes.
    C. The overall statistical crime rate would increase because police would probably be clearing more crimes by arrest.
    D. The overall statistical crime rate would decrease because police would be less likely to arrest offenders for minor violations.
    E. Increased public confidence in police would have no effect on the overall statistical crime rate because this depends on the number of crimes committed, not public attitude toward police.

25. Individual differences in the capabilities of high ranking officers might possibly be taken into consideration when a new commander is planning changes in the organizational structure of a precinct.
Which one of the following choices BEST states both the extent to which differences in capabilities should be considered and also the best reason therefor? Individual differences

    A. *should not be* taken into account, because they open the door to charges of favoritism
    B. *may be* taken into account, only if there are serious differences in the capabilities of the high-ranking officers

C. *must be* taken into account, because the purpose of organization is to make the best use of all available talent
D. *may be* taken into account, provided that all of the positions in the organizational structure are equally attractive assignments
E. *should not be* taken into account, because it is impossible for commanding officers to accurately measure individual differences

---

# KEY (CORRECT ANSWERS)

| | | | |
|---|---|---|---|
| 1. | A | 11. | E |
| 2. | E | 12. | A |
| 3. | B | 13. | A |
| 4. | E | 14. | B |
| 5. | C | 15. | E |
| 6. | D | 16. | D |
| 7. | A | 17. | B |
| 8. | E | 18. | A |
| 9. | A | 19. | B |
| 10. | C | 20. | C |

| | |
|---|---|
| 21. | E |
| 22. | C |
| 23. | A |
| 24. | B |
| 25. | C |

---

# TEST 2

DIRECTIONS: Each question or incomplete statement is followed by several suggested answers or completions. Select the one that BEST answers the question or completes the statement. *PRINT THE LETTER OF THE CORRECT ANSWER IN THE SPACE AT THE RIGHT.*

1. One method of organizing police record-keeping is to establish a central records system. The alternative is a decentralized system in which patrol, traffic, and other divisions maintain their own records.
   Which one of the following choices both BEST evaluates the desirability of centralized or decentralized records and also states the MOST important reason therefor?

    A. *Decentralized* records are better, because this method permits each unit to control its own recording.
    B. *Centralized* records are better, because the records are available to fewer people.
    C. *Decentralized* records are better, because this method places responsibility closest to the level of operating management.
    D. *Centralized* records are better, because with decentralized records there is less assurance that an accurate accounting of police work is being made.
    E. *Decentralized* records are better, because with centralized records there is less assurance that an accurate accounting of police work is being made.

2. A certain police administrator finds that he is directly supervising fourteen persons, many of whom perform different kinds of functions.
   Which one of the following *undesirable* effects is MOST likely to occur if he substantially narrows his span of control?
   The effect of

    A. hampering communications
    B. hampering unit of command
    C. narrowing the chain of command
    D. curtailing the length of the chain of command
    E. decreasing the total amount of authority delegated

3. A police administrator changed the way the follow-up investigation responsibilities were organized. He greatly reduced the size and scope of the centralized detective division. He reassigned detectives to precincts to provide investigative capabilities under the direct command of the precinct commander. In making this change, he has changed from one accepted organizational principle for grouping tasks to another principle.
   Which one of the following BEST states the change in organization theory made by the administrator?
   He has changed from grouping tasks

    A. by their *function and purpose* to grouping tasks by the *methodology required*
    B. by the *methodology required* to grouping tasks by the *place of execution*
    C. on the basis of *clientele served* to grouping tasks on the basis of *function and purposes*
    D. on the basis of *clientele served* to grouping tasks on the basis of *methodology required*
    E. by the *place of execution* to grouping tasks on the basis of the *level of authority required*

4. One of the important tasks of any administrator is the development of a proper filing system for classifying written documents by subject. Following are three suggested rules for subject cross-referencing which might possibly be considered proper:
    I. All filed material should have at least one subject cross-reference
    II. There should be no limit on the number of subject cross-references that may be made for a single record
    III. The original document should be filed under the primary classification subject, with only cross-reference sheets, not considered as records, being filed under the cross-reference subject classifications

Which one of the following choices MOST accurately classifies the above into those that are proper rules for cross-referencing and those that are not?

   A. I is a proper rule, but II and III are not.
   B. I and III are proper rules, but II is not.
   C. II and III are proper rules, but I is not.
   D. III is a proper rule, but I and II are not.
   E. None of I, II, and III is a proper rule.

5. Wherever gambling, prostitution, and narcotics distribution openly flourish, they are usually accompanied by community charges of *protection* on the part of local police.
Which one of the following BEST states both whether or not such charges have merit, and also the BEST reason therefor?
Such changes

   A. *do not* have merit, because the nature of these operations makes them very difficult to detect
   B. *have* merit, because such operations cannot long continue openly without some measure of police protection
   C. *have* merit, because offenses of this type are among the easiest to eliminate
   D. *do not* have merit, because the local patrol forces probably do not have responsibility for large scale vice enforcement
   E. *do not* have merit, because vice flourishes openly only in a community which desires it; therefore, it is the community that is providing the protection

Questions 6-10.

DIRECTIONS: The following selection is to be used as the SOLE basis for answering Questions 6 through 10. Read the selection carefully and base your answers ONLY on the information contained therein.

While training large groups of rookie police officers in fingerprinting, we discovered that it was convenient to use portable stands, rather than attaching ink plates and card holders permanently to table tops. Unfortunately, our original design stands were awkward to store.

A simplified fingerprinting stand was designed to replace the old ones for our training purposes. To make a stand, we started with a sheet of one-sixteenth inch thick aluminum, one and one-half feet wide and two feet long, with eight inches of the two foot length bent at a ninety degree angle. It cost $37.70 for the material, cutting and bending, less card holder and inking plate. The new version weighed about 1.5 pounds and a stack of ten occupied the space of two older models.

The new stands were put to use in May and used by some one hundred students to print an average of three fingerprint cards each, during a trial period. Student use revealed two problems: (1) the slope of the working surface was too great, and (2) sometimes the stands slipped onto the floor because they were so light.

The first problem was corrected by bending a six-inch section of the longer *leg* to an inside angle of 110 degrees. Thus, the finished stand, in cross-section, looked like this:

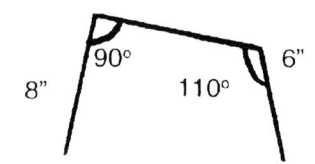

8"  90°  110°  6"

Storage and handling was not affected by the change. The additional cost of the modification wasn't determined.

The second problem, slippage, hasn't been solved. No material tried, including a coat of liquid latex, had adhered to the metal with any degree of permanency. The main reason for this is that when the stands were stacked, the latex on the edges that rested on a shelf surface was caught, pulled, pushed, and finally torn loose. Of course, wooden or metal stops could be mounted on a shelf, cabinet or table top, if a stand were permanently installed. The lack of a solution hasn't caused any appreciable problem.

An average of two stands will be dropped from a table to the floor in a forty-man class, during a two-hour block of instruction on taking rolled prints. Thirty of these stands have been in use since July to train some 2,400 students, most of whom have no prior fingerprint or police experience. So stands have been dropped a total of about 120 times, or an average of four times per stand. No observable damage has appeared during this period.

The ink plates and card holders were originally mounted on the working surface with a double-stick adhesive tape to allow for easy modification and replacement of parts. This has worked well with the plates, but the larger and thicker card holders bear most of the pressure when the stands are stacked for storage. This sometimes causes considerable shifting of their position. As a result, in July, they were bolted to their stands. These accessories together take up about 10% of the working surface area. The rest is clear working space.

We shortly found that the bolt ends strike the card holders of lower stands when they are stacked. The unused wooden part of the holders has been marred, but this hasn't affected their use.

6. According to the selection, the number of square inches of clear working surface of each finished fingerprinting stand of the new design is _____ square inches.

    A. 18        B. 162        C. 259        D. 389        E. 432

7. According to the selection, which one of the following is the MOST important advantage of the new fingerprinting stands over older models?
They

   A. are much lighter
   B. are less expensive
   C. take up less storage space
   D. can be used for training purposes
   E. are easier to fit with ink plates and card holders

7.____

8. Which one of the following is the MOST important reason why the slippage problem hasn't been solved?

   A. The liquid latex was continually being torn loose.
   B. The liquid latex would not adhere at all to the edges of the stands.
   C. The liquid latex got caught on the wooden stops and was torn off.
   D. Nothing would adhere to the slippery metal surface of the stands.
   E. The liquid latex would not adhere to the slippery metal surface of the stands.

8.____

9. Assume that what has occurred while the stands were in use between May and July is a good indicator of what will occur during future use of the stands.
Based on this assumption, which one of the following is MOST likely to happen if a new batch of stands of the same shape is put into use to train a similar group of students?
The

   A. ink plates will be bolted to the stands
   B. stands will be permanently installed on the tables
   C. stands will regularly fall onto the floor
   D. card holders on the stands will have to be replaced before they wear out
   E. card holders will be attached to the stands with double-stick adhesive tape

9.____

10. According to the selection, _____ ACTUAL modifications were made to the new stand that originally cost $37.70 and weighed 1.5 pounds.

    A. 1   B. 2   C. 4   D. 5   E. 6

10.____

Questions 11-13.

DIRECTIONS: The following graph is to be used as the SOLE basis for answering Questions 11 through 13. Study the graph carefully and base your answers ONLY on the information contained therein.

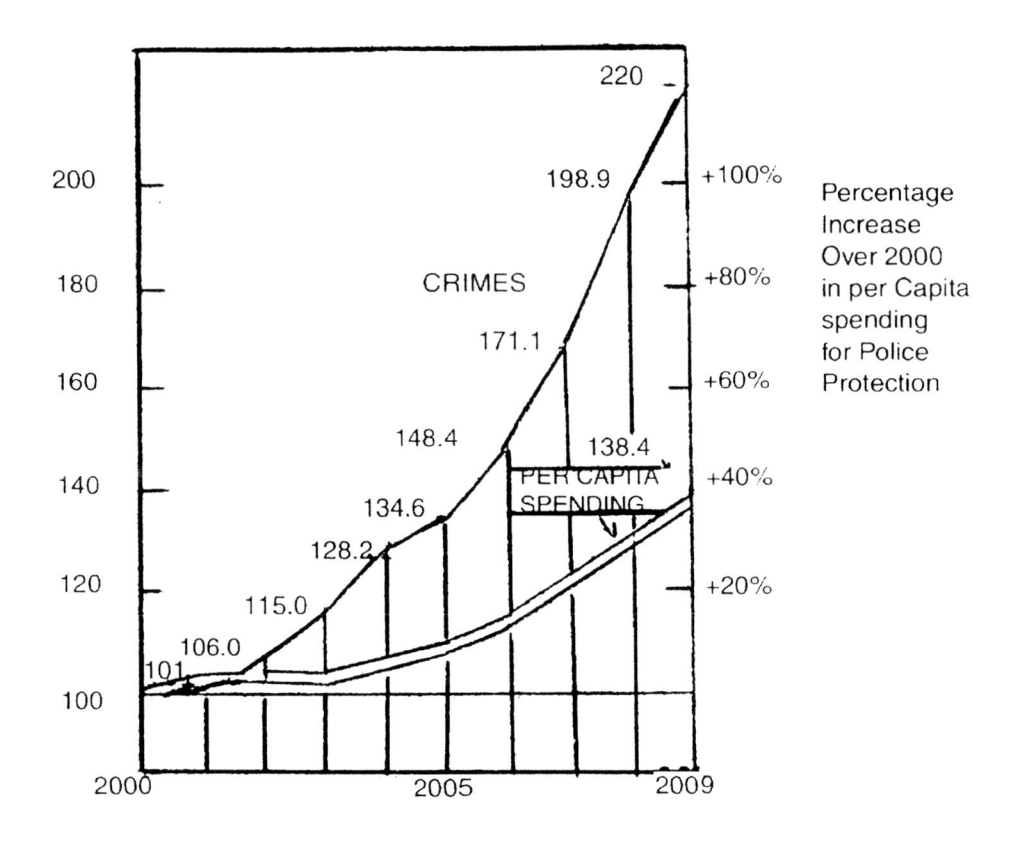

[Graph showing CRIMES rising from 101 (2000) to 220 (2009), with intermediate values 106.0, 115.0, 128.2, 134.6, 148.4, 171.1, 198.9; and PER CAPITA SPENDING rising to about 138.4 by 2009. Right axis shows Percentage Increase Over 2000 in per Capita spending for Police Protection, from +20% to +100%. X-axis spans 2000 to 2009.]

CLEARANCE RATES FOR ROBBERIES
2000 - 26.9%    2009 - 41.5%

11. Which of the following is MOST NEARLY the increase in robberies from 2000 to 2009?  11.

   A. 12.0   B. 21.1   C. 120.0   D. 211.0   E. 120,000

12. Which one of the following choices MOST accurately compares the percentage change   12.
    between 2000 and 2009 in the number of robberies cleared, the number of robberies
    committed, and the per capita spending.
    The percentage increase in the number of robberies cleared is

   A. *greater than* both the percentage increase in robberies committed and the percentage increase in per capita spending
   B. *less than* both the percentage increase in robberies committed and the percentage increase in per capita spending
   C. *greater than* the percentage increase in per capita spending and *less than* the percentage increase in robberies committed
   D. *greater than* the percentage increase in robberies committed and *less than* the percentage increase in per capita spending
   E. *about the same* as the percentage increase in per capita spending and *less than* the percentage increase in robberies committed

13. The GREATEST increase in thousands of robberies committed occurred in _____ in comparison with _____.

   A. 2004; 2003
   B. 2006; 2005
   C. 2007; 2006
   D. 2008; 2007
   E. 2009; 2008

Questions 14-18.

DIRECTIONS: The following selection is to be used as the SOLE basis for answering Questions 14 through 18. Read the selection carefully and base your answers ONLY on the information contained therein.

In a study of Federal probationers, two researchers found a relationship between age and success on probation. Their study was based on 190 cases which were selected by taking every second male receiving a term of one year or more of probation between January 1, 2007 and July 1, 2008 in the U.S. District Court for the Northern District of Illinois. These researchers found that the older a man was at the time of first arrest, the better candidate he was for probation. In contrast to a failure rate of almost half for those under 20 years of age at first arrest, only 6 of 81 (7%) who were between 30 and 50 years of age at the time of first arrest were unsuccessful on probation.

A different research team subsequently did another statistical study with respect to probation. In contrast to the first study, these researchers made a distinction between *straight probation* and *probation under suspended sentence*. Their findings, concerning the first category, straight probation, agree with those of the first study cited, and are as follows: From the twenty-seventh year, behavior on probation improves and remains at about the same level throughout the later years. The picture is less clear in regard to probation under suspended sentence. The failure rate remains rather high until age thirty-two; from thirty-two to forty-two years, there is marked improvement; after that age, however, there is a *slump*.

14. Based on the results of the first study cited, which one of the following inferences is MOST likely regarding the probation failure rate for those subjects between 20 and 29 years of age at the time of first arrest?
The failure rate

   A. is greater than 50%
   B. is between 1% and 7%
   C. is between 7% and 50%
   D. is between 45% and 55%
   E. gradually increases with increasing age

15. A certain man was convicted in the U.S. District Court for the Northern District of Illinois of assaulting a Federal officer. On January 3 of the following year, he was given a five-year term of probation from the same court.
Which one of the following is the MOST likely reason why this man was NOT a subject in the first study cited in the selection?
Because

   A. the study only selected every other man
   B. he was under 20 at the time of his arrest
   C. he was convicted in another district
   D. his term of probation was not of the appropriate length
   E. he was in the category *probation under suspended sentence*

16. According to the selection, which one of the following statements, regarding the persons (cases) used in the two studies, is MOST accurate?
    They

    A. were all males
    B. were all convicted of a crime
    C. were all Federal probationers
    D. all received at least one year's probation
    E. all were sentenced in the U.S. District Court for the Northern District of Illinois

17. Which one of the following omissions in the selection is MOST serious, in comparing the two studies?
    The

    A. date of the second study
    B. place of the second study
    C. identity of the researchers in both studies
    D. reference point to which the ages mentioned in the second study apply
    E. crimes in both studies for which they were placed on probation

18. Which one of the following statements about the failure rates, among the 190 cases in the first study, for each year of age between 30 and 50 is MOST accurate, based on the data in the selection?

    A. In each year of age between 30 and 50, the failure rate is 7%.
    B. The failure rate for some years of age between 30 and 50 was zero.
    C. In each year of age between 30 and 50, the same percentage of failure occurred.
    D. The failure rate for ages close to 30 is higher than 7% and, for ages close to 50, lower than 7%, but in no year of age is the failure rate below 4%.
    E. The failure rate for ages close to 31 is higher than 7% and, for ages close to 49, lower than 7%, but in no year of age is the failure rate below 4%.

Questions 19-21.

DIRECTIONS: The following graph is to be used as the SOLE basis for answering Questions 19 through 21. Study the graph carefully and base your answers ONLY on the information contained therein.

MONTHS IN 2008 COMPARED WITH
THE SAME MONTHS IN 2007

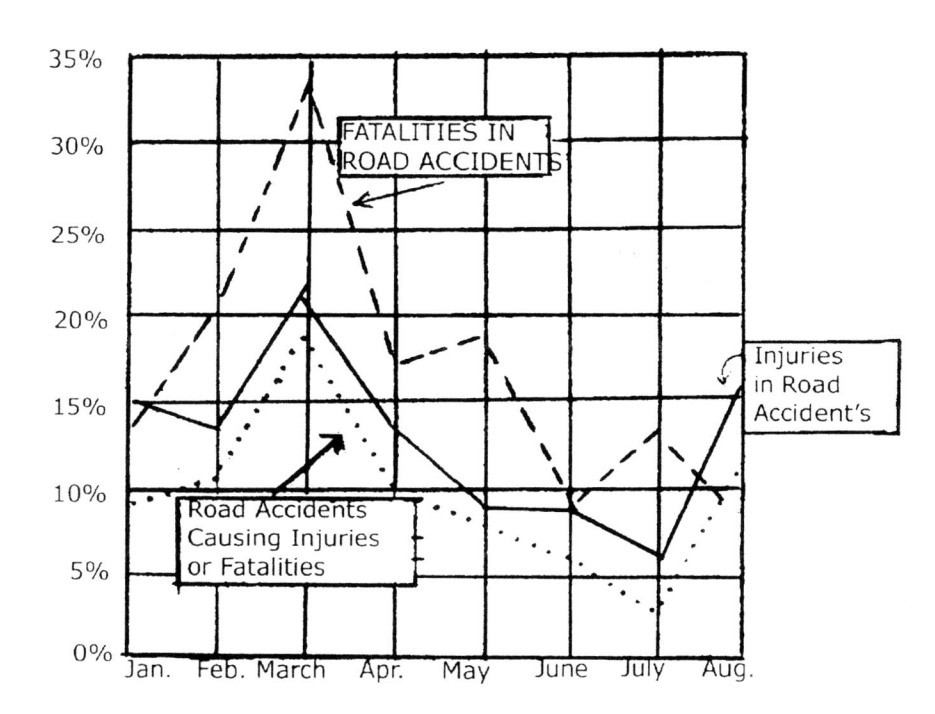

19. From the chart, it is possible to compare the number of fatalities in any month of 2007 with the same month in 2008.
Which one of the following statements is the MOST accurate comparison?
The number of fatalities in

A. each month in 2008 was less than the same month in 2007
B. each month in 2008 was more than the same month in 2007
C. 2008 was less than the same month in 2007 only in the months of March, May, and July
D. 2008 was more than the same month in 2007 only in the months of March, May, and July
E. 2008 was less than the same month in 2007 only in the months of January, April, June, and August

19.____

20. If the ratio of fatalities to road accidents causing injuries or fatalities in July 2007 was one fatality to 10 such road accidents, which one of the following, if any, can be determined to be the RATIO of fatalities to road accidents in July 2008?

A. One fatality to about 15 road accidents
B. One fatality to about 11 road accidents
C. One fatality to about 9 road accidents
D. 12 fatalities to about 3 road accidents
E. The 2008 ratio cannot be determined from the facts given

20.____

21. Based on the graph, in which one of the following months of 2008 did the GREATEST percentage improvement occur in the number of road fatalities, in comparison with the same month of the previous year?

    A. May          B. June          C. July
    D. April         E. August

Questions 22-25.

DIRECTIONS: The following selection is to be used as the SOLE basis for answering Questions 22 through 25. Read the selection carefully and base your answers ONLY on the information contained therein.

The community often sees the police as employees of the state, not as public servants, and rarely, if ever, as the formal guardians of the community's sentiments.

The police are given, the community generally feels, legal power only. Although it is true that the police officer does not employ more rights, privileges, or power than the ordinary citizen, the police officer does perform a role that brings together certain rights, responsibilities, and power that the citizen has only in a very general and uncommitted sense. That is, the police officer, when he takes a salary and signs up for the job, is committed to performing certain limited activities that express legal power, while the citizen who is working in a factory, an office, or a classroom does not use this same power. The investment of time, labor, and personal involvement makes the difference.

However, if the police officer has power concentrated in his role, he also wants authority— that is, rightful or moral authority. It is this kind of authority the community often appears unwilling to grant. Power itself is not necessarily rightful. As has been said elsewhere, legal power itself *gives one man the ability to force another to do his will. But if this power is seen as rightful, as authority, the second man will probably comply with the police officer's wishes because he feels morally obliged to do so.* In these terms, police officers could possess both authority and power. However, many criminals and many lawbreakers do not consciously recognize police officers as having moral authority over them.

In most situations, the police expect that the persons with whom they deal will regard the police as being morally justified in dealing with them as they do. The police try to get offenders to recognize what the norm of proper conduct is and to agree to observe it in the future. If the *client* must be made a *captive,* the police really prefer that the offender believe that he deserved it.

This is the reason why the police officer is generally reluctant to make arrests, as well as why he feels called upon to argue with the persons he arrests - to confirm his moral authority. When he must make an arrest, the police officer is often in a conflict situation and is almost in one sense *betraying* the arrestee.

The situation is similar to that of the agents in society who are responsible for having persons committed to a mental hospital. This unattractive role requires restricting a man's freedom while at the same time trying to suggest that it is for his own good and for the good of others.

When the police are rebuffed, they can no longer be seen or see themselves as executing the will of the community. When this happens, their moral authority is chipped away until only legal power, which is in itself ineffective, remains. The motorist who is stopped comes then to be intimidated by the legal power of the police to make an arrest but does comply with requests out of a belief in the officer's rightful authority to require conformity. The more society is in this condition, the weaker are the police, the more alienated they become, the less secure is the community.

22. According to the selection, which one of the following is MOST likely to occur if police are granted more moral authority by the community?

    A. Police will be more reluctant to make arrests.
    B. Police will become the formal guardians of the community's sentiments.
    C. The police will have more privileges and power than they have now.
    D. A person committed to a mental hospital will see that it is for his own good.
    E. Warnings will be more effective as deterrents to traffic violations than they are now.

23. According to the selection, which one of the following is the MOST important reason why legal power alone may not be enough to enable a police officer to enforce the law effectively?

    A. Most lawbreakers do not recognize legal power.
    B. Legal power is not necessarily seen as rightful by the community.
    C. Police have had their legal power chipped away and weakened in recent years.
    D. Private citizens do not invest enough time, labor, and personal involvement in backing legal power.
    E. Police are required to spend too much time performing duties not related to crime prevention, such as handling psycho cases.

24. While it is true that police generally expect people with whom they deal to grant them moral authority, many lawbreakers in fact do not.
    According to the selection, which one of the following is the MOST serious effect this fact has on police officers' feelings about making arrests?
    They feel

    A. that their legal authority is threatened
    B. that they have to justify the arrest to the public
    C. like captives of the overly-restrictive legal system
    D. that they have to justify the arrest to their superiors
    E. that they are being betrayed by lawbreakers they arrest

25. Which one of the following definitions of moral authority is MOST in keeping with the selection?
    Power

    A. to enforce laws against lawbreakers
    B. which is seen as rightful by the community
    C. to force another person to do one's own will
    D. to force another person to comply with the law
    E. which comes from the strength of one's own character

## KEY (CORRECT ANSWERS)

| | | | | |
|---|---|---|---|---|
| 1. | D | | 11. | E |
| 2. | A | | 12. | A |
| 3. | B | | 13. | D |
| 4. | C | | 14. | C |
| 5. | B | | 15. | A |
| 6. | B | | 16. | B |
| 7. | C | | 17. | D |
| 8. | A | | 18. | B |
| 9. | C | | 19. | A |
| 10. | B | | 20. | B |

21. A
22. E
23. B
24. B
25. B

# EXAMINATION SECTION
## TEST 1

DIRECTIONS: Each question or incomplete statement is followed by several suggested answers or completions. Select the one that BEST answers the question or completes the statement. *PRINT THE LETTER OF THE CORRECT ANSWER IN THE SPACE AT THE RIGHT.*

1. The one of the following which is the MOST serious draw-back of the traffic violation procedure whereby a violator pays the fine by mail or to a court clerk is that the

   A. police officers tend to encourage such payment to avoid court appearances
   B. deterrent effect of facing a judge is lost
   C. ignoring of such summonses is encouraged
   D. mechanism of checking returns becomes complicated and often unwieldy
   E. pleas of *not guilty* are virtually eliminated

   1.____

2. Good traffic accident investigation has a number of major objectives.
   Of the following, the one that is LEAST important is to

   A. provide the basis for evaluation of existing traffic flow control
   B. protect the city from negligence suits at all times
   C. obtain facts required as the basis of accident prevention programs
   D. determine whether violations of law occurred and to gather evidence for prosecution of violators
   E. get facts needed by those involved in accidents to exercise their rights under civil law

   2.____

3. The effectiveness of a traffic law enforcement program is BEST measured by

   A. an increase in traffic enforcement actions
   B. the concentration of available forces in areas and at times of major traffic violations
   C. a decrease in the ratio of convictions to enforcement actions
   D. an increase in the ratio of convictions to enforcement actions
   E. a reduction of traffic accidents and delays

   3.____

4. A statutory exception whereby a police officer may make an arrest for a misdemeanor though not committed in his presence is

   A. smoking in the subway        B. keeping a disorderly house
   C. jostling                     D. peddling without a license
   E. leaving scene of an accident

   4.____

5. James Ford, finding the door of the Sanford Warehouse unlocked, pushed it open and went inside the warehouse. When apprehended by Patrolman Wilson, he was examining the contents of the safe which he had apparently opened.
   Of the following, the MOST appropriate charge against Ford is that of

   A. burglary          B. trespass
   C. petty larceny     D. malicious mischief
   E. robbery

   5.____

6. A robbed B of his diamond ring valued at $250 and hid it in C's home with C's knowledge and consent. C *double-crossed* A and offered to sell the ring to D for one-half its value, telling D that it had been stolen by A. D purchased the ring.
On the basis of these facts,

   A. C is guilty of a felony and D of a misdemeanor
   B. D is guilty of no crime
   C. C is guilty of both a felony and a misdemeanor
   D. C and D are both guilty of a felony
   E. C and D are both guilty of a misdemeanor

7. A takes $50 at 1:00 A.M. from B's pocket while B is asleep on the porch of his home.
Of the following, the crime that has been committed is MOST accurately described as

   A. grand larceny, 1st degree
   B. grand larceny, 2nd degree
   C. petty larceny
   D. robbery, 1st degree
   E. robbery, 2nd degree

8. Jones and Black were partners in a business venture. According to their agreement, each was allowed to draw checks on the funds of the partnership. Jones drew a check to himself for $200 against the funds of the partnership and cashed the check, using the $200 for his personal pleasure.
Of the following, the statement which is MOST correct concerning this situation as stated is that

   A. Jones is guilty of embezzlement of funds of the partnership
   B. Jones could not be held on a charge of embezzlement
   C. only a charge of robbery could be placed against Jones
   D. Jones could be prosecuted for obtaining money under false pretenses
   E. premeditated grand larceny could be charged against Jones

9. J, in great pain and believing himself to be dying, said, *My brother R did not murder K. I murdered K.* J died the next day. At the trial of R for the murder of K, the statement of J was not admitted as a dying declaration. This was so PRIMARILY because

   A. the great pain of K probably affected his mental processes and judgment
   B. J's statement did not concern his own death
   C. J did not die shortly after the confession
   D. J was a relative of R
   E. it could be proved that shortly before he died, J thought he was recovering

10. On checking the prints of a burglary suspect against whom there is little evidence, it is found that he is listed as wanted in Pennsylvania for assault with intent to commit murder.
Of the following, the FIRST thing to do is to

   A. ascertain if there is a mutual agreement on extradition between the states of Pennsylvania and New York
   B. determine if he is still wanted in Pennsylvania
   C. question the man closely to obtain facts necessary for extradition
   D. have Pennsylvania send the necessary extradition papers immediately
   E. have the necessary evidence sent to determine if the man can be held

11. As soon as practicable after an arrest, the arresting officer should inform the arrested person of the offense or conduct for which the arrest is made.
Of the following, the MOST appropriate reason for this procedure is that

   A. such procedure will usually prevent resistance on the part of the person being arrested
   B. the person being arrested will have his fear of assault or robbery allayed
   C. a good public relations policy dictates the need for full communication between officer and the arrested person
   D. immediate disclosure of the reason for arrest will reduce possible complaints of improper police conduct
   E. it affords the arrested person an opportunity to determine his legal rights or defense, or both

11.____

12. If a surety wishes to obtain the return of cash bail but was not present at the time the defendant was arraigned, the surety must make personal application

   A. at the station house to any officer on duty above the rank of sergeant
   B. to the office of the City Treasurer for the return
   C. to the magistrate or judge before whom the defendant was arraigned
   D. at the station house to the desk officer who originally accepted the cash bail
   E. to the clerk of the court where the defendant was arraigned

12.____

Questions 13-14.

DIRECTIONS: Questions 13 and 14 are to be answered on the basis of the following paragraph.

A person who, with the intent to deprive or defraud another of the use and benefit of property or to appropriate the same to the use of the taker, or of any other person other than the true owner, wrongfully takes, obtains or withholds, by any means whatever, from the possession of the true owner or of any other person any money, personal property, thing in action, evidence of debt or contract, or article of value of any kind, steals such property and is guilty of larceny.

13. The definition from the Penal Law has NO application to the act of

   A. fraudulent conversion by a vendor of city sales tax money collected from purchasers
   B. refusing to give proper change after a purchaser has paid for an article in cash
   C. receiving property stolen from the rightful owner
   D. embezzling money from the rightful owner
   E. stealing property which the rightful owner intends to give away

13.____

14. According to the above paragraph, an auto mechanic who claimed to have a lien on an automobile for completed repairs and refused to surrender possession until the bill was paid

   A. *cannot* be charged with larceny because his repairs increased the value of the car
   B. *can* be charged with larceny because such actual possession can be construed to include intent to deprive the owner of use of the car
   C. *cannot* be charged with larceny because the withholding is temporary and such possession is not an evidence of debt

14.____

D. *can* be charged with larceny because he is wrongfully withholding the car from the true owner by questionable means
E. *cannot* be charged with larceny because intent to defraud is lacking

15. The peak hour for motor vehicle accidents involving death or personal injury is GENERALLY from _____ P.M.

   A. 2 to 3     B. 4 to 5     C. 6 to 7
   D. 8 to 9     E. 10 to 11

16. When an arrest for a robbery is made, the suspect is routinely questioned concerning narcotics addiction.
   Of the following, the MOST important value derived from such interrogation at this time is that the

   A. background of the suspect can be more accurately determined and recorded
   B. basis for further questioning as to intent and commission of the crime can be established
   C. suspect can be referred for treatment of the cause of his delinquency
   D. narcotics squad can immediately enter the situation to ascertain the source
   E. narcotics addict is usually an active criminal

17. It has been frequently suggested that the sale of narcotics be made legal under strict governmental control. In this way, it is asserted, the narcotics black market and attendant crime will be ended.
   The MAJOR objection to this suggestion is that

   A. the evils that are involved in licensing users and controlling selling places will defeat the purpose of the plan
   B. crime resulting from addiction will not be reduced since the cause is not eliminated
   C. legalized sale will increase rather than decrease control costs
   D. the problems of addiction are not ended, but are merely legalized
   E. there is no evidence to indicate that such control will affect bootlegging and associated crime

18. When a bullet is fired at fairly close range through a glass window, the direction from which it has been fired can be determined.
   Of the following, the statement that is CORRECT concerning such determinations is that

   A. lateral fractures will form first on the side opposite the one from which the bullet was fired
   B. the hole is wider on the side facing the source of the bullet
   C. numerous small flakes are found blown away from the side opposite the one from which the bullet was fired
   D. numerous small flakes are found blown away from the side from which the bullet was fired
   E. the more acute the angle, the fewer flakes will be blown away

19. Of the following, the MOST common form of suicide is by

   A. hanging     B. shooting     C. slit wounds
   D. poisoning     E. drowning

20. When the Emergency Service Truck and Bomb Squad and other required units arrive at the scene of a bomb or explosive discovery, heavy lubricating oil and a container are brought to the location of the bomb or explosive.
Of the following, the statement that is CORRECT with respect to the use of lubricating oil is that

   A. the heavy oil reduces the explosion hazard of any bomb or explosive
   B. heavy oil penetrates the surface of projectiles or bombs, reducing the possibility of explosions
   C. shells should be completely immersed in the oil to kill the enclosed detonator
   D. oil should be used only when the bomb has a stem detonator
   E. metal-covered grenades should not be immersed in the oil

20.____

21. One of the findings of criminologists regarding the cause and incidence of juvenile delinquency is that the

   A. number of lone-wolf crimes among boys is double that among girls
   B. delinquent tends to be less active in social participation and group play than the nondelinquent
   C. delinquent and the nondelinquent exhibit fairly equal interest in gang or group activities
   D. initial delinquency of a juvenile offender generally results from exposure to criminal associations
   E. occurrence of companionate crimes outweighs lone-wolf offenses by at least two to one

21.____

22. The problem of criminal and antisocial behavior among the young requires the use of varied resources for orienting youth to life in the community.
In this connection, the fundamental task of the Juvenile Aid Bureau today is to

   A. supervise the work of youth squads, youth councils, and cooperating community agencies
   B. train precinct youth patrolmen to dispose of minor instances of misconduct on the precinct level
   C. investigate and report on neglect cases referred to it by the children's court or family court
   D. investigate to determine the proper referral to other agencies for appropriate treatment
   E. undertake treatment in those cases where juvenile delinquency arrests are not indicated

22.____

23. The MOST important reason for requiring that detectives work during normal business hours insofar as this is possible is that

   A. persons involved in the investigation are more likely to be mentally alert during day hours
   B. check of performance and attendance to assignments are more effectively maintained
   C. during those hours it is easiest to get in touch with victims, witnesses, and others
   D. the percentage of crimes that occur after midnight and require continued investigation are relatively few
   E. mobility of suspects is greatest during day hours

23.____

24. Questions put to a suspect or a witness should not be so formulated as to lead the questioned person to answer in a certain direction or suggest the answer to him.
Of the following, the MOST important reason for this principle is that such questioning

   A. usually implies guilt on the part of the questioned person
   B. tends to diminish the possibility of ascertaining the true facts
   C. will cause the denial of knowledge by the person questioned
   D. draws the interrogation away from relevant matters
   E. indicates bias on the part of the questioner

25. The FIRST stage in the transformation of a collection of separate individuals into a potentially dangerous mob is the

   A. involvement of insecure or frustrated persons eager to transfer their feelings to others
   B. presence of very large groups of individuals in close contact with each other
   C. occurrence of some exciting episode
   D. existence of opposing viewpoints among the individuals concerned
   E. loss of ability to act independently by the individuals involved

## KEY (CORRECT ANSWERS)

| | | | |
|---|---|---|---|
| 1. | B | 11. | E |
| 2. | B | 12. | D |
| 3. | E | 13. | C |
| 4. | E | 14. | E |
| 5. | A | 15. | B |
| 6. | D | 16. | B |
| 7. | A | 17. | D |
| 8. | B | 18. | C |
| 9. | B | 19. | B |
| 10. | B | 20. | E |

21. E
22. D
23. C
24. B
25. C

# TEST 2

DIRECTIONS: Each question or incomplete statement is followed by several suggested answers or completions. Select the one that BEST answers the question or completes the statement. *PRINT THE LETTER OF THE CORRECT ANSWER IN THE SPACE AT THE RIGHT.*

1. A, a resident of county X, reported the theft of his automobile in county Y. The automobile was subsequently found in the possession of B in Z county.
An indictment for the larceny of the automobile may be found in

    A. X county or Z county
    B. Y county or Z county
    C. Y county *only*
    D. Z county *only*

    1._____

2. As an officer interested in the promotion of traffic safety, you should know that according to recent statistics the one group which has the HIGHEST number of deaths as a result of being struck in traffic is

    A. adults over 55 years of age
    B. adults between 36 and 55 years of age
    C. adults between 22 and 35 years old
    D. children up to 4 years old

    2._____

3. As an intelligent officer, having a knowledge of the various types of crimes, you should know that in recent years the age group 16 through 25 showed the GREATEST number of arrests for

    A. grand larceny from highways and vehicles
    B. burglary
    C. rape
    D. homicide

    3._____

4. The corroboration necessary for a first degree rape conviction is supplied by

    A. statements made by the complainant to a policeman within a half hour after the commission of the act
    B. an admission by the defendant that he *fooled* with the defendant
    C. evidence of the birth of a child within one year after the alleged crime
    D. a confession made by the defendant

    4._____

5. If an erasure appears on an application for a pistol license, the desk officer should

    A. require the applicant to initial the change
    B. require the applicant to file a new application
    C. obtain a satisfactory explanation from the applicant before accepting it
    D. compare it with the duplicate before accepting it

    5._____

6. Investigation of the character of applicants for miscellaneous licenses or permits issued by the city and state agencies other than the police department is under the supervision of the superior officer in charge of the

    A. Pistol License Bureau
    B. Bureau of Special Service and Investigation
    C. Statistical and Criminal Investigation Bureau
    D. Main Office Squad

    6._____

7. Where there is evidence or suspicion of accidental food poisoning or food infection in a restaurant, notification should be promptly made to the

   A. police laboratory
   B. Chief Medical Examiner
   C. Department of Health
   D. Emergency Service Division

8. The terms *happy dust* and *snow* are frequently used by drug addicts as synonyms for

   A. opium     B. morphine     C. cocaine     D. heroin

9. That part of a teletype message which reads, *The following temporary assignments are ordered to take effect immediately,* would be indicated by Code Signal No.

   A. 16     B. 17     C. 18     D. 19

10. Where a complaint is received of lost or stolen property and the complainant does not know definitely where the loss or theft occurred, the place of occurrence will be deemed to be the

    A. place where the complainant first became aware that the property was missing
    B. home address of the complainant
    C. place where the property is usually kept
    D. place where the complainant last recalls having seen the property

11. In the operation of two-way radio sets in radio motor patrol cars, in order to indicate that a message has been received satisfactorily, the operator should signal

    A. K
    B. ten-four (10-4)
    C. roger
    D. over and out

12. Where a defendant, who had been admitted to bail by a desk officer, appears in court but the surety fails to appear thereat, the cash bail will be

    A. forfeited by the surety
    B. deposited with the court clerk to be returned to the surety after the proper affidavits have been signed and attested by the presiding magistrate
    C. returned to the surety upon personal application to the desk officer who originally accepted the bail
    D. invoiced and forwarded immediately to the Property Clerk

13. A desk officer may take bail in the case of a person charged with

    A. unlawfully soliciting alms on a public street
    B. keeping a bawdy house
    C. vagrancy
    D. eavesdropping

14. If a bail bond is made by a surety company, the desk officer should require the representative of the bonding company to identify himself and present a

    A. power of attorney and a certified copy of the company's license
    B. power of attorney and a financial statement of the bonding company
    C. financial statement of the bonding company and a certified copy of the company's license
    D. power of attorney, a certified copy of the company's license, and a financial statement of the bonding company

15. *Our most accurate crime statistics indicate that crime rates rise and fall on the tides of economic, social, and political cycles with embarrassingly little attention to the most determined efforts of our police.*
    Of the following, the MOST reasonable deduction to make from this observation is that

    A. crime rates are not necessarily a reflection of police performance
    B. better law enforcement has minor significance in the control of crime even in periods of economic stability
    C. greater recognition of police objectives by the police agencies rather than the public is necessary to cope with increasing crime rates
    D. crime rates depend primarily on the complexity of societal organization

16. The delivery of an arrested person to his sureties, upon their giving security for his appearance at the time and place designated to submit to the jurisdiction and judgment of the court, is known as

    A. bail
    B. habeas corpus
    C. parole
    D. probation

17. Jones was charged with the murder of Smith. Brown, Jones' landlord, testified at the trial that Jones had in his home a well-equipped laboratory which contained all the necessary chemicals for producing the poison which an autopsy showed caused Smith's death. Brown's testimony constitutes what is called _____ evidence.

    A. corroborative
    B. opinion
    C. hearsay
    D. circumstantial

18. The procedure whereby a defendant is brought before a magistrate, is informed of the charge against him, and is asked how he pleads thereto is called

    A. arraignment
    B. indictment
    C. presentment
    D. inquisition

19. A minor who commits an offense that would be a felony if committed by an adult can be found guilty of juvenile delinquency ONLY if he is

    A. 18 years of age or under
    B. under 18 years of age
    C. 16 years of age or under
    D. under 16 years of age

20. A written accusation of a crime presented by a grand jury is called a(n)

    A. commitment
    B. arraignment
    C. indictment
    D. demurrer

21. The one of the following statements made by a prisoner that is CORRECTLY called an alibi is:

   A. He struck me first
   B. I didn't intend to hurt him
   C. I was miles away from there at the time
   D. I don't remember what happened

22. A person who, after the commission of a crime, conceals the offender with the intent that the latter may escape from arrest and trial is called a(n)

   A. accessory    B. accomplice
   C. confederate    D. associate

23. A sworn statement of fact is called a(n)

   A. affidavit    B. oath
   C. acknowledgment    D. subpoena

24. A drug addict whose arm shows many scars from the injection of a hypodermic needle is MOST apt to be addicted to

   A. heroin    B. cocaine    C. opium    D. marijuana

25. All of the following drugs are derived from opium EXCEPT

   A. cocaine    B. heroin    C. morphine    D. codeine

## KEY (CORRECT ANSWERS)

| | | | |
|---|---|---|---|
| 1. | B | 11. | B |
| 2. | A | 12. | C |
| 3. | B | 13. | D |
| 4. | D | 14. | B |
| 5. | B | 15. | A |
| 6. | A | 16. | A |
| 7. | C | 17. | D |
| 8. | C | 18. | A |
| 9. | B | 19. | D |
| 10. | A | 20. | C |

21. C
22. A
23. A
24. A
25. A

# TEST 3

DIRECTIONS: Each question or incomplete statement is followed by several suggested answers or completions. Select the one that BEST answers the question or completes the statement. *PRINT THE LETTER OF THE CORRECT ANSWER IN THE SPACE AT THE RIGHT.*

Questions 1-10.

DIRECTIONS: Column I lists certain crimes or offenses. In the space at the right next to the number of the crime or offense in Column I, place the letter preceding the statement in Column II which MOST accurately describes it.

COLUMN I

1. Coercion
2. Abandonment
3. Public nuisance
4. Malicious mischief
5. Robbery
6. Rape
7. Riot
8. Sodomy
9. Sending threatening letters
10. Vagrancy

COLUMN II

A. is always a felony
B. is always a misdemeanor
C. may be a felony or a misdemeanor
D. is neither a felony nor misdemeanor

11. Fingerprints should be taken of any person arrested and charged with

    A. libel
    B. exposure of person in a public place
    C. soliciting alms on a public street
    D. adultery

12. A child under the age of sixteen could be convicted of the crime of

    A. felony murder
    B. murder, 2nd degree
    C. manslaughter, 1st degree
    D. manslaughter, 2nd degree

13. There are no degrees of the crime of

    A. sodomy    B. perjury    C. forgery    D. fraud

14. A person could be convicted of an attempt to commit burglary who
    A. planned a burglary and started in an automobile to commit it but was arrested before he reached the building he intended to break and enter
    B. attempted to break and enter a building but who became frightened and ran away before effecting either a break or entry
    C. approached a house with the intent of breaking and entering it but who, upon reaching it, changed his mind and burned it instead
    D. not knowing the purpose for which they would be used, furnished another with the tools employed in breaking and entering burglarized premises

15. A person who wilfully in any manner encourages or assists another person in taking his life is guilty of
    A. murder in the 2nd degree
    B. manslaughter in the 1st degree
    C. manslaughter in the 2nd degree
    D. suicide

16. In order to establish the crime of kidnapping, it is NOT necessary to show
    A. that actual force was used
    B. the existence of a specific criminal intent
    C. that the taking was against the will of the victim
    D. that there was no lawful authority for the taking

17. A person who made oral threats in order to obtain property of another can be convicted of the felony of extortion only if it is shown that the
    A. threats were to injure the person or property of the person threatened of another
    B. victim actually parted with property
    C. victim parted with his property against his will
    D. threats were made under color of official right

18. The corroboration required in the case of the testimony of an accomplice
    A. must be sufficient to establish the corpus delicti
    B. must refer to all the material elements of the crime charged
    C. need only show that the crime has been committed
    D. need only connect the defendant with the commission of the crime

19. A public officer who, unlawfully and maliciously under color of official authority, does an act whereby another person is injured in his person, property, or rights, commits the crime of
    A. embracery
    B. champetry
    C. coercion
    D. oppression

20. The crime of arson in the first degree can be committed
    A. in the daytime
    B. by burning an unoccupied dwelling house
    C. by burning a building other than a dwelling house
    D. by burning an uninhabited building in the night time

21. As an officer interested in the reduction of unnecessary traffic accidents, you should know that two of the chief sources of such accidents to pedestrians in recent years were crossing a street

   A. against the light and crossing past a parked car
   B. at a point other than the crossing and crossing against the light
   C. at a point other than the crossing and running off the sidewalk
   D. against the light and failing to observe whether cars were making right or left turns

22. A *modus operandi* file will be MOST valuable to an officer as a means of showing the

   A. methods used by criminals
   B. various bureaus and divisions of the police department
   C. number and nature of vehicular accidents
   D. forms used by the police department

23. An officer is frequently advised to lie down before returning fire if a person is shooting at him.
   This is PRIMARILY for the reason that

   A. a smaller target will thus be presented to the assailant
   B. he can return fire more quickly while in the prone position
   C. the assailant will think he has struck the officer and cease firing
   D. it will indicate that the officer is not the aggressor

24. In making arrests during a large riot, it is the practice of the police to take the ringleaders into custody as soon as possible.
   This is PRIMARY because

   A. the police can obtain valuable information from them
   B. they deserve punishment more than the other rioters
   C. rioters need leadership and, without it, will disperse more quickly
   D. arrests of wrongdoers should always be in order of their importance

25. You observe two men running toward a parked automobile in which a driver is seated. You question the three men and you note the license number.
   You should

   A. let them go if you see nothing suspicious
   B. warn them not to be caught loitering again
   C. arrest them because they have probably committed a crime
   D. take them back with you to the place from which the two men came

26. You find a flashlight and a screwdriver lying near a closed bar and grill. You notice further some jimmy marks on the door.
   You should

   A. note in your memorandum book what you have seen
   B. arrest any persons standing in the vicinity
   C. try to enter the bar and grill to investigate whether it has been robbed
   D. telephone the owner of the bar and grill to inform him of what you have seen outside the door

27. The driver of a vehicle engaged in an accident must, without delay, report the accident to the nearest police station

   A. if the accident results in damage to property of the city
   B. only if he is operating the vehicle for hire
   C. if the accident results in injury to the person who was responsible for the accident
   D. only if the death of a person results from the accident

28. A MAJOR advance in our legal concepts of crime and of juvenile delinquency was brought about by certain state legislation which

   A. placed in the court discretion as to whether a fifteen year old child charged with a crime punishable by death or life imprisonment should be treated as a criminal or as a juvenile delinquent
   B. provided that murder, 1st degree, committed by a defendant under 18 shall be punished as murder, 2nd degree
   C. allowed prisoners to be released on parole and to receive discretionary reduction of definite sentences for certain convictions as 2nd and 3rd offenders
   D. provided that violations for sale of alcoholic beverages to minors shall apply when it is apparent or known that the minor is under the age of 18, instead of actually or apparently under that age

29. The task of protecting the President and his family while in residence at the White House is entrusted PRIMARILY to the

   A. Federal Bureau of Investigation
   B. United States Secret Service
   C. Central Intelligence Agency
   D. District of Columbia Police Department

30. The coordinating organization for the various federal agencies engaged in intelligence activities is the

   A. Federal Bureau of Investigation
   B. Federal Security Agency
   C. Mutual Security Agency
   D. Central Intelligence Agency

# KEY (CORRECT ANSWERS)

| | | | |
|---|---|---|---|
| 1. | B | 16. | A |
| 2. | C | 17. | B |
| 3. | B | 18. | D |
| 4. | C | 19. | D |
| 5. | A | 20. | C |
| 6. | C | 21. | B |
| 7. | C | 22. | A |
| 8. | C | 23. | A |
| 9. | B | 24. | C |
| 10. | D | 25. | A |
| 11. | B | 26. | C |
| 12. | B | 27. | C |
| 13. | D | 28. | A |
| 14. | B | 29. | B |
| 15. | B | 30. | D |

# TEST 4

DIRECTIONS: Each question or incomplete statement is followed by several suggested answers or completions. Select the one that BEST answers the question or completes the statement. *PRINT THE LETTER OF THE CORRECT ANSWER IN THE SPACE AT THE RIGHT.*

1. Police department statistics show that the vast majority of grand larcenies involve

    A. residences
    B. stores
    C. pickpockets
    D. automobiles

2. A court order MUST be obtained if the police department wants a postmaster to

    A. place covers on mail
    B. furnish tracings of mail
    C. provide forwarding addresses of persons who have moved
    D. open a letter when a federal crime is suspected

3. Under the portrait parle system of identification, of the following, the MOST important part of a description of a person is the

    A. dress, since it is the most noticeable
    B. ears, since no two are alike
    C. eyes, since they cannot be altered
    D. nose, since it is most distinctive

4. The caliber of a gun is

    A. its barrel length
    B. the diameter of its barrel
    C. the size of the ammunition used
    D. none of the above

5. Identifying markings or imprint are NOT left on a bullet by the

    A. firing pin
    B. ejector
    C. extractor
    D. hammer

6. Homicide cases may be classified as *closed* when

    A. the perpetrator is presumed dead
    B. the statute of limitations has run
    C. no further results can be obtained by continuing the investigation
    D. the Grand Jury failed to indict on the grounds the homicide was justifiable

7. Sexual intercourse is a necessary element of

    A. abduction, seduction, and statutory rape
    B. abduction and seduction
    C. seduction and statutory rape
    D. abduction and statutory rape

8. No person can be convicted of murder or manslaughter unless there is direct proof rather than circumstantial evidence of the

   A. accused's responsibility for the death of the victim
   B. death of the victim
   C. identity of the victim
   D. corpus delicti

9. To be a homicide, statutes require that the killing result from another's act, procurement, or omission.
   Under the provisions of the penal laws, one whose *procurement* was responsible for a homicide would be punishable as a(n)

   A. accomplice          B. conspirator
   C. principal           D. accessory

10. A conviction for 1st degree murder requires proof of

    A. a design to effect death
    B. deliberation and premeditation
    C. malice, express or implied
    D. motive for the killing

11. In general, the MAIN difference between murder and manslaughter is that in the latter there is no

    A. premeditation and deliberation
    B. design to kill
    C. use of a dangerous weapon
    D. felonious intent

12. It is NOT an essential element of the crime of blackmail that the

    A. threat be in writing
    B. accused had the intent to extort or gain money or property
    C. contents of the written threat be known to the accused
    D. threat be calculated to inspire fear or produce terror

13. It is ESSENTIAL to constitute the crime of forgery that the

    A. person in whose name it purports to be made have the legal capacity to make the instrument
    B. person to whom it is directed be bound to act upon it if genuine, or have a remedy over
    C. person whose name is forged be an actual living person
    D. forged instrument would be valid if genuine

14. No person shall park a vehicle within fifty feet of a

    A. fire hydrant        B. railroad crossing
    C. car stop safety zone D. fire station

15. If a witness in a criminal prosecution is solicited by two persons to give false testimony but refuses and is therefore threatened or intimidated, the solicitors could be charged with all of the following crimes EXCEPT

    A. coercion
    B. conspiracy
    C. suppressing evidence
    D. subornation of perjury

16. Robbery differs from larceny in that to constitute the former,

    A. property must be taken from the person of the victim
    B. the victim must be the owner of the property taken
    C. the taking must be accomplished by violence, threats, or terror
    D. there need be no consent to the taking

17. A, intending to steal from the store of B, bored a hole through the door with a centerbit but before he could proceed any further he was discovered and arrested. Part of the chips were found on the inside of the store, indicating that the end of the centerbit had penetrated into the house.
    A can be convicted of

    A. burglary, since penetration by the centerbit constituted a sufficient breaking and entry
    B. unlawful entry only, since penetration by the center-bit constituted an entry but not a breaking
    C. attempted burglary, since there was a sufficient breaking but not entry
    D. no crime, since the instrument was used for the purpose of effecting an entry, and not for the purpose of committing the contemplated felony

18. The crime of burglary, 1st degree can be committed

    A. by an unarmed person
    B. in the daytime
    C. in a building other than a dwelling house
    D. without intent to commit burglary

19. The willful transmission of a false fire alarm is classified in the penal law as

    A. disorderly conduct
    B. a public nuisance
    C. malicious mischief
    D. a crime involving public safety

20. A *public nuisance,* as defined in the penal law, consists in unlawfully doing an act, or omitting to perform a duty, which act or omission

    A. results in the hurt or annoyance of the lands, tenements, or hereditaments of another
    B. results in annoyance or injury to the comfort, repose, health or safety of the community as a whole
    C. while not amounting to an assault or battery, annoys or interferes with any person in any place or with the passengers in any public conveyance
    D. results in the wanton and reckless destruction of property or the willful perpetration of injury to the person

4 (#4)

21. It would NOT be a violation of the accused's constitutional right against self-incrimination for the police to require him without his consent to

   A. submit to a blood test for alcoholic intoxication
   B. furnish a specimen of his handwriting
   C. exhibit his body for scars or wounds
   D. submit to the use of a stomach pump

21.____

22. The fact that the defendant was armed with a dangerous weapon does NOT affect the degree of the crime with which he is charged when he is accused of

   A. larceny          B. manslaughter
   C. robbery          D. burglary

22.____

23. In order to sustain a prosecution for criminal libel,

   A. the person libeled must be living
   B. there must be evidence of malice on the part of the defendant
   C. the libelous matter must have been seen by at least one third party
   D. the matter published must be false

23.____

24. A person who influences or attempts to influence improperly a juror in a civil or criminal action or proceeding commits the crime of

   A. embracery        B. barratry
   C. champetry        D. coercion

24.____

25. No agreement amounts to a conspiracy, unless some overt act besides such agreement be done to effect the object thereof by one or more of the parties to such agreement if its object is to commit

   A. larceny          B. arson
   C. burglary         D. felonious assault

25.____

26. Maiming differs from assault in that

   A. the injury inflicted must disable as well as dis-figure the victim
   B. the injury must be premeditated
   C. there must be proof of an intent to inflict a particular kind of injury
   D. the means or instrument used is material

26.____

27. The principal distinction between first and second degree assault is that the former requires

   A. intent to kill or commit a felony
   B. use of a dangerous weapon
   C. actual battery or consummation of the offense
   D. premeditation

27.____

28. Regardless of intent, it is a felony merely to possess

   A. a Browning automatic
   B. a Thompson submachine gun
   C. a .45 caliber revolver
   D. any explosive substance

28.____

29. A was shot by B and, having given up all hope of recovery, stated to the arresting officer that several days before he was shot, he had been held up and robbed by C of $2,000. This dying statement is inadmissible in evidence against C because

    A. the statement is not part of the res gestae
    B. A was not shown to have been in extremis
    C. dying declarations are admissible only in homicide cases
    D. dying declarations must be statements of fact rather than opinion

30. It is in all cases essential to extradition that the

    A. accused departed from the state for the purpose
    B. accused was present in the demanding state at the time of commission of the crime alleged
    C. crime charged is a felony
    D. requisition be accompanied by a copy of the indictment or information supported by affidavit, or affidavit made before a magistrate

## KEY (CORRECT ANSWERS)

| | | | |
|---|---|---|---|
| 1. | D | 16. | C |
| 2. | D | 17. | C |
| 3. | B | 18. | A |
| 4. | D | 19. | C |
| 5. | D | 20. | B |
| 6. | D | 21. | C |
| 7. | C | 22. | A |
| 8. | B | 23. | D |
| 9. | C | 24. | A |
| 10. | B | 25. | A |
| 11. | B | 26. | C |
| 12. | D | 27. | A |
| 13. | D | 28. | B |
| 14. | B | 29. | C |
| 15. | D | 30. | D |

# EXAMINATION SECTION
## TEST 1

DIRECTIONS: Each question or incomplete statement is followed by several suggested answers or completions. Select the one that BEST answers the question or completes the statement. *PRINT THE LETTER OF THE CORRECT ANSWER IN THE SPACE AT THE RIGHT.*

1. As the desk officer, Lieutenant Jones is responsible for

    A. accepting service of civil process for a member of the service and notifying the member's command
    B. examining reports and forms prepared during the previous twenty-four hours and processing them as required when performing duty with the second platoon
    C. making sure that a sergeant conducts an investigation and submits required reports when a member of the service is injured and/or department property is damaged
    D. interviewing visitors only in the absence of the commanding officer

    1.____

2. An operations coordinator is responsible for

    A. recommending redeployment of personnel, if necessary, to precinct commander, executive, or desk officer
    B. apportioning communications among sergeants for investigation based only on each sergeant's abilities
    C. insuring that the proper entries are made in the barrier record book
    D. inspecting and signing activity logs of patrol sergeants at least once each month

    2.____

3. The telephone switchboard operator is responsible for maintaining all of the following EXCEPT

    A. telephone dispatch log
    B. highway condition record
    C. telephone record
    D. outgoing toll calls

    3.____

4. Which of the following is NOT a responsibility of a desk officer?

    A. Visiting and inspecting all areas of the station house at least twice per tour
    B. Inspecting and signing the activity log of patrol sergeants at least once each month
    C. Inspecting and verifying the return roll call
    D. All police operations within the command during the tour

    4.____

5. Which of the following personnel are under the direct supervision of the desk officer?

    A. All precinct personnel assigned to perform duty in uniform
    B. Robbery identification program personnel
    C. The attendant
    D. Personnel assigned to election details

    5.____

6. When a uniformed member of the service returns to the command from court, the desk officer should make entries in the command log, interrupted patrol log, the telephone dispatch log, and the

    A. front of the roll call
    B. arrest log
    C. activity log
    D. roll call recapitulation

    6.____

7. Lieutenant Clark, who is serving as desk officer, anticipates a lot of activity in about an hour. She decides to change her meal and go now. There is one patrol supervisor on patrol who will be relieved for meal by the anti-crime supervisor when he comes off meal in one-half hour. The lieutenant tells Officer Cooper, the station house relief, to take the desk duty while she is on meal. She informs the officer that an assistant district attorney will be coming in regarding a homicide arrest and that it is alright for the assistant district attorney to be behind the desk. The lieutenant also instructs Officer Cooper to notify the telephone switchboard operator of all post changes.
Which of the following actions taken by the lieutenant should be considered INCORRECT?

   A. Changing her assigned meal period
   B. Assigning a police officer as meal relief for desk duty
   C. Permitting an assistant district attorney to go behind the desk
   D. Directing that the telephone switchboard operator be notified of all post changes

8. Police Officer Smith is assigned to a fixed post at the beginning of her tour. Two hours later, she telephones you, the desk officer, and informs you that there are no unusual circumstances at the post and that the conditions requiring the post have been corrected. You trust her judgment and assign her to a patrol post in a shopping district.
You should now record the post change in the

   A. command log and telephone record
   B. command log and then notify the radio dispatcher
   C. command log and roll call, and then notify the telephone switchboard operator
   D. telephone dispatch log and roll call

9. The desk officer is inspecting the property locker at the start of his tour and finds a large amount of property. In this situation, the desk officer should do all of the following EXCEPT

   A. use the property index and compare entries against actual property invoices
   B. inspect seals of all plastic security envelopes for tampering
   C. enter results of the inspection of property and evidence seals in the command log
   D. check the lead seal on the narcotics safe and record the results on the brown page in the rear of the command log

10. Operations coordinators are responsible for all of the following EXCEPT

    A. coordinating the early intervention monitoring system
    B. reviewing all orders and preparing summaries of pertinent information for presentation to members of the command at unit training or roll call instruction
    C. preparing written instructions for sergeants and police officers
    D. reviewing and supervising the maintenance of records and files of the command

11. Which of the following is responsible for supervising election details?

    A. Desk officer                    B. Commanding officer
    C. Integrity control officer       D. Precinct planning officer

12. The operations coordinator is responsible for all of the following EXCEPT

    A. supervising the maintenance of the precinct library
    B. insuring the proper maintenance of the subpoena receipt book
    C. supervising performance of the patrol wagon operator
    D. checking the property voucher book and property on hand in the precinct

13. The precinct's integrity control officer observes a male detective assigned to the precinct's detective squad entering a social club in the company of two females. Two hours later, he observes the detective exit the club and leave the area.
The integrity control officer should

    A. warn and admonish the detective
    B. initiate an investigation of the social club and the detective
    C. determine if the visit was authorized by the detective's commanding officer
    D. notify the borough detective area command of the observation

14. Which of the following statements is CORRECT regarding notifications to crime victims who may be entitled to compensation under the Crime Victim's Compensation Law?
The

    A. crime prevention officer reviews all complaint reports and attempts to make telephone notifications to all such victims
    B. member of the service taking the initial report is responsible for notifying such victims and advising them to contact the victim services agency for applications
    C. community affairs officer reviews all complaint reports and mails out crime victim compensation law booklets to such victims
    D. detective assigned to conduct a follow-up investigation notifies such victims who were not personally notified, and notes such fact on a complaint follow-up informational

15. With regard to the use of deadly physical force by police officers to effect arrests or prevent escapes, it would be INCORRECT to state that

    A. only the minimum amount of force will be used which is consistent with the accomplishment of a mission
    B. every other reasonable alternative means will be utilized before a police officer resorts to the use of his firearm
    C. the firearm shall be viewed as an offensive weapon, to be used solely as a tool of apprehension
    D. to minimize the possibility of accidentally discharging a weapon, firearms shall not be cocked

16. As a desk officer instructing the platoon, which of the following guidelines regarding department policy on the use of firearms does NOT allow for exceptions?

    A. Firearms should be fired double action
    B. The discharge of a firearm at dogs or other animals
    C. Discharging a firearm to summon assistance
    D. Discharging a firearm from or at a moving vehicle

17. You, the desk officer, receive a call from the patrol supervisor from the scene of an incident where he was requested to respond by an off-duty member of the service. The patrol supervisor tells you that a female has just made an allegation of corruption against the officer.
In this situation, you should tell the sergeant to

   A. have the off-duty officer and the complainant brought to the station house where the integrity control officer or field internal affairs investigators will be the only members to interview the complainant
   B. instruct the off-duty officer to report this allegation of corruption to his commanding officer or directly to the internal affairs division, action desk
   C. interview only the complainant and then confer with the internal affairs division, action desk before interviewing the officer concerning the allegation
   D. investigate, prepare a complaint report, and forward the complaint report to the commanding officer, internal affairs division, within 24 hours

18. Which one of the following statements regarding vacation policy is CORRECT?

   A. Accrued vacation carried into the following year may be used by only 2% of precinct personnel at the same time during the month of December.
   B. Only 2% of patrol services personnel may take individual vacation days at the same time.
   C. Police officers may not select the following holidays as an individual vacation day: Independence Day, Labor Day, Thanksgiving Day, Christmas Day, or New Year's Day.
   D. Members of the service who wish to exchange vacations with one another may do so at their own discretion.

19. The members of a precinct club wish to form a softball league. They plan to run a benefit and raffle through the precinct community council to raise funds for the team. They have printed tickets with the words *Help Form the 27th Precinct Softball Team, Donation $2.00.*
In order to properly carry out such a plan, the club members must FIRST seek the approval of the

   A. chief of patrol
   B. chief of inspectional services
   C. commanding officer, internal affairs division
   D. commanding officer, personnel bureau

20. As a precinct integrity control officer, it is your responsibility to know that only certain awards may be accepted by members of the service.
Which one of the following awards may NOT be accepted?
A(n)

   A. monetary award from the city employee's suggestion board
   B. award of departmental recognition
   C. monetary award from a local civic organization
   D. award from a metropolitan newspaper to a member of an officer's family for a brave or meritorious act

21. Sergeant Smith approaches the desk and asks you, the desk officer, for some help in answering some questions regarding the carrying of firearms, while off duty.
Which of the following statements regarding the carrying of firearms while a member is off duty is INCORRECT?
He

   A. may be unarmed at his own discretion while off duty and on vacation
   B. must be armed while engaging in authorized off duty employment
   C. must not store a firearm in an unattended motor vehicle
   D. must carry the service revolver, authorized special weapon, or authorized off duty revolver, when required to carry a firearm

22. Regarding uniforms and equipment, it would be CORRECT to state that

   A. the nameplate should be worn 1/4 inch below and centered under the shield on the outermost garment, including raincoat
   B. the shield and identification card must be carried at all times and both be presented when necessary to establish identification
   C. uniformed members of the service utilizing the option of not carrying their firearm off duty, as described under *equipment firearms*, must carry the shield and identification card
   D. the shield and identification card should be presented when a member is wearing either the uniform or civilian clothes, while delivering or withdrawing evidence from property clerk division

23. Which one of the following statements regarding the possession of firearms both on and off duty is CORRECT?

   A. A member of the service who is permitted to carry special weapons in lieu of regulation firearms while on duty must carry regulation firearms while off duty.
   B. The department makes no provision for allowing the modification of any authorized firearm, except for rubber grips.
   C. All handguns purchased by a member of the service should be tested by the firearms and tactics range officer prior to use.
   D. If a member of the service is appearing in Family Court as a respondent, he should safeguard his weapon at a safe location other than Family Court.

24. The desk officer is instructing the outgoing platoon on the preparation of duplicate aided cards.
She should state that a duplicate aided card should NOT be prepared if

   A. cardio-pulmonary resuscitation is administered
   B. a person is killed in a boating accident
   C. a child is neglected, abused, or maltreated
   D. a person is hospitalized and an uncared-for child is left with friends residing in the household

25. Mrs. Simon comes into the station house and tells you, the desk officer, that she just purchased an expensive bottle of perfume from a local merchant. When she used it, she developed a rash. She gives you the perfume and tells you that she wants the police to analyze it.
Which of the following actions should you take?

A. Notify Mrs. Simon that in civil negligence cases private laboratories should conduct the necessary analysis.
B. Have the perfume vouchered in order that an analysis may be performed by the Department of Health
C. Refer Mrs. Simon's complaint to the Department of Health, Food Poisoning Investigation Unit.
D. Have the perfume vouchered and forwarded to the police laboratory with a *request for laboratory analysis*.

26. An aided report and a complaint report are prepared when a person who lived alone is found deceased at his residence.
If no relative of the deceased person can be located, the desk officer should direct the officer concerned to prepare a _____ report.

    A. complaint follow-up
    B. duplicate aided
    C. missing/unidentified persons
    D. second complaint

27. The single parent of a nine year-old child is hospitalized. The child is left in the care of a relative residing at an address different from the child's.
Of the following, the desk officer should make or direct notification to the

    A. state central registry
    B. missing persons unit
    C. County Society for the Prevention of Cruelty to Children
    D. Bureau of Child Welfare

28. Lieutenant Johnson is reviewing reports for accuracy. In one incident, a pedestrian was struck by a bicycle and both parties were injured.
Which of the following should have been filed for this incident?

    A. One police accident report with an accident number, prefixed with *B*
    B. Two aided reports, one with an aided number and the other with an accident number, both prefixed with *B*
    C. Two police accident reports, each with a separate aided number and prefixed with *B*
    D. One aided report and one police accident report, each with a separate aided number and prefixed with *B*

29. A nine year-old child is injured in an accident with a bicycle. The child is hospitalized, and his relatives cannot be located for notification.
The desk officer should insure that which of the following reports are prepared?

    A. Police accident report, missing/unidentified person report, and juvenile report
    B. Aided report, missing/unidentified person report, and juvenile report
    C. Aided report, missing/unidentified person report, and police accident report
    D. Police accident report, aided report, and juvenile report

30. A police officer advises the desk officer that she is in the precinct to make a notification to the relatives of an elderly deceased person who lived alone. After making inquiries, the officer was able to obtain the name, address, and telephone number of an older brother residing in Yonkers.
In discussing the notification with the police officer, the desk officer should insure that the notification was made by telephoning the _____ making the notification

   A. inter-city correspondence unit and requesting their assistance in
   B. Yonkers police department and requesting their assistance in
   C. brother and tactfully
   D. missing persons unit and requesting their assistance in

31. A police officer responds to a vehicle accident in his sector. When the officer returns to the station house, he informs the desk officer that two motor vehicles and a bicyclist were involved in the accident resulting in two minor injuries. The parties were taken to a hospital before his arrival at the scene.
The desk officer should direct the police officer to determine the location of the injured parties and obtain the information needed to prepare a(n)

   A. police accident report
   B. police accident report and an aided report for the bicyclist
   C. complaint report and a police accident report for each person injured, with the accident numbers prefixed with the letter *B*
   D. accident report - city involved

32. The desk officer is reviewing a police accident report concerning a vehicle accident. Which of the following statements is INCORRECT?
If the vehicle

   A. accident involves personal injury and the operator of one of the vehicles has fled the scene without reporting the incident, then a complaint report is also required
   B. operator leaves the scene of the accident and is then apprehended and issued a summons for the traffic offense (leaving the scene of an accident without reporting) prior to the preparation of a complaint report, then a complaint report is not required
   C. accident involves property damage only and the operator of one of the vehicles has fled the scene without reporting the incident, a universal summons returnable to Department of Motor Vehicles, Traffic Violations Bureau may not be served because the officer did not observe the offense
   D. accident involves property damage only and the operator of one of the vehicles has fled the scene without reporting the incident, a complaint report is not required

33. A man sustains what appears to be a minor injury in a vehicle accident. He reports the accident to the police but refuses medical aid. The desk officer at the precinct of record is notified the following day that the man died as a result of injuries sustained in the accident.
Which of the following reports must be prepared in this situation?
A(n) _____ report.

   A. unusual occurrence report and a supplementary police accident
   B. complaint report and a supplementary aided
   C. unusual occurrence report and a supplementary aided
   D. complaint report and a supplementary police accident

34. A police department vehicle is involved in an accident resulting in minor property damage only. The patrol supervisor notified the precinct desk officer of the pertinent facts.
In this situation, the desk officer should immediately request which one of the following to respond to the accident scene?

   A. Operations unit, precinct highway safety officer
   B. The precinct commander/duty captain
   C. The accident investigation squad
   D. The operations coordinator

35. A highway patrol investigation reveals a mechanical defect in a vehicle that is going to be held as investigation evidence. The vehicle was involved in an accident resulting in death.
In this situation, the desk officer should

   A. permit removal of the vehicle when the defect is corrected
   B. make a command log entry concerning the mechanical defect and the identity of the highway unit officer
   C. have the police officer preparing the police accident report also prepare the motor vehicle accident mechanism report
   D. permit removal of the vehicle by an authorized private tow truck equipped with a crane

## KEY (CORRECT ANSWERS)

| | | | | | | | |
|---|---|---|---|---|---|---|---|
| 1. | C | 11. | A | 21. | B | 31. | A |
| 2. | A | 12. | C | 22. | D | 32. | D |
| 3. | C | 13. | C | 23. | D | 33. | D |
| 4. | A | 14. | D | 24. | D | 34. | B |
| 5. | C | 15. | C | 25. | A | 35. | B |
| 6. | A | 16. | A | 26. | C | | |
| 7. | B | 17. | C | 27. | D | | |
| 8. | C | 18. | B | 28. | C | | |
| 9. | D | 19. | B | 29. | A | | |
| 10. | A | 20. | C | 30. | A | | |

# TEST 2

DIRECTIONS: Each question or incomplete statement is followed by several suggested answers or completions. Select the one that BEST answers the question or completes the statement. *PRINT THE LETTER OF THE CORRECT ANSWER IN THE SPACE AT THE RIGHT.*

1. The patrol supervisor advises the desk officer that he is at the residence of a confirmed missing eight year old. In this situation, the desk officer should IMMEDIATELY

    A. check precinct records to determine if the missing child was the subject of a police action
    B. direct the patrol supervisor to plan, but not commence, the search pending the arrival of the duty captain
    C. notify the youth service division
    D. notify the Bureau of Child Welfare

    1._____

2. As a desk officer, you should advise a police officer to prepare a missing persons report in which one of the following cases?
A

    A. 19-year-old female who resides in the city and left home because of domestic problems with her father
    B. 10-year-old child who lives in New Jersey, reported missing by his mother, who had been shopping with him at a city mall
    C. 17-year-old female staying at a local hotel for the past week who is reported missing by her boyfriend
    D. 62-year-old male who lives in the city, had an argument with his wife, and has not returned home for two days

    2._____

3. Lieutenant Lane receives a telephone call from a police officer who states that he has discovered an illegal drug laboratory in an abandoned building on his post. Lieutenant Lane, realizing that volatile substances may be present, should without delay notify the

    A. arson and explosion squad
    B. police laboratory
    C. aviation unit
    D. crime scene unit

    3._____

4. While you are serving as desk officer, a probationary police officer reports a past robbery at a bank located in your precinct. The perpetrator threatened a teller with a gun and escaped with $25,000.
In reviewing the officer's paperwork for this robbery, you should insure that which one of the following notifications has been made?

    A. Central robbery division
    B. Detective borough task force
    C. City joint robbery task force
    D. Major case squad

    4._____

5. As desk officer, you should tell the concerned police officer that it was IMPROPER to prepare a juvenile report on a(n)

    A. 14-year-old for jostling on the subway

    5._____

B. 8-year-old declared *uncontrollable* by his parents, with the words *Person In Need of Supervision* printed across the top of the report
C. 15-year-old found intoxicated on the street
D. 13-year-old for criminal trespass with a school security officer listed as the complainant

6. With regard to the duties of a precinct desk officer, it would be CORRECT to state that the desk officer will

   A. make necessary entries in command log, interrupted patrol log, and roll call when required, indicating the arresting officer's time of arrival at central booking
   B. forward the original copy of the property clerk's invoice to central booking whenever evidence has been vouchered
   C. allow an attorney who represents a prisoner to interview the prisoner in the precinct muster room and will assure that a uniformed member of the service keeps the prisoner and attorney under observation at all times
   D. notify the Department of Correction and make a telephone record entry whenever a prisoner is admitted to the hospital

7. Which of the following statements regarding the release of prisoners is CORRECT?

   A. The desk officer need not always be notified when a prisoner is released.
   B. Under no circumstances will a police officer release a prisoner without the prior approval of the patrol supervisor.
   C. A person may be released by the police department at any time from initial custody until arraignment.
   D. In cases where a dispute arises regarding the release of prisoners, the desk officer must confer with the district attorney's office.

8. An attorney is present at the station house where a prisoner is lodged and requests to interview the prisoner. The attorney states that he does not know the prisoner's name, but was present at the prisoner's arrest and feels that the arrest was unjustified.
   In this situation, the desk officer should

   A. refuse to permit the attorney to visit the prisoner because he is unable to give the prisoner's name
   B. advise the attorney that he may see the prisoner at the central booking facility
   C. direct the communications operator to transmit a message to all commands advising that prisoner may not be questioned without approval of said attorney
   D. permit the attorney to visit the prisoner in the precinct detention cell for 15 minutes

9. Mr. Jones, who resides in New Jersey, is arrested within New York City for possession of a stiletto. The arresting officer notifies the desk officer that a check with the identification section discloses that Mr. Jones has a previous conviction for falsely reporting an incident. With regard to desk appearance ticket and bail procedures, it would be CORRECT to state that Mr. Jones

   A. does not qualify for a desk appearance ticket or bail because he lives in New Jersey
   B. qualifies for a desk appearance ticket but does not qualify for bail because of the possession of a weapon

C. does not qualify for a desk appearance ticket or bail because of the current charge and previous conviction
D. qualifies for a desk appearance ticket and bail because the current charge is not a photographible offense

10. A police officer advises the desk officer that he has made an off-duty arrest of a 14 year-old male for robbery. The complainant is hospitalized with injuries suffered in the crime, which was witnessed by the police officer.
Which of the following actions should the desk officer take?

    A. Assign this arrest to an on-duty officer.
    B. Notify the duty captain or commanding officer to respond to the station house to determine the validity of this arrest.
    C. Direct the police officer to take the juvenile to Family Court directly if it is in session.
    D. Instruct the police officer to release the juvenile to his parents on personal recognizance.

10.____

11. Police Officer Larsen enters the station house with a prisoner arrested for third degree assault, a misdemeanor.
In this situation, the desk officer should do all of the following EXCEPT

    A. inform the prisoner that he may be issued a desk appearance ticket if he qualifies
    B. deny a desk appearance ticket if the prisoner resides out of state
    C. have the arresting officer prepare a warrant investigation report
    D. make a final determination as to whether a desk appearance ticket will be issued, based on verification information, crime circumstances, and the suspect's criminal record

11.____

12. A prisoner arrested for grand larceny was legally in possession of a prescription drug. The arresting officer is now holding the drug.
In order to alert detention facility personnel that the prisoner may require a prescription drug, the desk officer should direct the arresting officer to

    A. invoice the drug for safekeeping and prepare a medical treatment of prisoner form
    B. return the drug to the prisoner and make a notation on the on-line booking system arrest worksheet
    C. invoice the drug for safekeeping and make a notation on the on-line booking system arrest worksheet
    D. return the drug to the prisoner and prepare a medical treatment of prisoner form

12.____

13. A police officer advises the desk officer that he is detaining a 15 year-old youth who has frequently harrassed an elderly woman by verbally threatening her and accusing her of constantly calling the police on him. The officer states that this has been a continuing problem with this youth, for whom he has previously prepared numerous juvenile reports. The officer further states that the juvenile's mother is present and states that her son is uncontrollable.
In this situation, the desk officer should direct that the

    A. officer prepare a juvenile report
    B. youth be arrested and charged with juvenile delinquency
    C. youth be taken into custody as a person in need of supervision
    D. officer prepare a complaint report and refer the elderly woman to court

13.____

14. The desk officer of the 82nd precinct permits an attorney to visit a prisoner lodged in the 82nd precinct detention facility. The prisoner was arrested in the 63rd precinct. The facts relating to the visit by the attorney should be telephoned to which one of the following?

    A. Central booking supervisor
    B. Arresting officer
    C. Station house clerk, precinct of detention
    D. Desk officer, precinct of arrest

15. The desk officer should assign which of the following to guard a hospitalized female prisoner who is a juvenile?

    A. Only a female officer in uniform
    B. Either a male or female officer in uniform
    C. Only a female officer in civilian clothes
    D. Either a male or female officer in civilian clothes

16. Which of the following prisoners should the precinct desk officer permit to be lodged in the same prisoner holding pen?

    A. A juvenile and his father arrested for criminal possession of a controlled substance
    B. A pregnant woman and her mother arrested for petit larceny
    C. Two intoxicated brothers arrested for criminal mischief
    D. A husband and wife team arrested for fraudulent accosting

17. During arrest processing at a station house, a prisoner begins to act irrationally. He starts to cry and yells that he cannot face going to jail and will try to commit suicide. The arresting officer has reliable and independent information that the prisoner has attempted suicide in the past.
    Upon being informed of this, the desk officer should

    A. remove the prisoner to central booking where a determination will be made regarding psychiatric treatment
    B. request an ambulance and have the prisoner removed to a hospital for psychiatric treatment, accompanied by a police officer
    C. direct the arresting officer to make frequent observations of the prisoner while he is in the holding pen and record these observations in the arrest log
    D. notify the duty captain or commanding officer

18. A prisoner is being lodged temporarily in a precinct holding pen.
    The desk officer should designate a member of the service to inspect and check the condition of the prisoner every _____ minutes.

    A. 10     B. 30     C. 45     D. 60

19. An arresting officer reports to the desk officer that the prisoner's attorney insists that the prisoner NOT be handcuffed.
    The desk officer should inform the officer that

    A. all prisoners must be handcuffed behind the back without exception
    B. prisoners charged with non-violent misdemeanors do not have to be handcuffed
    C. a prisoner who surrenders at a law enforcement facility accompanied by his attorney should not be handcuffed
    D. a precinct desk officer may authorize an arresting officer not to use handcuffs in certain cases

20. A police officer is at the station house with a prisoner arrested for attempted robbery involving the use of a simulated firearm. The simulated firearm is a toy gun. The desk officer should advise the police officer to voucher the toy gun

    A. on a separate voucher and send it to the property clerk for storage
    B. with all other evidence on the same voucher for use in future court proceedings
    C. in the same manner as a real gun would be vouchered
    D. and store it in the precinct gun locker until the district attorney determines the charges

21. A desk officer receives a plastic security envelope that is sealed in his presence by a police officer.
    The desk officer should next complete which of the following?

    A. Captions on the plastic security envelope
    B. Entries in the property inventory log
    C. Entries in the property index log
    D. Entries in the security envelope log

22. A police officer arrests a man for robbery who was driving a stolen car that is now disabled. A previously reported stolen .38 caliber revolver is found on the front seat of the stolen car. The arresting officer is processing the arrest and invoicing the recovered property at the station house while another officer waits for department tow to pick up the stolen car.
    In reviewing the arresting officer's work, the desk officer should make sure that the officer notifies the

    A. owner of the stolen vehicle that the vehicle has been recovered
    B. Alarm Board to cancel the alarm on the vehicle
    C. Bureau of Alcohol, Tobacco and Firearms of the recovery of the revolver
    D. Alarm Board to cancel the alarm on the firearm

23. A desk officer is reviewing the actions taken by a sergeant who supervised a search of the apartment of a deceased female who lived alone.
    Which of the following actions taken by the sergeant should be considered CORRECT?

    A. Requesting that the brother of the deceased take the cemetery deed found in the apartment
    B. Directing that only a female police officer search the deceased female
    C. Requesting the property clerk's assistance in releasing a large valuable sculpture
    D. Directing that at least one responsible civilian be located to witness the search

24. A citizen walks into the station house, properly identifies himself, and claims that the registration plates were removed from his derelict vehicle earlier that day. The desk officer checks the expired registration log and verifies that the plates were removed and are now in police custody.
    The desk officer should deliver the plates

    A. to the Department of Motor Vehicles and deny the claimant's request for the plates even though he has proper identification

B. with one copy of registration plate removal notice to the registered owner
   C. with property clerk's motor vehicle/boat invoice to the property clerk division within five days
   D. to the registered owner or representative upon presentation of a current registration certificate and sticker for the vehicle

25. When a desk officer must open a sealed plastic security envelope containing evidence, he should

   A. discard the opened envelope, use a new envelope, and record the new envelope's serial number on the property index sheet and on the property clerk's invoice under *Remarks*
   B. place the opened envelope and the property into a yellow property envelope, seal it, and sign it across the seal
   C. reseal the envelope with clear plastic tape and enter the reason for opening the envelope on the property clerk's invoice
   D. place the opened envelope into a new envelope and enter the serial number of the new envelope on the property clerk's invoice

26. A police officer calls the desk officer for guidance in determining what to do with the pushcart and goods of a licensed food vendor. The officer has served an environmental control board notice of violation and hearing because the vendor returned to a congested fire scene several times in one hour after being instructed not to return.
    The desk officer should instruct the officer to do all of the following EXCEPT

   A. seize the pushcart and goods
   B. tell the vendor he may not assist in the removal of the property
   C. seize the vendor's license and prepare a property clerk's invoice
   D. place all seized property into large plastic bags, and close them with plastic security seals, in the presence of the peddler

27. The integrity control officer should examine roll calls from the preceding week to identify uniformed members who made appearances in court, grand jury, etc.
    The court attendance records of members who made such appearances should be compared with the

   A. command log              B. telephone record
   C. time and record report   D. arrest report

28. Police Officer Smith is assigned to patrol post 1 on a day tour and has been placed on stand-by telephone alert for a court appearance.
    The desk officer should

   A. activate the telephone alert that day if it is received by 1400 hours
   B. notify the precinct commander in writing if Officer Smith appears in court without being called
   C. notify the precinct commander in writing if Officer Smith fails to appear when called
   D. direct Officer Smith if not equipped with portable radio to call the station house every 30 minutes between 1000 and 1300 hours

29. A police officer responded to a dispute on her patrol post and observes two large groups of people shouting racial epithets and brandishing bottles and bricks at one another. She immediately notifies the desk officer and requests the patrol supervisor to respond. The desk officer notifies the commanding officer/duty captain to respond.
Which one of the following actions should the desk officer perform NEXT?

    A. Notify the community affairs unit to respond without waiting for complete details.
    B. Notify the operations unit without waiting for complete details.
    C. Inform the public information unit of the details of the preliminary investigation.
    D. Inform the chief of patrol's office of the details of the preliminary investigation.

30. A patrol car responds to a radio run *assault in progress*. A traffic enforcement agent at the scene reports that he was assaulted by a motorist to whom he had issued a summons. He also reports that the motorist threatened him with a tire iron. The motorist is arrested and charged with assault, 3rd degree and menacing.
In this situation, the desk officer should

    A. not release the defendant on a desk appearance ticket unless agreed to by the traffic enforcement agent
    B. not release the defendant on a desk appearance ticket or station house bail
    C. release the defendant on a desk appearance ticket if he meets eligibility requirements
    D. release the defendant on station house bail if he is ineligible for a desk appearance ticket

31. At the start of the 8x4 tour, the desk officer reviews the roll call and observes no coverage for section C in the precinct. She takes Police Officer Adams, patrol post 1, meal - 1130 hours, and Police Officer Bates, patrol post 2, meal - 1300 hours, and assigns them to Sector C.
In this situation, the desk officer should also

    A. designate a location in the adjoining precinct where meals can be obtained if no suitable location is available in the precinct
    B. verify that meal locations are listed on the desk copy of roll call
    C. make appropriate adjustments so that members are not deprived of a meal
    D. advise Sector C that if meal is taken in the patrol car, no more than two cars may be parked in the same place at the same time

32. As desk officer, you receive an intelligence report on a suspected narcotics location.
In this situation, you should do all of the following EXCEPT

    A. notify the narcotics division
    B. record the information in the precinct command log
    C. have the details entered in the intelligence report record
    D. deliver the intelligence report to the commanding officer

33. Lieutenant Diaz is assigned precinct patrol duties because the only patrol sergeant has been designated *limited duty* and is assigned to the desk. While on patrol, Lieutenant Diaz hears the following radio transmission: *Two Charlie in pursuit of a black sedan with New Jersey plates 744XYZ, proceeding northbound on 6th Ave. at 38th Street.*
Based on this information, Lieutenant Diaz should

A. direct and control the pursuit and the apprehension effort and terminate the pursuit if warranted
B. direct all precinct patrol cars to participate in the pursuit in order to effect an apprehension
C. direct precinct vans and scooters to participate in the pursuit in order to effect an apprehension
D. terminate pursuit immediately because vehicle pursuits are in violation of department policy

34. Mr. Plunkett arrives at the station house and tells the desk officer about a conversation he recently overheard among members of a radical group. They talked about assassinating a visiting foreign dignitary who will be arriving in New York the following week during an official visit.
In this situation, the desk officer should IMMEDIATELY notify by telephone the

A. unified intelligence unit
B. special investigations division
C. intelligence division
D. operations unit

35. The desk officer is notified that a department vehicle has been involved in a minor accident within the confines of the precinct.
The desk officer should notify the

A. patrol borough command of the accident and respond to the scene, conduct an investigation, and review the actions taken by the patrol supervisor
B. patrol borough command of the accident and request the duty captain to respond to the scene of the accident
C. highway unit and request a highway unit officer to respond to the scene of the accident and conduct an investigation
D. division commander of the accident and request that the division commander respond to the scene of the accident

## KEY (CORRECT ANSWERS)

| | | | | | | | |
|---|---|---|---|---|---|---|---|
| 1. | A | 11. | B | 21. | D | 31. | C |
| 2. | C | 12. | A | 22. | A | 32. | B |
| 3. | B | 13. | A | 23. | D | 33. | A |
| 4. | C | 14. | D | 24. | D | 34. | C |
| 5. | A | 15. | D | 25. | D | 35. | B |
| 6. | C | 16. | B | 26. | C | | |
| 7. | C | 17. | B | 27. | A | | |
| 8. | A | 18. | B | 28. | D | | |
| 9. | C | 19. | D | 29. | B | | |
| 10. | B | 20. | C | 30. | B | | |

# TEST 3

DIRECTIONS: Each question or incomplete statement is followed by several suggested answers or completions. Select the one that BEST answers the question or completes the statement. *PRINT THE LETTER OF THE CORRECT ANSWER IN THE SPACE AT THE RIGHT.*

1. Which one of the following statements concerning the scene of a hostage/barricaded person incident is INCORRECT?  1.____

    A. The patrol borough commander should attempt to establish contact with the barricaded person, pending arrival of the hostage negotiators.
    B. If the barricaded person is contained and poses no immediate threat or danger, no additional action will be taken without the authorization of the precinct commander/ duty captain at the scene.
    C. The ranking emergency service unit supervisor on the scene is in command and will coordinate all patrol operations.
    D. The emergency service unit supervisor must insure that only properly equipped and designated personnel enter the inner perimeter.

2. A precinct desk officer receives a call from an angry citizen who claims that two officers and a sergeant are refusing to take action in connection with an alleged unlawful eviction. The citizen claims that her mother-in-law, who is also her landlord, removed her possessions from the dwelling and changed the locks. The desk officer then asks to speak to the sergeant.
In this situation, which of the following statements by the desk officer concerning unlawful evictions would be INCORRECT?  2.____

    A. When an arrest is necessary, the violator shall be brought to criminal court for prompt arraignment.
    B. The protective provisions of the Unlawful Eviction Law apply to individuals who have unlawfully occupied a dwelling unit for 30 or more consecutive days.
    C. Officers may decline to issue a summons or effect an arrest for unlawful eviction in domestic violence cases.
    D. Removal of an occupant's possessions from a dwelling or changing locks does not qualify as unlawful eviction unless force is used or threatened in the process.

3. Which one of the following CORRECTLY names those personnel who are required to carry off-duty mobilization cards at all times?  3.____

    A. All members of the service below the rank of captain
    B. Only uniformed members of the service
    C. All uniformed and civilian members of the service
    D. All uniformed and designated civilian members of the service

4. There is an emergency mobilization of off-duty members of the service. Police Officer Grant lives in Brooklyn but is in Suffolk County when he learns of the mobilization.
In this situation, Officer Grant should report to  4.____

    A. his permanent command
    B. Special Operations Division Headquarters, Flushing Meadow Park
    C. 113th Precinct, Queens
    D. the mobilization point designated by the borough command in which the mobilization has been called

5. A sergeant is planning to explain the procedures for reporting sick to the outgoing platoon.
When she asks the desk officer for assistance, the desk officer should tell the sergeant to instruct the police officers that they should

   A. report sick by telephone, either in person or by competent messenger, at least three hours before the start of a scheduled tour, unless disability occurs during this period
   B. notify the sick desk before notifying assigned patrol command if they are reporting sick within two hours of commencement of tour
   C. remain at their residence or other authorized location unless permission to leave is granted by the precinct commanding officer
   D. inform the member to whom they are reporting sick of any pending arraignment or scheduled appearance in court

6. A desk officer should NOT offer *administrative return from sick report* to a uniformed member of the service when the member

   A. has a minor non-line-of-duty injury
   B. has a dental problem
   C. is designated chronic absent - category A
   D. is reporting sick less than two hours before the tour

7. Police Officer Williams informs the desk officer that she was escorting an injured complainant into the station house when blood from the complainant's injuries dripped on the floor of the sitting room.
The desk officer should instruct Officer Williams to have the spill cleaned with a mixture of ten parts water and one part

   A. ammonia           B. bleach
   C. baking soda       D. detergent

8. In order to be excused from an appearance, a member of the service on the Traffic Violation Bureau's *Must Appear List* or *Alert Status List* must present which one of the following reasons?

   A. Medical check-up
   B. Civilian complaint review board hearing
   C. Regular day off
   D. Appearance for training

9. A rapid mobilization code 10-47 has occurred while you are performing an 8x4 tour as the desk officer. Two patrol car teams are preparing to leave the station house and ask you for instructions.
In this situation, you should instruct the patrol car teams to

   A. respond directly to the precinct mobilization point, picking up members assigned to special posts along the way
   B. take a detail roster to prepare upon arrival
   C. request barriers upon arrival, if they are required, through communications division radio dispatcher
   D. respond directly to the precinct mobilization point

10. According to the relevant interim order, a desk officer is required to supervise all prisoner  Q 10.____
    removals from the precinct.
    In order to comply with this directive, the desk officer should

    A. direct the patrol supervisor to check that all prisoners are secured to transport chains or are rear handcuffed
    B. direct a police officer to check the cell area to make sure all cells are vacated
    C. personally check that all prisoners are secured to transport chains or are rear handcuffed
    D. personally check all cell areas to make sure all cells are vacated

11. Which one of the following patrol services bureau units is NOT authorized to carry a shotgun?   11.____

    A. Patrol supervisor's patrol car          B. Highway officer patrol car
    C. Precinct one-officer patrol car         D. Emergency service unit

12. John Bates and Joe Norris intend to rob the owner of a supermarket as he leaves the   12.____
    store after closing. They stand at the entrance to the supermarket after it closes. Bates is looking through the glass door and Norris is keeping watch. At this point, they are interrupted by the arrival of a police car. Police Officer Jones, observing their behavior, takes both men into custody and appears before you, the desk officer. Officer Jones states that he wishes to charge Bates and Norris with attempted robbery.
    You should tell Officer Jones that _____ be charged with attempted robbery.

    A. John Bates and Joe Norris should
    B. John Bates and Joe Norris should not
    C. only John Bates should
    D. only Joe Norris should

13. Joe steals a ring from Mary at knifepoint. Moments later, Ray steals the same ring from   13.____
    Joe at gunpoint.
    In this situation, which one of the following should be considered a CORRECT statement?
    Ray should

    A. not be charged with robbery of Joe because Joe was not the legal owner of the ring
    B. be charged with robbery of Mary through the theory of transferred intent
    C. be charged with attempted robbery, rather than robbery, of Joe because of a factual impossibility
    D. be charged with robbery of Joe but not robbery of Mary

14. One morning, Phil is jogging in a park when he happens upon a man holding a knife to a   14.____
    child's throat. The man threatens to kill the child unless Phil gives him money. Phil then gives the man some money, the child is released unharmed, the man flees, and is later apprehended.
    Of the following, it would be MOST appropriate to charge the man with

    A. robbery of Phil                    B. robbery of the child
    C. grand larceny by extortion         D. coercion

15. A derelict enters a prominent city art gallery, produces a can of spray paint, and threatens to deface a priceless masterpiece unless the gallery owner gives him $500. The owner does so and no damage is done to the painting. When the derelict is later apprehended, it would be MOST appropriate to charge him with

    A. scheme to defraud
    B. petit larceny
    C. grand larceny
    D. robbery

16. Henry approaches Tim and says, *Give me $10 right now or I'll break your arm when I see you tomorrow.* Tim gives Henry the $10 and immediately spots a police officer. Tim has Henry arrested on the spot.
    Of the following, Henry should be charged with

    A. grand larceny
    B. petit larceny
    C. robbery
    D. fraudulent accosting

17. Lieutenant Reed, the operations coordinator in his precinct, is advising police officers concerning weapons that require an intent to use unlawfully before the possessor can be arrested.
    Which of the following weapons requires such intent?

    A. Chuka stick
    B. Blackjack
    C. Electronic dart gun
    D. Kung fu star

18. A police officer tells the desk officer that he is somewhat confused by the law on vehicular assault.
    In explaining the law to the police officer, the desk officer should state that vehicular assault

    A. requires physical injury caused by criminal negligence, coupled with intoxicated operation of a vehicle
    B. requires serious physical injury caused by recklessness or criminal negligence, coupled with intoxicated operation of a vehicle
    C. requires only serious physical injury caused by intoxicated operation of a vehicle
    D. always requires criminal negligence and a serious physical injury

19. The sergeant seeks direction from you, a lieutenant in the public morals division, regarding the proper execution of search warrants.
    Of the following, you should tell the sergeant that a search warrant

    A. must be executed within ten days after the date of issuance, excluding Sundays and holidays
    B. which is not endorsed for *nighttime service* may be executed anytime if it can later be demonstrated that property will be destroyed if not immediately seized
    C. may be executed between 0600 hours to 2100 hours, including Sundays and holidays
    D. that is unexecuted must be returned within twenty days from the date of issuance

20. Lieutenant Rogers, recently assigned to a narcotics division unit, observed the unit execute a search warrant of a suspected crack house. He called the unit together to commend them on the procedures that were followed during the execution of the warrant.
    Of the following, it would be APPROPRIATE for the lieutenant to tell the officers that

A. permitting the occupant of the premises to leave was correct since detention would have been improper
B. searching the occupant of the premises was correct since the warrant conveys such authority
C. detaining the occupant of the premises until the completion of the warrant was correct since such detention is proper
D. arresting the occupant of the premises when he asked to leave was correct since the issuance of a search warrant establishes probable cause

21. Police Officer Sullivan arrests a male for possession of an illegal firearm recovered during a search of the suspect's vehicle within the city. The vehicle matched a detailed description transmitted by the communications unit. The communications dispatcher had broadcast the description of the male and his vehicle twenty minutes earlier, indicating that the male had just committed an armed robbery with a sawed-off shotgun in Newark, New Jersey. The communications unit also advised that the message had been received by teletype from the Newark Police Department.
Of the following, a desk officer should tell Officer Sullivan that the arrest and search were

   A. *proper,* since the radio message established probable cause
   B. *improper,* since the radio message established only mere suspicion
   C. *proper,* only if the search of the vehicle was made with the consent of the driver
   D. *improper,* since the police officer did not comply with the Uniform Close Pursuit Act

21._____

22. Lieutenant Claster is a precinct detective squad commander. A detective in his squad has just arrested a suspect for a crime which has attracted media attention. A well-known newspaper reporter is at the station house seeking to interview the arresting officer. Lieutenant Claster should instruct the detective to release which of the following information?

   A. Admissions, confessions, or the contents of a statement or alibi attributable to the accused person
   B. The substance or text of the charge, for example, complaint, indictment, information, and the identity of the complainant where appropriate
   C. The results of evidentiary tests or the refusal of the accused to take such test
   D. Statements concerning the anticipated testimony of prospective witnesses

22._____

23. Certain distinctions must be kept in mind when a defendant is to be charged with either robbery or grand larceny.
Of the following, it would be APPROPRIATE to charge a defendant with

   A. *grand larceny* if, in using force to grab a woman's pocketbook from her arm, he causes the woman to slip, fall, and as a result sustain a physical injury
   B. *robbery* if he rips a woman's purse from her hand as she tries to hold on to it
   C. *grand larceny* if he puts one arm around the neck of the victim and, with the other hand, takes property from the victim
   D. *robbery* if he secretly picks the pocket of another and the victim does not know it

23._____

24. The desk officer receives a call from the recorder of a patrol car who has responded to a dispute at an automotive repair shop, registered with the State Department of Motor Vehicles. The recorder tells the desk officer that a motorist drove his car into the repair shop earlier in the day and requested that the repair shop owner tune-up the car. The motorist has now returned to the repair shop to get his car, but refuses to pay the bill because the repair shop owner is charging an unreasonable amount for the tune-up. The motorist wants his car and wants the repair shop owner arrested if he continues to keep the car. The repair shop owner says he is only charging his regular reasonable price for the tune-up. He absolutely refuses to give the motorist his car until he has been paid. Although he has not been to court, the shop owner claims to have a lien on the car. The desk officer should instruct the recorder to advise the

    A. motorist that the repair shop owner has a valid lien and does not have to return the car until the repair charges are paid
    B. repair shop owner that a lien does not arise automatically and that a court order is necessary
    C. repair shop owner that he must return the car to the motorist and then sue him for any charges claimed
    D. repair shop owner and the motorist that since this is a civil matter, the police department does not get involved

25. A sector car team brings three prisoners who were arrested for robbery into the station house. The officers inform the desk officer that a woman was robbed three hours earlier and gave them a physical description of the three men. She knew two of the men from the neighborhood as Ernest and Vernon. The third was a stranger to her.
As the officers are standing at the desk, with the prisoners in handcuffs, a field training unit team walks in and tells the desk officer that they have the complainant with them. They ask if they should bring her in to confirm the identity of the prisoners.
In this situation, the desk officer should

    A. instruct the field training unit officers that the complainant may not view any of the suspects in the station house without a line-up
    B. allow a showup only if the handcuffs are removed and the suspects are not the only persons present in civilian clothes
    C. direct the arresting officers to take the suspects outside and casually walk them past the complainant
    D. allow the complainant to confirm the identity only of Ernest and Vernon without a line-up

26. Which of the following statements regarding *stop, question and frisk* is INCORRECT?

    A. Any questioning situation that is based on mere suspicion is considered by the courts to be improper.
    B. The movement of a suspect for even a short distance may constitute an arrest.
    C. Exigent circumstances may permit a police officer to move a suspect a short distance from the place where he was actually stopped.
    D. If the police officer has developed probable cause for an arrest, a suspect may be moved.

27. It would be CORRECT for a desk officer who is instructing roll call formations regarding *stop, question, and frisk* to make which one of the following statements?
If an officer has _____ suspicion that a felony has been committed, _____.

   A. mere; he may not ask a suspect questions concerning his conduct
   B. reasonable; a suspect must answer the officer's questions
   C. mere; force may be used to detain a person
   D. reasonable; force may be used to detain a person

28. Which one of the following statements regarding eyewitness identification procedures is INCORRECT?

   A. There is no right to counsel at an on-the-scene show-up procedure.
   B. There is no right to counsel at a photo identification procedure.
   C. A person arrested pursuant to an arrest warrant has no right to counsel at a lineup held prior to arraignment.
   D. An attorney who is present at the lineup site must be allowed to view the lineup.

29. A bullet was fired through the floor of an apartment striking a man in the apartment below. Arriving police officers entered the apartment from which the shot was fired without a search warrant. No one was present when they entered the apartment. They found three weapons, including a sawed-off shotgun during the search. One of the officers noticed two sets of expensive stereo components which appeared out of place in the otherwise poorly furnished apartment. Suspecting the components were stolen, the officer moved the components and recorded the serial numbers. While at the scene, the officer telephoned to check whether the items had been reported stolen and was advised that the turntable had been reported stolen. The officer seized it immediately.
In reviewing the actions of the officers afterward, the desk officer should tell them that

   A. the entry into the apartment without a search warrant and the seizure of the turntable violated the Fourth Amendment
   B. the entry into the apartment without a search warrant was permissible because there were exigent circumstances, but the movement of the equipment to see and record the serial numbers violated the Fourth Amendment
   C. the entry into the apartment without a search warrant was permissible because there were exigent circumstances, and the seizure of the turntable was permissible because it was in plain view
   D. they had a right to move the equipment to check the serial numbers because they reasonably suspected that the equipment was stolen

30. An operations coordinator is conducting training for handling emotionally disturbed persons at a precinct supervisor's conference.
During the group discussion, it would be INCORRECT for a sergeant to make which one of the following statements?

   A. Even though a housing or transit police supervisor is at the scene, a patrol supervisor may also respond.
   B. Emergency service unit personnel will obtain the permission of the emergency service supervisor prior to using a taser/stun device, except in emergencies.
   C. The patrol supervisor will establish a *zone of safety* around an emotionally disturbed person after the emotionally disturbed person has become stationary.
   D. The patrol supervisor or emergency service personnel using a taser/stun device will prepare a *taser/stun device report*.

31. A police officer makes an arrest during his scheduled third platoon tour of duty. As a result, he works continuously beyond the normal expiration of the tour and reaches the district attorney's complaint room (pre-arraignment) at 0630 hours. The officer calls the desk officer for instruction because he is scheduled for a third platoon tour of duty that day.
The desk officer should tell him that

   A. he is rescheduled to the second platoon
   B. his overtime ends as of 0630 hours
   C. his overtime ends when he signs out of court
   D. he is dismissed when he signs out of court

32. The Administrative Code requires that most persons who enter city service on or after September 1, 1986 must be or become a resident of the city.
According to the relevant operations order, this provision

   A. applies only to members of the service above the rank of captain
   B. does not apply to uniformed members of the service
   C. applies only to members of the service above the rank of deputy chief
   D. does not apply to civilian employees of the police department

33. When a member of the service is involved in a shooting incident, disaster, or other violent occurrence resulting in death or injury, the desk officer is required to notify the

   A. sick desk supervisor
   B. operations unit
   C. trauma counseling unit
   D. department chaplain's office

34. A lieutenant is directing operations at the scene of an incident in which one of his officers has been shot. Which of the following instructions given by the lieutenant to his sergeant would be INCORRECT?

   A. An emergency medical service ambulance should be the means of transportation.
   B. If police personnel are transporting the officer, make sure that they request communications to direct them to the nearest trauma center.
   C. The decision to transfer the officer from one hospital to another will be made by the ranking patrol services bureau supervisor after conferring with emergency service personnel.
   D. The police surgeon at the hospital will be a party to determining transfer to other facilities.

35. A desk officer is completing an inspection of the invoiced property at the station house. Which of the following statements regarding such inspections is INCORRECT?

   A. Inspect the property locker and all areas within the station house where invoiced property is held at the commencement of each tour.
   B. Inspect seals on all security envelopes present for tampering and notify the precinct commander/duty captain to conduct an investigation if seal is violated.
   C. Utilize the property index to determine what property has been invoiced.
   D. Enter the results of the inspection of the invoiced property and seals in the command log and safeguard the key and invoiced property during the tour.

## KEY (CORRECT ANSWERS)

| | | | | | | | |
|---|---|---|---|---|---|---|---|
| 1. | C | 11. | A | 21. | A | 31. | A |
| 2. | D | 12. | B | 22. | B | 32. | B |
| 3. | D | 13. | D | 23. | B | 33. | B |
| 4. | A | 14. | A | 24. | A | 34. | C |
| 5. | D | 15. | C | 25. | D | 35. | B |
| 6. | B | 16. | A | 26. | A | | |
| 7. | B | 17. | D | 27. | D | | |
| 8. | C | 18. | D | 28. | C | | |
| 9. | D | 19. | C | 29. | B | | |
| 10. | C | 20. | C | 30. | C | | |

———

# EXAMINATION SECTION
# TEST 1

DIRECTIONS: Each question or incomplete statement is followed by several suggested answers or completions. Select the one that BEST answers the question or completes the statement. *PRINT THE LETTER OF THE CORRECT ANSWER IN THE SPACE AT THE RIGHT.*

Questions 1-6.

DIRECTIONS: Questions 1 through 6 pertain to the fact pattern below. Answer the questions based on appropriate procedures.

A major winter snowstorm accompanied by strong winds has just passed through a section of the city. Several tornado-like windstorms developed from this storm, knocking down power lines, destroying homes, and damaging businesses. In addition, many storefronts were blown out, scattering merchandise throughout the area. As a result, looting has become a major problem. Lieutenant Reynolds has just arrived at the scene and is considered the superior officer in charge.

1. After arriving at the scene, Lieutenant Reynolds' FIRST priority is to

   A. prepare a Detail Roster/Assignment Sheet
   B. alert the Civil Defense Headquarters
   C. leave the scene to pick up members performing foot patrol in the immediate vicinity
   D. determine if additional personnel/equipment is required

2. Who has the responsibility of establishing a temporary headquarters?

   A. The senior police officer at the scene
   B. Lieutenant Reynolds
   C. The duty captain
   D. The station house supervisor

3. The MAJOR reason for establishing a temporary headquarters is to

   A. improve efficiency of operation by having direct telephone communication and record keeping available
   B. provide working space for supervisory officers as they arrive at the scene
   C. provide a storage area for recovered property
   D. provide a detention area for containing prisoners

4. In order to effectively mobilize police service, Lieutenant Reynolds should direct responding vehicles to park

   A. as closely as possible to the emergency scene to reduce response time
   B. in an area removed from the emergency scene so as not to interfere with operations
   C. in an area that affords easy access to members
   D. at the nearest precinct station house

5. A member of the service is not assigned to precinct patrol, but is performing duty in a department vehicle within this command.
This officer should take which of the following actions in response to the situation (i.e., the winter storm)?

   A. Respond to the scene and report to the ranking officer in charge.
   B. Call in to the dispatcher to request permission to respond to the scene.
   C. Respond to the scene, but upon arrival of patrol officers be relieved.
   D. Contact the station house supervisor with any information the member may add, but not respond personally.

6. According to proper temporary headquarters procedure, which of the following actions should Lieutenant Reynolds take once the temporary headquarters has been discontinued?

   A. Reassign personnel after conferring with the individual members.
   B. Reassign personnel since he is the ranking officer in charge.
   C. Reassign personnel after conferring with the station house supervisor.
   D. Direct personnel to return to the precinct assignments they had prior to the emergency.

Questions 7-9.

DIRECTIONS: Questions 7 through 9 pertain to the fact pattern below. Answer the questions based on appropriate procedures.

A criminal court warrant for the arrest of John Amato has been issued. This warrant is delivered to the precinct in which Lieutenant Malecki is the Operations Coordinator. Officer Brown is assigned to execute this arrest warrant.

7. Officer Brown proceeded to Amato's residence.
Assuming that no factors exist that make normal procedures impractical (e.g., Amato does not try to escape, etc.), Officer Brown must ALWAYS follow which procedure at the time of arrest?

   A. Search Amato's residence for evidence.
   B. Show Amato the warrant.
   C. Allow Amato to make a phone call.
   D. Inform Amato of the charge.

8. Lieutenant Malecki should receive which of the following with the warrant from the station house officer?
   I. Warrant Division Summary Sheet
   II. Warrants Forwarded for Investigation Sheet
   III. Central Warrant Unit's Computerized List
   IV. Outstanding Warrant Sheet from Central Booking
   The CORRECT answer is:

   A. I, II        B. II, III        C. III, IV        D. I, IV

9. In order to ensure that no additional warrants are outstanding against Amato, Officer Brown should contact

   A. Lieutenant Malecki or the central booking supervisor
   B. the Central Warrant Division/ FATN System
   C. the station house supervisor in the precinct of arrest
   D. the officer at the court from which the warrant was issued

10. An officer was sent to make an arrest outside of the city limits. Necessary and proper police action was taken in order to effect the arrest. A lawsuit was then brought in a United States District Court against the officer as a result of his action.
    According to State General Municipal Law, which of the following is MOST accurate?
    The

    A. city would save harmless and indemnify the officer
    B. city would not save harmless or indemnify the officer
    C. state would save harmless and indemnify the officer
    D. officer would be solely liable

11. Assume an officer, while off-duty, arrested a drunk driver outside the city and, as a result, is sued under Section 1983 of Title 18 of the United States Code.
    Which of the following statements is ACCURATE?
    The

    A. officer is not liable for his actions
    B. state would save harmless and indemnify this officer
    C. city may not be liable for the officer's actions
    D. plaintiff in the lawsuit must prefer criminal, rather than civil, charges

Questions 12-14.

DIRECTIONS: Questions 12 through 14 are to be answered on the basis of the fact pattern below.

A sergeant calls the station house officer from the scene of an accident. He reports that an automobile was observed going through a red traffic signal. The car struck a parked unoccupied vehicle and then left the scene. The radio motor patrol crew, who made the observation, pursued and apprehended the driver. The officers then noticed that the automobile bore diplomatic license plates. The driver stated that he was a staff member for a foreign legation.

12. The station house officer should inform the sergeant that the PROPER course of action for the radio motor patrol crew is to

    A. serve a summons for the appropriate traffic infraction
    B. arrest the staff member for reckless driving if the damage to the parked car exceeds $250
    C. arrest the staff member for leaving the scene of an accident, regardless of the extent of the damages
    D. prepare an accident report and, after verification of the name, title of diplomat, and the government he represents, take no further action

13. In this case, the lieutenant operations officer has responsibility for

    A. immediately notifying the Action Desk and the police commissioner of the occurrence by telephone
    B. contacting the city commission for the United Nations
    C. investigating the incident by interviewing witnesses
    D. visiting the headquarters district of the United Nations to interview the staff member

14. If a vehicle bearing *DPL* or *FC* license plates was illegally parked by a staff member of a foreign legation and was creating a safety hazard violation, what should a member of the service be expected to do?

    A. Verify the ownership and registration of the vehicle and take no further action.
    B. Issue a parking summons.
    C. Await the return of the staff member and administer an oral reprimand.
    D. Summon authorized tow and have the car towed away and impounded.

Questions 15-17.

DIRECTIONS: Questions 15 through 17 pertain to the fact pattern below. Answer the questions based on appropriate procedures.

A station house officer, in reviewing an arrest report of a subordinate, notes that the prisoner, Benjamin Pierce, was arrested for driving while intoxicated. Pierce was arrested and convicted for the same offense eight years ago.

15. What effect, if any, would the previous record have in this case?

    A. It would have no effect since the conviction was more than seven years ago.
    B. If the prior arrest was for DWI (Narcotics or Controlled Substances), the current charge should be a misdemeanor offense.
    C. It changes the current charge to a felony.
    D. Mr. Pierce must suffer the immediate revocation of his driver's license by the Department of Motor Vehicles.

16. Mr. Pierce refused to submit to a chemical (breathalyzer) test.
    Officers must inform Mr. Pierce that the consequence of this refusal is that he

    A. will be compelled to sign a Chemical Test Refusal Report (CTRR)
    B. will have his driver's license suspended and subsequently revoked
    C. will forfeit the possibility of issuance of a DAT
    D. must consent to blood and urine analysis tests instead

17. Mr. Pierce was disqualified for a DAT.
    One possible reason for such disqualification was that

    A. he was charged with a felony
    B. he was undergoing methadone maintenance treatment at the time of arrest
    C. he was not a citizen
    D. his reported address could not be verified

Questions 18-21.

DIRECTIONS: Questions 18 through 21 pertain to the fact pattern below. Answer the questions based on appropriate procedures.

Lieutenant O'Donnell, while conducting a spot inspection tour in the precinct, observed Officer Warren behaving in an unusual manner while on duty. Upon approaching this officer, the lieutenant determined that the cause of Officer Warren's behavior was the influence of alcohol. Lieutenant O'Donnell ordered Officer Warren to report to the station house. Officer Warren refused to obey this order.

18. Because of Officer Warren's apparent intoxication, Lieutenant O'Donnell should

    A. direct Officer Warren to report to his commanding officer
    B. reprimand Officer Warren in writing within 3 days
    C. orally reprimand Officer Warren only
    D. remove Officer Warren's firearms

19. An investigation to determine Officer Warren's fitness for duty should be conducted by

    A. the precinct commander or the duty captain
    B. the reserve surgeon
    C. an HP technician
    D. Lieutenant O'Donnell

20. Because Officer Warren did not obey the lieutenant's direct order, Lieutenant O'Donnell informed Officer Warren that he was suspended.
In this case, did Lieutenant O'Donnell have the authority to suspend Officer Warren?

    A. Yes; he is not required to obtain prior approval from a higher ranking officer
    B. No; he must first obtain approval from the reserve surgeon
    C. No; he must first obtain approval from Officer Warren's commanding officer
    D. No; he must first inform the Department Advocate of the facts of the case

21. Assume that Officer Warren was officially suspended from duty.
Which of the following rules must Officer Warren follow?
    I. Report in person each day to the precinct during his suspension.
    II. Report in person every Friday to his resident precinct.
    III. Surrender all department property upon suspension.
    IV. Wear his uniform for his appearances at the precinct during the suspension.
The CORRECT answer is:

    A. I, II      B. II, III      C. III, IV      D. I, IV

Questions 22-24.

DIRECTIONS: Questions 22 through, 24 pertain to the fact pattern below. Answer the questions based on appropriate procedures.

Lieutenant Almond receives the following information: Officer Simpson responded to a complaint concerning a man who had locked himself in his room at a boarding house and was causing damage to boarding house property. Officer Simpson judged that the subject, an occupant of a second story room, was at least temporarily deranged. The boarding house proprietor supplied no identification of the subject.

22. After deciding that the subject might be emotionally disturbed, Officer Simpson should

   A. attempt to identify the man by questioning other occupants of the boarding house
   B. request the patrol supervisor and the emergency service unit to respond to the scene
   C. attempt to force entry into the room and use whatever force necessary to restrain the subject
   D. request permission from the patrol supervisor to force entry and restrain the subject

23. Eventually, the subject jumps from the window, knocking himself unconscious. Lieutenant Almond should direct subordinates to do all of the following EXCEPT

   A. render reasonable aid
   B. interview witnesses in an attempt to identify the aided
   C. remove any Medic Alert emblems from the subject for delivery to ambulance attendants
   D. request an ambulance and wait in view to direct the ambulance

24. Once the ambulance arrives, Lieutenant Almond should direct Officer Simpson to

   A. remain at the scene pending the arrival of his patrol supervisor
   B. accompany the subject to the hospital in the back of the ambulance
   C. follow the ambulance to the hospital in a patrol car
   D. remain at the scene to question the boarding house staff and boarders concerning the subject

25. Assume you are a desk officer and the sergeant on patrol calls you with the following problem: A burglar alarm in a building in a non-residential area has malfunctioned. It has been ringing for the last ten minutes.
   Are the police authorized by the noise control provisions of the city administrative code to disconnect the alarm?

   A. *Yes;* the burglar alarm may be immediately disconnected.
   B. *No;* the burglar alarm may not be disconnected because this is a non-residential area.
   C. *No;* the burglar alarm may not be disconnected because the administrative code does not authorize the police to do so in a building.
   D. *Yes,* but the burglar alarm may be disconnected only after the lapse of fifteen minutes of uninterrupted operation.

## KEY (CORRECT ANSWERS)

| | | | | |
|---|---|---|---|---|
| 1. | D | | 11. | C |
| 2. | B | | 12. | D |
| 3. | A | | 13. | C |
| 4. | B | | 14. | B |
| 5. | A | | 15. | C |
| 6. | C | | 16. | B |
| 7. | D | | 17. | A |
| 8. | B | | 18. | D |
| 9. | B | | 19. | A |
| 10. | A | | 20. | A |

21. B
22. B
23. C
24. B
25. C

# TEST 2

DIRECTIONS: Each question or incomplete statement is followed by several suggested answers or completions. Select the one that BEST answers the question or completes the statement. *PRINT THE LETTER OF THE CORRECT ANSWER IN THE SPACE AT THE RIGHT.*

Questions 1-5.

DIRECTIONS: Questions 1 through 5 pertain to the fact pattern below. Answer the questions based on appropriate procedures and laws.

As an administrative lieutenant, you are reviewing reports on the following incident: An informant called the station house around midnight and said, *A white male dressed in a green jacket, blue jeans, western boots, and a cowboy hat, walking with the assistance of a cane, is on the corner of Gretchen and Kilburn. He is carrying a gun.* The caller would not identify himself. Officer Mary Wilson, a uniformed officer, responded to this tip.

1. Assume that Officer Wilson observed a man fitting this description at the corner of Gretchen and Kilburn. No one else was in the area.
   Under these conditions, what is the extent of Officer Wilson's authority?
   She can

   A. stop this suspect at gunpoint and conduct a complete search
   B. stop this suspect at gunpoint and pat down his outer garments
   C. make an immediate summary arrest
   D. remove the suspect to the station house and conduct a search thereat

2. Assume that the caller had said, *A white man with a gun is on Gretchen Street.*
   Officer Wilson, in this case, should

   A. subject any white male on Gretchen Street to a stop and frisk
   B. stop any white male on Gretchen Street at gunpoint and frisk him
   C. forcibly stop only white males who conduct themselves in a suspicious manner
   D. conduct a further investigation

3. Assume that Officer Wilson approached the man who fit the description in the original fact pattern, and this man said, *I'm a police officer assigned to the 50th precinct. My name is Bob O'Keefe, and I'm off duty right now.* Officer Wilson wanted to see the suspect's identification. O'Keefe should react, according to procedures, by

   A. telling Officer Wilson where his identification is located before producing it
   B. requesting his supervisor to respond to the scene
   C. requesting Officer Wilson to call his patrol supervisor for verification of the suspect's status as a police officer
   D. requesting Officer Wilson to call his commanding officer for verification of the suspect's status as a police officer

4. Assume that Officer Wilson was dissatisfied with O'Keefe's credentials.
   Under these circumstances, Officer Wilson should

   A. request additional patrol officers and a patrol supervisor to respond to the scene
   B. request a supervisory officer in her precinct to respond to the scene

1.___

2.___

3.___

4.___

C. request O'Keefe's supervisory officer to respond to the scene
D. arrest the suspect, then request Officer Wilson's patrol supervisor to respond to the scene

5. Assume that a supervisory officer has responded to the scene. 5.____
The PROPER course of action for this supervisor would be to
   I. arrest the suspect and question him further at the station house
   II. direct Officer Wilson and O'Keefe to report to the station house in the precinct of occurrence
   III. request assistance from the borough commander in identifying the suspect
   IV. determine O'Keefe's duty status if the supervisor is satisfied with O'Keefe's credentials

The CORRECT answer is:

A. I, IV         B. II, III         C. II, IV         D. III, IV

Questions 6-8.

DIRECTIONS: Answer Questions 6 through 8 based on the following fact pattern and applicable procedures.

Lieutenant McCauley is the station house officer in the 10th Precinct in Manhattan. At about 8:15 A.M., Mrs. Busby visits the precinct and tells the lieutenant the following story. Last night she was unable to sleep so she was sitting at her bedroom window, on the second floor, watching the traffic go by At about 3:30 A.M., a police car with the logo *10th Precinct* and *883* stenciled on it pulled up and stopped across the street from her apartment. The car was parked in front of 527 West 14th Street, a television and appliance store. Both officers got out of the patrol car and appeared to assault a pedestrian who was standing in the doorway. The officers calmly got into their patrol car and drove away. No one else was on the street to witness the incident. Mrs. Busby refuses to take any further action but feels Lieutenant McCauley should know about the incident.

6. What should be Lieutenant McCauley's FIRST course of action based on these facts? 6.____

   A. Thank Mrs. Busby for coming in to share the information but do nothing further.
   B. Have a copy of a civilian complaint report prepared.
   C. Determine who was assigned to the patrol car and have a supervisory complaint report prepared.
   D. Take the information from Mrs. Busby, then turn the entire matter over to the Internal Affairs Division.

7. If the complainant in this situation had telephoned her complaint anonymously, what should be the PROPER method for processing this complaint? 7.____

   A. The same way that it would be handled if the complaint were personally made.
   B. Forward complaint, through channels, to the Chief of Operations' office for filing in the *Anonymous Complaint File.*
   C. Record complaint in the station house log, then forward, with endorsement, to the borough office concerned.
   D. File in precinct's *Anonymous Complaint File.*

8. Several hours after the original complaint was lodged by Mrs. Busby, Mr. Hellman comes into the station house and tells Lieutenant McCauley he was assaulted by two uniformed police officers at 3:30 A.M. at 527 West 14th Street. Mr. Hellman further states that he knows the police officers were members of the Transit Authority police department.
In this case, Lieutenant McCauley should interview Mr. Hellman and
   I. refer Mr. Hellman to the Transit Authority police department
   II. enter Mr. Hellman's statement in the activity log
   III. have Mr. Hellman prepare a civilian complaint report
   IV. prepare a civilian complaint report and have it forwarded to the Transit Authority police department
The CORRECT answer is:

   A. I, III  B. II, IV  C. III, IV  D. I, IV

Questions 9-11.

DIRECTIONS: Answer Questions 9 through 11 based on the following fact pattern and applicable procedures.

After closing his store for the night, a grocer comes into the station house and turns in a well-worn leather wallet he states was found in a vegetable bin. Upon examining the wallet, a member of the service finds that it contains old, torn bills totaling $22, faded snapshots, but no identification.

9. The member of the service who is in possession of this property at this point should

   A. give the wallet back to the grocer since no identification was found
   B. issue a receipt to the grocer for the wallet
   C. have the grocer complete and sign a Report of Found Property and issue a copy to him
   D. have the grocer sign the Property Index and issue a copy to him

10. In order to process this wallet, the station house officer should have the following prepared:

   A. Report of Unclaimed Property
   B. Found Report on official letterhead
   C. Found Currency Report on official letterhead
   D. A statement from the grocer

11. The station house officer should forward the original of the document prepared in the above question to the

   A. property clerk
   B. duty officer
   C. precinct commanding officer
   D. stolen property inquiry section

Questions 12-15.

DIRECTIONS: Answer Questions 12 through 15 based on the following fact pattern and applicable procedures.

As supervisory officer of a unit, you have just been informed of the following: An official department investigation is to be held following the receipt of allegations that one of the officers under your supervision, Officer Fischer, has misappropriated confiscated drugs.

12. Prior to questioning, Officer Fischer must be given the opportunity to

    A. submit refuting evidence for review
    B. obtain counsel
    C. meet with the complainant
    D. submit his resignation

13. The interrogation of Officer Fischer must be

    A. concluded within one hour
    B. conducted during the officer's off-duty time
    C. conducted in the presence of Officer Fischer's commanding officer
    D. officially recorded for future review/referral

14. Information gained from Officer Fischer during the interrogation relating directly to the allegations against him may

    A. not be used against Officer Fischer in any subsequent criminal proceedings
    B. be used against Officer Fischer even if given *off the record*
    C. not be used against Officer Fischer in relation to subsequent departmental charges
    D. be used against Officer Fischer even if given under duress

15. If Officer Fischer refuses to answer questions during the interrogation specifically directed and narrowly related to his official duties, he will be

    A. subject to no punitive action (Fifth Amendment)
    B. subject to departmental charges
    C. immediately dismissed
    D. administratively transferred

Questions 16-17.

DIRECTIONS: Answer Questions 16 and 17 based on the following fact pattern and applicable procedures.

As a detective squad commander, you have received the following information from one of your undercover officers: Ramona Lincoln, a 55 year old female, owns a home in which fifteen (15) males and females between the ages of 12 and 20 reside. There is probable cause to believe that Lincoln is taking money and gifts from one of her residents (a fifteen year old girl) in return for permitting this girl to participate in prostitution activity within the premises.

16. The MOST appropriate charge for Ramona Lincoln would be

    A. promoting prostitution, misdemeanor
    B. permitting prostitution, felony
    C. promoting prostitution, felony
    D. patronizing a prostitute, felony

17. Under these circumstances, the MOST appropriate charge for the fifteen year old girl is  17.___

   A. prostitution, misdemeanor only
   B. promoting prostitution, misdemeanor
   C. promoting prostitution, felony
   D. juvenile delinquency

Questions 18-21.

DIRECTIONS: Answer Questions 18 through 21 based on the following fact pattern and the applicable laws and procedures.

Lieutenant Sanders arrives on the scene and is advised by uniformed officers from his precinct that shots were fired in front of a grocery store. As the officers approached the scene, they observed a group of four people split up and run. A man was lying on the sidewalk, bleeding and apparently unconscious. They further observed two women run from the man and hide in a nearby doorway. One officer drew his revolver but held it at his side with the barrel pointing toward the ground and ordered the women to come out from the doorway. When both women emerged with their hands in the air, the officer reholstered his weapon. The other officer then asked, *What happened here?* One of the women cried out, *I shot him! I shot him! Please, just get me out of here!* The other woman thrust a small handgun at the officer and said, *I took that away from her. She used it to shoot him.*

18. Lieutenant Sanders should advise the officers to FIRST notify the  18.___

   A. crime scene unit
   B. patrol services bureau
   C. precinct detective unit/detective specialty squad concerned
   D. ballistics unit

19. The officer's question, *What happened here?* should be interpreted as  19.___

   A. constituting a custodial interrogation
   B. not constituting interrogation
   C. improper because the Miranda warnings were not given
   D. coercive

20. The action of the police officer in drawing his revolver  20.___

   A. did not make the encounter custodial because his action was a necessary safety measure
   B. did not make the encounter custodial because he reholstered his firearm before the other officer asked, *What happened here?*
   C. made the encounter custodial but, under the circumstances, the officers could ask questions designed to clarify the nature of the situation confronting them without giving Miranda warnings
   D. made the encounter custodial but interrogation would be permissible because the encounter took place on a public sidewalk and the suspect's friend was present

21. Assume that the officers advise the suspect that she is under arrest and give her Miranda warnings. The suspect states that she wishes to talk to a lawyer.  21.___
If the officers wish to interrogate the suspect, they would be

A. required to wait until the suspect changes her mind and decides to answer their questions
B. required to limit their questioning to crimes other than the shooting
C. permitted to do so if the suspect's attorney refuses to come to the station house
D. permitted to do so only if the suspect waives her right to counsel in the physical presence of an attorney representing her

22. A young woman was walking along the street when Wagner grabbed her pocketbook. Because of the force Wagner used in grabbing the pocketbook, the woman slipped, fell to the ground, and sustained a physical injury.
In this case, it is MOST appropriate to charge Wagner with

22._____

A. grand larceny and criminal mischief
B. robbery
C. grand larceny *only*
D. petit larceny

Questions 23-25.

DIRECTIONS: Answer Questions 23 through 25 based on the following fact pattern and the applicable procedures.

As station house officer, you are responsible for processing several firearms that were used in a bank robbery and recovered at the scene of the crime which is within your precinct.

23. These firearms came into the possession of an officer at the scene.
Which of the following statements ACCURATELY reflects processing procedures?

23._____

A. Each weapon should be marked for identification with the officer's initials.
B. The weapons should be bundled and then marked with a security lead seal.
C. Only weapons with indistinguishable serial numbers need be marked for identification.
D. A security lead seal should be affixed to every weapon.

24. You are required to list cumulatively all the firearms invoiced at command on a(n)

24._____

A. intelligence report
B. weapons processing report
C. unusual occurrence report
D. letter of transmittal - evidence

25. In which one of the following situations should a request for laboratory examination of ammunition and weapons coming into police custody be prepared?

25._____

A. Following the arrest and arraignment of perpetrators
B. As part of the standard processing procedure for all firearms coming into the possession of the department
C. If the weapons and ammunition were in the possession of the arrested persons
D. Only at the written request of the commanding officer of the ballistics unit

# TEST 3

DIRECTIONS: Each question or incomplete statement is followed by several suggested answers or completions. Select the one that BEST answers the question or completes the statement. *PRINT THE LETTER OF THE CORRECT ANSWER IN THE SPACE AT THE RIGHT.*

Questions 1-3.

DIRECTIONS: Answer Questions 1 through 3 based on the following fact pattern and applicable procedures.

As a station house supervisor, you are reviewing the following report: At 2025 hours, Patrol Officers Clifford and Wicks responded to a three-car collision at 21st Avenue and Midtown Expressway (located in your precinct). Preliminary investigation indicated that a 2005 Volkswagen, driven by a Horace Barker, M/W/74, entered the off-ramp going in the wrong direction. The off-ramp connects the Midtown Expressway to 21st Avenue. Mrs. Felicia Hines, F/W/26, was exiting said expressway when hit broadside by Mr. Barker. The third auto, driven by William Evans, M/W/38, was traveling parallel to the Hines auto and was struck head-on. Mr. Barker and Mrs. Hines appeared to be uninjured, but Mr. Evans sustained serious injury and is likely to die.

1. In addition to the patrol supervisor, who should Officers Clifford and Wicks request to respond to the scene?

   A. Emergency service
   B. Highway patrol
   C. District attorney
   D. Borough commander

   1.___

2. As station house supervisor, you should

   A. prepare complaint reports on all persons involved in the accident
   B. forward any complaint reports to the traffic division
   C. prepare a complaint report regarding Mr. Evans *only*
   D. prepare separate complaint reports on Mr. Barker and Mrs. Hines

   2.___

3. Assume that it was later discovered Mrs. Hines had indeed suffered a serious injury as a result of this accident and may die.
   Upon reception of this information, you should

   A. prepare a complaint report for Mrs. Hines
   B. revise all existing complaint reports regarding this occurrence to include the new information
   C. telephone the traffic division
   D. notify the central records division

   3.___

4. Kevin, a 19-year-old male, has sexual intercourse with a 16-year-old female, who consents to the act.
   Kevin should be charged with

   A. rape and endangering the welfare of a minor
   B. no crime since the female consented to the act
   C. sexual misconduct and unlawfully dealing with a child
   D. sexual misconduct *only*

   4.___

Questions 5-6.

DIRECTIONS: Answer Questions 5 and 6 based on the penal law and the following fact pattern.

As a desk officer, you have been asked to advise a police officer concerning the following situation: George and Janet Miller, the parents of a 6-year-old boy, Derek, have just been legally separated. Janet has been given legal custody of Derek, and both are living in the city. Upset over the court decision to give Janet legal custody of Derek, George took Derek from his home without Janet's consent. He did so with the intent to have Derek live with him in a different part of the city.

5. Based on the above information, George should be charged with

   A. custodial interference, misdemeanor
   B. custodial interference, felony
   C. kidnapping, felony
   D. unlawful imprisonment, felony

6. Assuming that Derek is sixteen years old and George removed him from Janet's custody by physical force, George should then be charged with

   A. kidnapping, felony
   B. unlawful imprisonment, misdemeanor
   C. custodial interference, felony
   D. custodial interference, misdemeanor

Questions 7-9.

DIRECTIONS: Questions 7 through 9 pertain to the following fact pattern. Answer the questions based on applicable procedures.

Based on a description supplied by the victim of a robbery, Bob Viola is arrested by Officer Kominsky a few minutes after the crime's occurrence. Officer Kominsky brings Viola to the station house. Meanwhile, another suspect is apprehended by Officer Poole. This person confesses to the crime and is identified by the victim as the perpetrator. Officer Kominsky is informed of this and has reasonable cause to believe that Viola, in fact, did not commit the robbery. He informs the station house officer of the above facts.

7. The PROPER course of action for the station house officer is to

   A. release Viola and void the arrest
   B. confer with the district attorney
   C. have Viola taken to the central booking facility
   D. process the arrest as usual and recommend dismissal at arraignment

8. Assume that Lieutenant Vindor had responded to the scene prior to the removal of Viola to the station house and has been informed that Officer Poole's prisoner had committed the crime.
The PROPER course of action for Lieutenant Vindor is to

   A. bring Viola to the station house for further investigation
   B. proceed directly to the central booking facility with Viola for release
   C. immediately release Viola
   D. have Officer Kominsky take Viola to the station house for identification and preparation for stop and frisk

9. Assume that Officer Kominsky was not aware of Officer Poole's apprehension of the alleged perpetrator. The following day, an assistant district attorney *343's* the charges against Viola (i.e., no complaint ordered).
Which of the following is NOT part of the procedure that should be followed under these circumstances?
   I. Officer Kominsky should obtain a copy of Court Form 343 from the assistant district attorney.
   II. Officer Kominsky should inform his commanding officer immediately after the release of Viola has been secured.
   III. Officer Kominsky should prepare an arrest disposition report after the release of Viola has been secured.
   IV. Court Form 343 and the file copy of the arrest report will be filed together.
The CORRECT answer is:

A. I, II      B. II, III      C. III, IV      D. I, IV

10. Greg Anderson, a resident of the city, informs Lieutenant Billdock that he plans to purchase a shotgun in Nassau County and store it at his home in Bronx County.
Lieutenant Billdock should advise Anderson that the law states he may

   A. not bring the weapon into the city because he does not have a permit and certificate of registration
   B. bring the weapon into the city but must surrender the weapon at his resident precinct and apply for a permit and certificate of registration within 48 hours after the purchase
   C. not bring the weapon into the city because he has not yet applied for a permit and certificate of registration
   D. bring the weapon into the city, but must surrender the weapon at his resident precinct and apply for a permit within 48 hours after bringing the weapon into the city

11. Assume that Greg Anderson, a resident of the city, has been issued a valid permit and certificate of registration for a shotgun. He is observed on a city street carrying the weapon, which is unloaded, in a transparent carrying case.
Is Anderson in compliance with the administrative code?

   A. *No,* since the weapon is not enclosed in a non-transparent carrying case
   B. *Yes,* since the weapon is enclosed in a carrying case
   C. *No,* since the weapon may not be carried on a public street
   D. *Yes,* since the weapon is unloaded

12. A desk officer has been asked by a police officer for advice pertaining to the distribution and handing out of commercial leaflets in the city.
The desk officer should state that

   A. such conduct would violate Section 755 (2) - 7.0 (5) of the Administrative Code of the city (Littering prohibited), and a summons should be served for violation of this section
   B. such conduct would violate Section 153.17 of the Health Code of the city (Handbills, cards, and circulars), and a summons should be served for violation of this section
   C. no police action is warranted
   D. the leaflets should be seized, and a summons issued for violation of Section 755 (2) - 7.0 (5) of the Administrative Code of the city (Littering prohibited)

13. Harrison shares an apartment with his wife, with whom he has just had an argument. The wife calls the police and informs them that her husband has a gun secreted in a cabinet to which she and her husband have mutual access. She admits the officers into the apartment and tells them the location of the cabinet. Mr. Harrison tells the officers that they have no right to search the cabinet, and he orders the officers to leave.
Under these circumstances, the police officers should

   A. immediately leave the apartment without searching the cabinet since they do not have the consent of the husband
   B. remain in the apartment and look in the cabinet since they have the consent of the wife
   C. discuss the matter with the husband and try to convince him to change his mind
   D. demand that the husband sign a form consenting to the search of the apartment

14. Lieutenant Dillon, a desk officer assigned to a patrol precinct, obtained the following reliable information from an undercover police officer: This officer saw James Jones, for whom an arrest warrant has been issued by a Justice of the State Supreme Court for the crime of grand larceny in the first degree, enter the house of his friend, Hickock. The undercover police officer further stated that he overheard Jones tell Hickock that he would be staying for a few days.
Under these circumstances, Lieutenant Dillon should

   A. direct the undercover officer to immediately enter the house to make an arrest of Jones
   B. direct uniformed officers to the scene but they are not to enter the house until the arrival of emergency service personnel
   C. direct plainclothes officers to the scene to enter the house and make an arrest of Jones
   D. ensure that the house is kept under surveillance until a search warrant is obtained

Questions 15-17.

DIRECTIONS: Answer Questions 15 through 17 based on the following fact pattern and applicable procedures.

Lieutenant Sepanski, while on meal period, walks by a construction site and notices a worker fall from a scaffolding. The worker gets up from the ground, staggers, and falls again to the ground. He appears to be seriously injured. When Lieutenant Sepanski asks him if he can help, the man repeatedly says, *I have to get back to work. I don't need any doctor.*

15. Lieutenant Sepanski should FIRST attempt to

   A. ascertain the identity of this apparently injured person
   B. call for an on-duty officer
   C. render aid to this person
   D. administer CPR to this person

16. The written record of this occurrence that would be APPROPRIATE in this case is a(n)

    A. unusual occurrence report
    B. construction site incident report
    C. aided and accident index entry *only*
    D. aided report

17. If the man is removed from the scene for medical attention by his friends, the APPROPRIATE notation to be made under the *Removed To* caption on the written record of this incident is

    A. *RMA*
    B. the name of the hospital
    C. the name of the ambulance attendant
    D. the name of the responding physician

18. Mr. Martin was arrested and his automobile was vouchered for safekeeping. During the course of the inventory of the vehicle, the arresting officer, Officer Kelly, found an unlocked gun case on the back seat.
    Under the circumstances, Officer Kelly would

    A. not be permitted to open the gun case without a search warrant
    B. be permitted to open the gun case without a search warrant because the gun case is in plain view
    C. not be permitted to open the gun case because it is a closed container
    D. be permitted to open the gun case because its contents may be inferred from its outward appearance

19. In which of the following cases should *command discipline* procedures be followed?
    The member concerned
    
    I. is subject to judicial punishment for this violation
    II. is on probation (due to previous proceedings before a trial commissioner)
    III. has been admonished or warned in writing by the commanding officer for this violation
    IV. requests a department trial
    
    The CORRECT answer is:

    A. I, II        B. II, III        C. III, IV        D. I, IV

20. If a violation was NOT specifically listed under Schedule *A* or *B*, but approved for handling under command discipline, under which schedule would it then fall?
    Schedule
    
    I. *A*
    II. *B*
    III. *C*
    
    The CORRECT answer is:

    A. I, II        B. II, III        C. I, III        D. I, II, III

## KEY (CORRECT ANSWERS)

| | | | | |
|---|---|---|---|---|
| 1. | B | | 11. | A |
| 2. | C | | 12. | C |
| 3. | A | | 13. | B |
| 4. | B | | 14. | D |
| 5. | A | | 15. | C |
| 6. | B | | 16. | D |
| 7. | A | | 17. | A |
| 8. | C | | 18. | D |
| 9. | B | | 19. | B |
| 10. | D | | 20. | B |

---

# EXAMINATION SECTION
# TEST 1

DIRECTIONS: Each question or incomplete statement is followed by several suggested answers or completions. Select the one that BEST answers the question or completes the statement. *PRINT THE LETTER OF THE CORRECT ANSWER IN THE SPACE AT THE RIGHT.*

Questions 1-5.

DIRECTIONS: Questions 1 through 5 contain a negative expression in that they call for consideration of an attribute such as *LEAST* likely. To emphasize this format, the word *LEAST* has been capitalized.

1. A police supervisor, responsible for training subordinates, should be aware of the usefulness of different teaching techniques. One of these is the group discussion technique. Which one of the following uses of the group discussion is LEAST likely to be appropriate?
To

    A. encourage problem solving on the part of students
    B. determine the extent of learning which has taken place
    C. bring together information from many different sources
    D. provide balance and vitality to the presentation of the subject
    E. adjust the pace of the instruction to the needs of individual students

1.____

2. A certain school child is found to be highly prejudiced.
Which one of the following is LEAST likely to be a belief held by the mother of this child?

    A. I prefer a quiet child to one who is noisy.
    B. There is more than one correct way of doing most things.
    C. Obedience is the most important thing a child can learn.
    D. A child should never be permitted to set his will against that of his parents.
    E. One should avoid doing things in public which seem wrong to others, even though one knows that these things are really all right.

2.____

3. In general, it is possible to say that persons who are highly prejudiced exhibit certain characteristics, while the less prejudiced exhibit certain other characteristics. Which one of the following is LEAST likely to be a characteristic of the highly prejudiced individual, as compared to the less prejudiced individual?
The highly prejudiced individual tends to

    A. be older
    B. earn a lower income
    C. have less formal education
    D. take a greater interest in civic affairs
    E. be a person involved in an unskilled occupation

3.____

4. The conduct of a police officer has an extremely important effect on community relations. 4.___
Which one of the following general rules of conduct for a police officer is LEAST likely
to improve community relations?
To

   A. require that the dress and appearance of the police officer is always in full accordance with regulations
   B. require courtesy towards all persons in the community, including suspects you may be questioning
   C. ignore verbal abuse directed at you, even though those around you will see someone get away with its use
   D. consciously resist accepting the word of those on your beat with whom you are friendly over those you do not know
   E. allow the use of profanity by officers when they deal with people who use profanity as an accepted way of communication

5. In many cases in which a citizen is offended by minor police misconduct, all the citizen 5.___
may desire is an apology or other informal resolution of the complaint. This procedure
saves the time and expense of a full investigation.
Which one of the following conditions is LEAST likely to result from this procedure?
It

   A. may be used by police supervisors to cover up more serious infractions
   B. minimizes the danger of creating unnecessary friction between the citizen involved and the police
   C. may result in police personnel misinterpreting departmental policy regarding what is justifiable conduct
   D. increases the need for field spot checks of police misconduct cases conducted by personnel from the division responsible for coordinating these investigations
   E. eliminates the need for preparing a written report for forwarding to the division responsible for coordinating department efforts in the area of police misconduct

Questions 6-15.

DIRECTIONS: Questions 6 through 15 contain a negative expression in that they call for consideration of such attributes as *LEAST* likely or most serious *ERROR*, etc. To emphasize this format, the words *LEAST* and *ERROR* have been capitalized.

6. A team of police officers is stopped by a resident who complains that he smells escaping 6.___
gas. The officers enter a small apartment house and do detect a heavy odor of the type
added to natural gas. The officers notify the gas company and call for police assistance.
Which one of the following additional steps taken by the officers is MOST likely to be in
ERROR?
The officers

   A. quickly open all windows and doors
   B. order all open fires or flames extinguished
   C. order all electric lights and appliances turned off
   D. evacuate all persons in the building and in neighboring buildings
   E. attempt to locate the source of the gas leak and determine the extent of it

7. A patrol team is directed to assist a city marshal in executing an eviction warrant. The officers examine the marshal's credentials and the eviction warrant and record the marshal's name and rank. They enter the premises with both the marshal and a representative of the landlord and remain with them until the entire eviction process is completed. The tenant does not arrive home during the eviction. The officers record the time of entry into the premises, names of drivers of the moving van the marshal has hired, and the address of the warehouse where the tenant's belongings will be taken.
Which one of the following, if any, is an ERROR committed by the officers in handling this eviction warrant assignment?

   A. Remaining on the scene throughout the entire eviction process
   B. Allowing the marshal to be responsible for the tenant's property
   C. Allowing the eviction to occur without the presence of the tenant
   D. Permitting anyone other than the landlord himself to direct the eviction
   E. None of the above is an error

8. Four officers in a patrol car are sent to set up a roadblock to halt a getaway car in an armed robbery. They select a portion of the road narrowed by a drain. They park the patrol car at an angle in the roadway, facing the direction from which the suspects are expected to come. The driver of the patrol car positions himself behind the engine block of the car. The other three officers position themselves behind cover a short distance ahead of the roadblock car. Two officers take the side of the road away from the officer behind the car and one officer takes the other side of the road.
Which one of the following, if any, is the most serious ERROR committed in setting up the roadblock?

   A. Positioning officers on opposite sides of the road
   B. Placing the car at an angle facing the oncoming traffic
   C. Setting up the roadblock at a narrow section of the roadway
   D. Positioning the three officers ahead of the roadblock car
   E. None of the above is an error in setting up the roadblock

9. In a certain precinct, tension between police and citizens is very high, and the potential for an outbreak of violence is also high. An angry crowd has begun to gather at the scene of an arrest.
Which one of the following is the LEAST appropriate command decision for a superior officer to make in this situation?
To

   A. order responding units not to use sirens and lights when traveling to the area
   B. respond immediately to the scene and give visible evidence that he is taking charge of the situation
   C. order police officers, with no extraordinary equipment, to the perimeter of the affected area
   D. order police officers, equipped with riot guns and helmets, into the center of the affected area
   E. remove all authority for independent action from the officers sent to the scene and to place it in the hands of a single superior officer

10. Which one of the following is the LEAST important consideration when deciding whether or not to *pat down* a suspect whom you have sufficient cause to detain?
The

    A. advanced age of the suspect
    B. emotional state of the suspect
    C. absence of presence of an assisting officer
    D. seriousness of the suspected criminal activity
    E. time of day and location where the *pat down* is to be conducted

11. A team of police officers is conducting a plainclothes foot surveillance of a suspect. Which one of the following actions would most likely be a MISTAKE on the part of the officer nearest to the suspect?

    A. Picking up a piece of paper discarded by the suspect
    B. Using a phone booth next to the one which the suspect is using
    C. Failing to use a disguise which alters completely the appearance of the officer
    D. Continuing to walk past the suspect, when he finds the suspect has stopped after turning a corner
    E. Waiting outside of a small shop which the suspect has entered, instead of entering and making a purchase

12. Only four patrol cars have been assigned to respond to a store robbery. A masked holdup man has fled on foot, heading south down the street in front of the store. Which one of the following actions, if taken by the responding units, would most likely be considered an ERROR?

    A. All four units first responded to the crime scene.
    B. One of the responding units stopped about two blocks from the scene and the two officers proceeded to the scene on foot.
    C. One of the responding units upon arriving at the scene took time to observe the onlookers to see if any fit the description of the robber.
    D. Three of the four units purposely did not respond directly to the scene, but approached the scene in a zigzag pattern from different directions.
    E. One of the units, before receiving a description of the robber, stopped and questioned a man who was hurriedly entering a car about two blocks from the scene.

13. Which one of the following is LEAST likely to be a symptom of amphetamine abuse?

    A. Anxiety             B. Euphoria
    C. Irritability        D. Slurred speech
    E. Hyperactive reflexes

14. Which one of the following is the LEAST appropriate justification for giving police patrol officers automobiles for the purpose of covering their assigned beats?
To

    A. provide protection against bad weather
    B. eliminate the need for patrol officers to cover their beats on foot
    C. provide assistance in the capturing of fleeing criminals
    D. allow them to respond to the scene of a call for service with greater speed
    E. help eliminate the fatigue from walking by providing occasional periods spent in driving from one location to another

15. In organizing a police department, the principle of specialization, that is, the assignment of particular tasks to special units or individuals, is often possible. Although specialization has advantages, it also has disadvantages.
Which one of the following is the most serious DISADVANTAGE of specialization?
Specialization may

    A. produce persons who have a narrowed field of interest and attention
    B. arouse an organized public interest in the area of specialized activity
    C. result in giving a few persons more intensive training than would be possible for the entire force
    D. create unjustified emphasis on special fields of police work and hamper the development of well-rounded police programs
    E. cause the specialized personnel to develop a proprietary interest in those departmental operations relating to their specialty

15._____

## KEY (CORRECT ANSWERS)

| | | | |
|---|---|---|---|
| 1. | E | 6. | C |
| 2. | B | 7. | E |
| 3. | D | 8. | A |
| 4. | E | 9. | D |
| 5. | E | 10. | A |

11. A
12. A
13. D
14. B
15. D

# TEST 2

DIRECTIONS: Each question or incomplete statement is followed by several suggested answers or completions. Select the one that BEST answers the question or completes the statement. *PRINT THE LETTER OF THE CORRECT ANSWER IN THE SPACE AT THE RIGHT.*

1. Much has been written about the causes of riots and civil unrest. Which one of the following widely held views as to the causes of rioting has actually been found to be ERRONEOUS?
   There is

   A. personal friction among members of the involved community, based on social differences
   B. an increase in the consumption of alcoholic beverages by prominent participants in riots
   C. a high degree of frustration in finding solutions to problems among prominent participants in riots
   D. a breakdown of respect for the police and the government in general, among prominent participants in riots
   E. a pathological syndrome in many of the prominent participants in riots in that they act without real underlying causes

1.___

2. Following are three general statements on group behavior which the overwhelming weight of evidence might possibly show to be true:
   I. Most judges and social workers are too lenient with juvenile offenders
   II. Generally speaking, people fall into two categories: good or bad
   III. Most men have destructive impulses which must be controlled by society
   
   Which one of the following choices lists ALL of the above generalities which have been shown to be true and NONE which have not, according to POLICE AND THE CHANGING COMMUNITY?

   A. I
   B. I and III
   C. I, II, and III
   D. none
   E. III

2.___

3. We hear quite a good deal today about community relations, human relations, public relations, etc. While many of these concepts are similar, there are recognized differences in direction and emphasis. Following is a definition of one of these concepts.
   The development of a favorable public impression of a given product (service), with a tendency to place more emphasis upon *looking good* than upon *being good*.
   Which one of the following labels is MOST often used to convey the above concept?
   _____ relations.

   A. Human          B. Public          C. Community
   D. Civil rights   E. Minority group

3.___

4. Prejudiced persons are often characterized by what psychiatrists call a weak self-image. They are fearful of their own impulses, they are insecure, become rigid minded in an attempt to get stability. It then becomes difficult for then to adapt and adjust to the forces of change.
This statement was made during a discussion on police professionalism in relationship to police-community relations.
Which one of the following ideas is it MOST significant for a police commander to understand from the above statement when he analyzes his community relations program?

    A. The importance of the attitude of the minority group members toward themselves
    B. The importance of the attitude of the individual police officer toward himself
    C. A recognition that police officers are actually more prejudiced than majority group members
    D. The importance of the attitude of the individual police officers toward minority group members
    E. A recognition that minority group members are actually more prejudiced than majority group members

5. A certain police commander has to select a man to head up the new community relations unit. A high degree of leadership ability is necessary in this position because a major part of the program involves reorienting the attitudes of men in the department as well as establishing communications between the minority community and the department.
He has narrowed his choice to the following three patrolmen, all of whom are of the same race. A description of the outstanding characteristics of each follows. Other than for the characteristics described, all three are equal.
    I. Patrolman W has considerable physical vitality and has always worked hard and been industrious. In addition, he has a high tolerance for frustration. He has no significant experience in community relations or in supervision.
    II. Patrolman S is young and tremendously ambitious to create a name for himself. He would literally do anything to make a success of any of his programs. He has had some slight supervisory experience but no community relations experience.
    III. Patrolman P has technical mastery of his job, so that he can give orders forcefully. He is reserved and avoids making personal contacts with his associates. He has had no experience in community relations or supervision.
Which one of the following choices BEST evaluates these three candidates for the leadership position of community relations officer, based on the facts given above?

    A. W is clearly better qualified than the others, with P second choice and S third choice
    B. P is clearly better qualified than the others, with W second choice and S third choice
    C. W and P are probably equally, but differently qualified and S is the third choice
    D. Although each offers different strengths, all three are equally well qualified for the position
    E. S is the best qualified and W or P, although different, are equally acceptable as the second choice

6. A former police inspector has clearly stated a police policy which he feels is the first requisite for good police-community relations.
Which one of the following should a police commander recognize as being the policy TRULY at the heart of a police-community relations program?
An enforced

   A. operational policy of equal treatment for all members of the community
   B. operational policy of equal enforcement of all laws imposed on the community
   C. organizational policy of establishing the staff function of community relations at the precinct level
   D. operational policy of matching whenever possible the ethnic background of police officers to the communities where they are assigned to patrol
   E. personnel policy of equal job opportunities and promotional opportunities for all religious, racial, language, and other groups within the community and the department

7. A police commander should be aware of the nature of the various organizations that represent or purport to represent minority groups in large cities. The following is a brief description of one such organization:
It is something more than a religious organization concerned with reforming the existing social order. At a minimum, they want a separate order in an autonomous society; and ideally, they anticipate a reversal of the existing caste arrangements in the existing order in this society.
Which one of the following is MOST likely to be the organization described above?

   A. CORE
   B. The NAACP
   C. The Black Muslims
   D. The Black Panthers
   E. The John Birch Society

8. A very important dilemma in law enforcement has been stated as follows: Some persons feel strongly that crime among minority groups ought to be stamped out, even at a high cost in the violation of civil liberties; others feel that civil liberties ought to be safeguarded, even at a high cost in crime.
Which one of the following BEST states who, in the long run, must be given final responsibility for solving this dilemma?

   A. The courts
   B. The individual beat patrolman
   C. Police commanders, at precinct and higher levels
   D. The community itself, through its legislature
   E. The leadership of those organizations that truly represent the minorities

9. Following are four statements concerning the assignment of police personnel to speak before community groups that might possibly be appropriate as guidelines for a police commander:
   I. A police department should resist use of its members as speakers and provide them only when it is absolutely necessary
   II. When a speaker is approved, the topic or subject of the speech should be dictated by the interests and wishes of the group requesting the speaker

III. In large departments, a public contact bureau or similar unit should be developed to match up speakers and groups
IV. All members of a police department should be prohibited from making any speeches without the express approval of the department

Which one of the following choices lists ALL of the above statements that are appropriate and NONE that is not?

A. II and III are appropriate, but I and IV are not.
B. I is appropriate, but II, III, and IV are not.
C. I and IV are appropriate, but II and III are not.
D. III is appropriate, but I, II, and IV are not.
E. II and IV are appropriate, but I and III are not.

10. A certain student of law enforcement has made the following comment: It does not take great reflection to understand that by permitting the police to use criminal tactics, we could not decrease the problem of crime - we increase it. No segment of the population, not the law enforcers, not even police commanders, can be permitted to flout the law. This statement was made as a rebuttal to a complaint frequently made by police commanders. Which one of the following is MOST likely this complaint?

A. Local courts are unable to make appropriate decisions in light of recent Supreme Court decisions.
B. The Supreme Court has greatly restricted the types of enforcement practices that the police can employ.
C. The increased professionalism and knowledge level of the habitual criminal makes many police efforts ineffective.
D. Police conditions encourage individual patrolmen to become corrupt and protect vice activities at the local beat level.
E. It is difficult to determine when the police have the right to arrest, for breach of the peace, during civil rights and other demonstrations.

11. A police commander is judged by many standards, such as the crime rate in his area, his arrest and clearance rates, and, to a lesser extent, his conviction rate. Many feel that the crime of aggravated assault should produce a high rate of arrest and conviction. Yet this is not the case, especially in the ghetto areas of large cities. Even when large numbers of these cases are reported to the police, in many instances no arrest is made or, if one is made, no prosecution is attempted. Which one of the following is the MOST serious problem police commanders experience in regard to the successful processing of a reported aggravated assault?
The

A. unwillingness of the courts to accept hearsay testimony
B. fact that no police officers have actually observed the crime
C. fact that the victim is often unwilling to cooperate with the police
D. rigid restrictions placed by the courts on the use of confessions
E. fact that the perpetrator of the crime is seldom known to the victim

12. There is much concern about the types of crimes committed by juvenile gang members. Which one of the following BEST states the types of crimes committed most frequently by juveniles and which very often accounts for up to 25% of all juvenile gang crimes?

A. Assaults
B. Drug use
C. Vandalism
D. Auto theft
E. Thefts (excluding auto theft)

13. Which one of the following is the MOST common direct cause of death due to narcotics overdosage, as opposed to deaths caused indirectly by narcotics usage?

    A. Hepatitis
    B. Heart damage
    C. Brain abcesses
    D. Blood poisoning
    E. Respiratory depression

14. The recent upsurge in juvenile delinquency problems has prompted efforts to find methods of predicting who will become delinquent.
    Which one of the following is the MOST important benefit that can be derived from the ability to make this prediction?
    Ability to

    A. recognize the family structures that create the highest incidence of delinquency
    B. analyze different environmental factors as they relate to juvenile crime and delinquency
    C. recognize potential juvenile delinquents before they commit delinquent acts, in order to take them out of their environment and place them in special schools
    D. deploy police enforcement efforts in those areas where juvenile crime is most likely to be committed
    E. concentrate programs designed to prevent delinquency toward those persons most seriously in need of such efforts

15. A certain police department is contemplating using evidence technicians, according to the procedures recommended by O.W. Wilson in his book, POLICE ADMINISTRATION. Following are three statements that might possibly be in accordance with Wilson's recommendations:
    The evidence technician shall be
    I. assigned directly to the patrol function and receive his direct supervision from patrol supervisors
    II. responsible only for the collection and preservation of physical evidence. The task of searching crime scenes should remain the responsibility of the investigating detective or beat patrolman
    III. responsible for performing work at both crime scenes and accident scenes.
    Which one of the following choices lists all of the above statements that are RECOMMENDED by Wilson and none that is NOT?

    A. I is recommended by Wilson, but II and III are not.
    B. I and II are recommended by Wilson, but III is not.
    C. I and III are recommended by Wilson, but II is not.
    D. I, II, and III all are recommended by Wilson.
    E. III is recommended by Wilson, but I and II are not.

16. Crime clearance is an important problem confronting police.  16.____
Following are three statements concerning the solution of crimes which may possibly be accurate:
    I. A single latent fingerprint is almost useless when there are no suspects to the crime
    II. The percentage of crimes which are cleared without a suspect being named by a witness usually is significantly below 20%
    III. If a suspect is not in custody within two hours after a crime has been committed, the chances of clearance decrease

Which one of the following choices lists all of the above statements that are ACCURATE and none that is NOT?

   A. I and II are accurate statements, but III is not.
   B. I and III are accurate statements, but II is not.
   C. I, II, and III all are accurate statements.
   D. II and III are accurate statements, but I is not.
   E. III is an accurate statement, but I and II are not.

17. Police commanders in large jurisdictions have had serious problems with juvenile gangs. POLICE WORK WITH JUVENILES reports on a study of juvenile gangs which appears to be appropriate for most large city gangs. This study has exploded some popular beliefs about gang leadership. Which one of the following beliefs on gang leadership is MOST likely to have been exploded?  17.____
Gang leadership

   A. usually falls to members of the gang who are noted for their *cool* behavioral style
   B. tends to fluctuate among various persons depending upon the gang activities in question
   C. usually falls to members of the gang who are able to bring benefits to the group
   D. tends to fall to those individuals with psychopathic tendencies (emotionally disturbed) owing to their aggressive behavioral patterns
   E. is usually stratified by age groups and younger members are influenced more by their peers than by the admired leaders of the oldest age group

18. A certain police commander, confronted with a high incidence of commercial breakings and enterings, instituted a program of *door shaking*. He determined that there were 7,098 store doors which, under his policy, were to be checked twice each night. A year later, his records disclosed that in the first year of the program, patrolmen found only 970 store doors unlocked. In other words, if police patrolled in accordance with policy, there should have been about 5,200,000 door shakes that year or one open premise for about every 12,000 *shakes*.  18.____
Based on this information, which one of the following is the MOST appropriate decision for a commander to make?
To

   A. continue the *door shaking* policy as it is presently constituted without any change
   B. discontinue the *door shaking* policy entirely and distribute all of these man-hours to routine patrol
   C. request additional manpower from his superior, so as to be able to maintain the *door shaking* procedure

D. modify his *door shaking* policy so as not to include all business places, but only a certain, much smaller percentage selected through analysis
E. continue the *door shaking* policy and to instruct his field supervisors to follow behind the man shaking doors in order to ascertain whether they are actually finding all the unsecure doors which exist

19. Following are three statements on the serious juvenile delinquency crime problem that might possibly be accurate:
    I.  There is a greater proportion of unreported delinquency and juvenile crime in middle-class areas as compared to lower socioeconomic areas
    II. There is a real and meaningful difference in the amount and type of juvenile crime committed in lower socioeconomic areas as compared to middle-class areas
    III. When factors of religion, nationality, and race are held constant and the factor *where one is growing up* is the only variable, then delinquency rates are constant

    Which one of the following choices lists all of the above statements that are ACCURATE and none that is NOT?

    A. I and II are accurate statements, but III is not.
    B. I and III are accurate statements, but II is not.
    C. I, II, and III all are accurate statements.
    D. None of I, II, and III is an accurate statement.
    E. II is an accurate statement, but I and III are not.

20. A sentiment often heard in law enforcement lately is:
    Based on arrest statistics, which admittedly is only a rough measure, youth (juveniles) are apparently responsible for a substantial and disproportionate part of the national crime problem.
    Which one of the following is the MOST accurate evaluation of this statement?

    A. It is most probably incorrect, since juveniles are more easily arrested than adults.
    B. It is most probably true and grossly understated, because a large percentage of juvenile arrests is not recorded.
    C. It is most probably incorrect, because juveniles usually operate in groups, thus producing large numbers of juvenile arrests.
    D. It is most probably incorrect, because the definition of a juvenile, in terms of age, is much more restricted than the definition of an adult.
    E. While probably slightly exaggerated, it is most probably true because persons between the ages of 15 and 20 are involved in a disproportionate number of crimes.

## KEY (CORRECT ANSWERS)

| | | | |
|---|---|---|---|
| 1. | E | 11. | C |
| 2. | D | 12. | E |
| 3. | B | 13. | E |
| 4. | B | 14. | E |
| 5. | A | 15. | C |
| 6. | A | 16. | C |
| 7. | C | 17. | D |
| 8. | D | 18. | D |
| 9. | A | 19. | A |
| 10. | B | 20. | E |

# EXAMINATION SECTION
## TEST 1

DIRECTIONS: Each question or incomplete statement is followed by several suggested answers or completions. Select the one that BEST answers the question or completes the statement. *PRINT THE LETTER OF THE CORRECT ANSWER IN THE SPACE AT THE RIGHT.*

Questions 1-5.

DIRECTIONS: The following selection is to be used as the SOLE basis for answering Questions 1 through 5. Read the selection carefully and base your answers ONLY on the information contained therein.

*As an example of the importance of social psychological concepts to law enforcement, let us consider stereotypes. Police officers must deal with stereotypes in a number of kinds of situations. First, they are themselves the victims of a vicious kind of stereotyping which runs the range from "idiot" to "sadist."*

*Secondly, they themselves have stereotypes of others in their minds, as a result of their backgrounds and socialization; these they must examine in the light of reason and experience, or they may be led into expressions of prejudice to the permanent destruction of their proper role in the community.*

*Finally, they need to do all that is possible to prevent the stereotyping of minority groups by others, and the stereotyping of others by minority groups - for here lie the seeds of civil disturbances, as stereotyping feeds prejudice, and prejudice creates tension.*

*The difficulty in trying to change such stereotypes is that there often seems to be a "kernel of truth" in most of them when they are drawn out of people who have first-hand knowledge of the group being stereotyped. It is this surface validity which cries out for more thorough assessment, otherwise a permanent prejudice may be created for the lack of true facts and the failure to appreciate the reason behind the attitude that was born in ignorance.*

*People who cherish stereotypes can be changed and they can be influenced to discard them. There are many social reinforcements that can be used to defeat the unwholesome stereotypes (and the behaviors they generate) that are omens of trouble.*

*Techniques for the control of human behavior have been developed by psychologists who have probed deeply into the science of behavior modification. Conditioning, modeling procedures, and insights into the learning process all offer meaningful measures to invoke the power of scientific knowledge toward human behavior modification.*

*For example, Watson has developed an approach called the process of reconditioning. Working with a small child in his crib, he conditioned the fear of anything furry by making a loud noise whenever he put a furry object in the crib with the child.*

*Then he reversed this by reconditioning the child to accept the furry object. Slowly, by placing the object across the room until the child could exist without fear of it, Watson would move the two closer together. Now, if the child is taken to represent a prejudiced person and the furry object, the "object" of his prejudice, one can easily see how this technique could be applied in a wide variety of situations, and with people of all age levels.*

*The effectiveness of behavior modification, involving manipulation, influence, and control of the environment, is such that the police should be concerned - if only from a negative standpoint. What is this new power that has been created by man, how might we use it and how do we prevent its abuse? These are questions to which law enforcement personnel might well address themselves.*

*Interpersonal contact between persons and groups helps to develop mutual attitudes of understanding. Whether favorable or unfavorable stereotypes will develop depends upon the perceptions of the participants and the testing of these perceptions against reality, but it has been demonstrated through scientific research that the proper degree of contact with many different races, nationalities, and cultures helps to break down the barriers of unwholesome stereotypes and prejudices.*

*Discussion groups with police and citizens from a variety of ethnic backgrounds have proven effective in combatting stereotypes. It is best in such groups not to talk about race, religion, politics, or other controversial topics; rather, topics of conversation should be of common interest to all participants. Crime problems, conditions in the community that encourage crime, and ways to protect against crime are topics which provide the proper environment for lively interaction, which in turn leads people toward a better understanding of their similarities and individual differences.*

1. The phrase *kernel of truth* appears in the fourth paragraph of the selection. Which one of the following phrases from that same paragraph means MOST NEARLY the same thing as *kernel of truth*?
   A. True facts
   B. Surface validity
   C. Firsthand knowledge
   D. Thorough assessment
   E. Reason behind the attitude

2. According to the conditioning principle set forth in the selection, which one of the following MOST accurately describes how stereotypes are formed?
People

A. are born uninformed, and stereotypes result from a failure to learn
B. learn to fear others when, as youths, they have contact with them
C. learn to fear others because they do not have the opportunity to get together with them
D. learn to fear others when they have contact with them under unpleasant circumstances
E. learn to fear others as a result of getting into an argument during which they are shouting at one another

3. A certain police department is conducting group discussions with Black, Hispanic, and White civilians, all participating along with several police officers. These discussions are aimed at combatting stereotypes and developing mutual understanding.
According to the selection, which one of the following topics of conversation is MOST likely to be effective in achieving this goal?
A. *Gun Registration and Control*
B. *Keeping Burglars Out of Your Home*
C. *Know Good English, Get a Good Job*
D. *What Your City Councilman Can Do For You*
E. *Contributions of Black Men in American History*

4. According to the selection, which one of the following results is MOST likely to occur if police officers show that they themselves are prejudiced?
The police
A. will be called *idiots* or *sadists*
B. will be subjected to behavior modification
C. will create tensions leading to a civil disorder
D. generally will become stereotyped by citizen groups
E. will be unable to fulfill their proper community role

5. According to the selection, which one of the following is the MOST serious obstacle encountered in trying to eliminate unwholesome stereotypes?
A. Psychologists have not yet developed techniques for changing stereotypes.
B. Stereotypes develop as a result of uncontrollable environmental influences.
C. Such stereotypes are basically accurate because they are based on first-hand knowledge.
D. Such stereotypes are generally inborn, or learned very young, and, in such cases, cannot be changed.
E. Such stereotypes have an appearance of truth which makes people less likely to examine the stereotypes closely.

Questions 6-10.

DIRECTIONS: The following selection is to be used as the SOLE basis for answering Questions 6 through 10. Read the selection carefully and base your answers ONLY on the information contained therein.

*Programs designed to reduce delinquency have been many and varied in approach. One can almost say that the pre-Lombroso era was one characterized as a total community approach.*

*Prior to the emergence of the Positive School of Criminology in 19th century Italy, criminology as a distinct scientific discipline did not exist. Crime was looked upon as one of the problems of the community, no different from the rest. Essentially, what the great doctor did was create a specialty, one which viewed the criminal among us as "different," a biologically distinct kind of human being, a "throwback" to earlier types of man.*

*From that point forward, in the history of man, wherever criminologists have gathered and organized themselves as separate from students of society in general, they have tended to study criminals as a type of group essentially different from other members in our society. Special ways of knowing tend to create special things to be known: new scientific disciplines generate new facts.*

*Lombrosoism has never completely died. It is still with us today, in a somewhat changed form, but nevertheless still there. The criminologist in the early 1900's changed the model of operation from the positivist school of thought, in which the idea of sin and willful corruption was stressed, to the individualistic or analytical school. The emphasis was shifted to single causes: physical disabilities, mental defects, etc. As one would suspect, our efforts at the art of crime prevention followed these theories. Coming full circle, we are now in the era of multiple causation, or a school that by and large places the blame for crime and delinquency back on the community.*

6. According to the selection, which one of the following choices MOST accurately describes the succession of schools of criminological thought?
   First the
   A. *analytical school* and, most recently, the positivistic school
   B. *positivistic school* and, most recently, the analytical school
   C. *analytical school*, followed by the positivistic school and, most recently, the multiple causation school
   D. *positivistic school*, followed by the individualistic school and, most recently, the multiple causation school
   E. *multiple causation school*, followed by the individualistic school, both of which superseded the positivistic school

6.____

7. Following are three statements about the history of Lombrosoism that might possibly be accurate:
   I. Lombrosoism replaced the Positive School of Criminology in the 19th century
   II. Lombrosoism served as the beginning point for criminology
   III. Some remainders of Lombrosoism still are left in modern theories of criminology

   Which one of the following choices MOST accurately classifies the above statements into those which are accurate and those which are not?
   A. I and II are accurate, but III is not.
   B. I and III are accurate, but II is not.
   C. II and III are accurate, but I is not.
   D. II is accurate, but I and III are not.
   E. All of I, II, and III are accurate.

8. Which one of the following was the MOST important belief held by the Positive School of Criminology?
   A. There is a single cause for criminal behavior.
   B. Blame for crime rests with the community.
   C. Criminology is not a distinct scientific discipline.
   D. Criminals are *throwbacks* to an earlier type of man.
   E. Crime results from a combination of causes which are present in every community.

9. The term *scientific discipline* appears near the end of the third paragraph of the selection.
   Which one of the following words or phrases from that same paragraph means MOST NEARLY the same thing as *scientific discipline*?
   A. Ways of knowing           B. Criminologists
   C. Generate new facts        D. Things to be known
   E. Students of society

10. A certain criminologist believes strongly that the theories of the analytical school of criminology are right.
    Which one of the following factors or combinations of factors is this person MOST likely to blame for crime?
    A. Heredity                 B. Sinfulness
    C. Mental illness           D. Community attitudes
    E. Unemployment and poverty

# KEY (CORRECT ANSWERS)

| 1. B | 6. D |
| 2. D | 7. C |
| 3. B | 8. D |
| 4. E | 9. A |
| 5. E | 10. C |

# TEST 2

DIRECTIONS: Each question or incomplete statement is followed by several suggested answers or completions. Select the one that BEST answers the question or completes the statement. *PRINT THE LETTER OF THE CORRECT ANSWER IN THE SPACE AT THE RIGHT.*

Questions 1-6.

DIRECTIONS: Questions 1 through 6 are to be answered on the basis of the following situation.

Lieutenant X has just been assigned as the commanding officer of a small departmental unit in which important administrative services are performed in the handling of departmental property and equipment records. Before assuming his new duties, Lieutenant X is informed by his superior officer that he has not been satisfied with the operation of this office under the previous commanding officer. Specifically, this superior officer informs the lieutenant that some, but not all, of the office personnel, consisting entirely of uniformed personnel, did not perform their work accurately enough nor did they produce the amount of work that could reasonably be expected of them. Further, the superior feels that the office routine in the handling of records was somewhat inefficient.

The first day in his new assignment, Lieutenant X calls the entire staff together for a meeting and proceeds to outline to them a completely revised office procedure which he has personally developed within the past few days and which is to be effective immediately. The lieutenant requests all staff members to give him their reactions to the revised procedure. The revised procedure is not in conflict with official departmental procedures. He also states that the office personnel will have to be more accurate in their work and not devote any of their working time to personal matters or needless conversation.

Sergeant Y, next in the line of command in the unit, hearing of the revisions in procedure for the first time at the meeting, feels that the revisions are too drastic and should be modified since, in his opinion, most of the previous inefficiency was due to the quality of work performed by some personnel in need of additional training and not to poor procedures as such. The sergeant, however, decides not to mention his views to the lieutenant since he thinks it may appear that he is trying to establish a personal defense of the previous procedures because he was involved in their operation.

Patrolman Z is disturbed by the lieutenant's statement concerning the need for greater attention to duty and speaks up vigorously at the meeting. He states that he has personally been very conscientious in the performance of his duties and implies that this may not hold true for everyone else in the office, glancing toward the *sergeant as he talks. The lieutenant, in an attempt to forestall a possible exchange of words between this patrolman and the sergeant, proceeds to take up some other matter. However, Sergeant Y feels compelled to defend himself and states that Patrolman Z is probably the individual most guilty of inattention to duty and that he spends a substantial part of the day in conversation of a personal nature with other office personnel. The lieutenant, feeling that the meeting is getting out of hand, states that this meeting is over, but that future meetings will be held regularly once every week.*

1. The action taken by Lieutenant X's superior officer in informing him of the reasons for his dissatisfaction with the operation of the records office under the previous commanding officer was
    A. *improper*; giving such information constitutes an unnecessary personal criticism of the previous commanding officer
    B. *proper*; the operation of the office is more likely to be improved by Lieutenant X if he has some specific indications of the previously prevailing conditions
    C. *improper*; the lieutenant is more likely to correct poor procedures if he is allowed to discover for himself the reason that such procedures were employed
    D. *proper*; it is an effective method of mildly disciplining the previous commanding officer

2. Lieutenant X's method of instituting the completely revised office procedure was
    A. *good*; the old procedures were not effective and had to be changed
    B. *poor*; he should have waited until he had established a friendly relationship with each of his subordinates
    C. *good*; the poor work performance of his subordinates is a clear indication that it would be a waste of time to obtain their views on the revision of procedures
    D. *poor*; the revisions are likely to be more effective and more acceptable to his subordinates if their views were considered before putting the revisions into effect

3. Lieutenant X's remarks at the meeting concerning the poor work performance of the office personnel and their devoting working time to personal matters were
    A. *appropriate*; Lieutenant X's superior officer knows definitely that some of the personnel did not perform their work in an acceptable manner
    B. *inappropriate*; these remarks serve to handicap supervisory relationships
    C. *appropriate*; staff morale is less likely to suffer if no particular individual is singled out
    D. *inappropriate*; any negative remarks concerning the work performance of the unit as a whole should be made privately to staff members

4. Sergeant Y's decision NOT to inform the lieutenant at this time of his opinion that the revisions of procedure are too drastic was
   A. *improper*; the sergeant should express his doubts concerning the revised procedure despite possible misinterpretation by the lieutenant
   B. *proper*; a sergeant must wait until a lieutenant addresses a question to him personally
   C. *improper*; the lieutenant's revisions of procedure should be reviewed and approved by all those affected before such changes are adopted
   D. *proper*; the sergeant's belief that the lieutenant does not really expect an expression of views is a realistic appraisal of the situation

5. The lieutenant's immediate action when Patrolman Z implies that the sergeant has not been very conscientious in the performance of his duties was
   A. *good*; the patrolman's statement is clearly biased and merits no further consideration
   B. *poor*; this situation provides a good opportunity for the lieutenant to determine to what extent the sergeant was responsible for the unit's poor performance
   C. *good*; an exchange of words between the officers is likely to become highly personal and tend to undermine unit discipline
   D. *poor*; the patrolman should be required to give details to support his implications of neglect of duty by the sergeant

6. Sergeant Y's answer to the charge of the patrolman was
   A. *appropriate*; an officer is justified in defending himself against unjust charges whatever their source may be
   B. *inappropriate*; the patrolman did not identify the sergeant by name as not being conscientious in the performance of his duties
   C. *appropriate*; a patrolman is never justified in criticizing the behavior of a superior in the presence of other staff members
   D. *inappropriate*; such a detailing of the patrolman's alleged misconduct should not be undertaken in the presence of other staff members

Questions 7-9.

DIRECTIONS: Questions 7 through 9 are to be answered SOLELY on the basis of the following paragraphs.

*Perhaps the most difficult administrative problem of the police records unit is the maintenance of cooperative relationships with the operating units in the department. Unless these relationships are completely accepted by the operating units, some records activities will result in friction. The records system is a tool of the chief administrative officer and the various supervising officers in managing personnel, police operations and procedures. However, the records unit must constantly check on the records activities of all members of the department if the records system is to serve as a really effective tool for these supervisory officers.*

*The first step in avoiding conflict between the records and the operating units is to develop definite policies and regulations governing the records system. These regulations should be prepared jointly by the head of the records unit and the heads of the operating units under the leadership of the chief administrative officer of the department. Once the records policies and regulations have been agreed upon, the task is to secure conformity. Theoretically, if a patrolman fails to prepare a report of an investigation, his commanding officer should be notified by the records unit and he in turn should take appropriate measures to secure the report. Practically, this line of command must be cut across in the case of such routine matters, or the commanding officer will spend time in keeping the records system going that should be devoted to the other police duties which comprise the major work of the department. However, if the patrolman is persistently negligent, or if a new policy or procedure is being initiated, the records unit must deal through the commanding officer.*

7. According to the above paragraphs, the one of the following situations in which the records unit would MOST likely contact a commanding officer of an operating unit is when
    A. a patrolman has expressed disagreement with a records unit policy and suggests a modification of the policy
    B. an important record, which involves more than one operating unit, has been carelessly prepared by a patrolman
    C. the commanding officer of the operating unit devotes little time to police duties which comprise the major work of the department
    D. the records unit has received orders from the chief administrative officer to institute several changes in previous records procedures

8. According to the above paragraphs, obtaining agreement as to definite policies and regulations governing the records system
    A. guarantees the avoidance of conflict between the records and operating divisions
    B. is of lesser importance than the maintenance of cooperative relationships thereafter
    C. should precede any active records division efforts to gain compliance with such policies and regulations
    D. should be preceded by an evaluation of the extent to which supervisory officers consider the system an effective management tool

9. According to the above paragraph, conflict between the records division and the operating divisions is MOST likely to result when the
   A. chief administrative officer denies to the records division the authority to check on the records activities of all members of the department
   B. operating divisions are not convinced that their work contacts with the records division are useful and desirable
   C. records division voluntarily attempts to establish productive relationships with operating divisions
   D. operating divisions understand the specific nature of records division duties

Questions 10-12.

DIRECTIONS: Questions 10 through 12 are to be answered SOLELY on the basis of the following paragraph.

*Early in the development of police service, legislators granted powers and authority to policemen beyond their inherent rights as citizens in order that they would be able to act effectively in the discharge of their duties. The law makers also recognized the fact that unless policemen were excused from complete obedience to certain laws and regulations they would be seriously encumbered in the effective discharge of their duties. The exemptions were specifically provided for by legislative action because of the danger of abuse of power involved in granting blanket privileges and powers. The public, however, has not been so discriminating and has gone well beyond the law in excusing policemen from full obedience to regulatory measures. The liberal interpretation that the public has placed upon the right of police officers to disobey the law has been motivated in part by public confidence in law enforcement and in part by a sincere desire of the public to assist the police in every way in the performance of their duties. Further, the average citizen is not interested in the technicalities of law enforcement nor is he aware of the legal limitations that are placed upon the authority of policemen. It is a regrettable fact that many policemen assume so-called rights of law that either do not exist or that are subject to well-defined legal limitations, because the public generally is unaware of the limitations placed by law upon policemen.*

10. According to the above paragraph, the one of the following statements which BEST explains the reason for granting special legal powers to policemen is that such powers were granted
    A. because the exercise of their inherent rights by citizens frequently conflicted with efficient law enforcement
    B. because the public has not been sufficiently vigilant in objecting to blanket grants of power
    C. in order to excuse policemen from full obedience to laws and regulations which they are unable to enforce
    D. in order to remove certain handicaps experienced by policemen in law enforcement operations

11. According to the above paragraph, specific legislative exemptions for policemen from complete obedience to certain laws and regulations
    A. are based largely on so-called rights of law that either do not exist or are misinterpreted by the public
    B. have not been abused by the police even though most individual policemen ignore proper legal limitations
    C. have not provided a fully effective limitation on the exercise of unwarranted police authority
    D. have been misunderstood by the police and the public partly because they are based on unduly technical laws

12. According to the above paragraph, the one of the following statements which BEST explains the liberal attitude of the public toward the special powers of policemen is that the public
    A. believes that the police are justified in disregarding the technicalities of law enforcement and also wants to assist the police in the performance of their duties
    B. feels that the laws restricting police authority are overly strict and also believes that the police are performing their duties in a proper manner
    C. is not aware of the legal restrictions on police authority and also believes that the police are performing their duties in a proper manner
    D. wants to assist the police in the performance of their duties and also feels that the laws on police authority are sufficiently restrictive

Questions 13-15.

DIRECTIONS: Questions 13 through 15 are to be answered SOLELY on the basis of the following paragraph.

*The use of modern scientific methods in the examination of physical evidence often provides information to the investigator which he could not otherwise obtain. This applies particularly to small objects and materials present in minute quantities or trace evidence because the quantities here are such that they may be overlooked without methodical searching, and often special means of detection are needed. Whenever two objects come in contact with one another, there is a transfer of material, however slight. Usually, the softer object will transfer to the harder, but the transfer may be mutual. The quantity of material transferred differs with the type of material involved and the more violent the contact the greater the degree of transference. Through scientific methods of determining physical properties and chemical composition, we can add to the facts observable by the investigator's unaided senses, and thereby increase the chances of identification.*

13. According to the above paragraph, the amount of material transferred whenever two objects come in contact with one another
    A. varies directly with the softness of the objects involved
    B. varies directly with the violence of the contact of the objects
    C. is greater when two soft, rather than hard, objects come into violent contact with each other
    D. is greater when coarse-grained, rather than smooth-grained, materials are involved

14. According to the above paragraph, the PRINCIPAL reason for employing scientific methods in obtaining trace evidence is that
    A. other methods do not involve a methodical search of the crime scene
    B. scientific methods of examination frequently reveal physical evidence which did not previously exist
    C. the amount of trace evidence may be so sparse that other methods are useless
    D. trace evidence cannot be properly identified unless special means of detection are employed

15. According to the above paragraph, the one of the following statements which BEST describes the manner in which scientific methods of analyzing physical evidence assists the investigator is that such methods
    A. add additional valuable information to the investigator's own knowledge of complex and rarely occurring materials found as evidence
    B. compensate for the lack of important evidential material through the use of physical and chemical analyses
    C. make possible an analysis of evidence which goes beyond the ordinary capacity of the investigator's senses
    D. identify precisely those physical characteristics of the individual which the untrained senses of the investigator are unable to discern

# KEY (CORRECT ANSWERS)

| | | |
|---|---|---|
| 1. B | 6. D | 11. C |
| 2. D | 7. D | 12. C |
| 3. B | 8. C | 13. B |
| 4. A | 9. B | 14. C |
| 5. C | 10. D | 15. C |

# EXAMINATION SECTION

# TEST 1

DIRECTIONS: Each question or incomplete statement is followed by several suggested answers or completions. Select the one that *BEST* answers the question or completes the statement. *PRINT THE LETTER OF THE CORRECT ANSWER IN THE SPACE AT THE RIGHT.*

1. Some superior police officers frequently issue orders to subordinates in such a way that it appears to be a request to perform a certain act rather than a direct order to perform it. This practice is GENERALLY
   A. *undesirable,* this method of issuing orders never carries the same weight as a direct command and implies a lack of self-confidence on the part of the superior officer
   B. *desirable,* this method of issuing orders carries almost the same weight as a direct command and is less likely to antagonize subordinates
   C. *undesirable,* this method of issuing orders leaves it up to the subordinate to establish his own priority of performance when several tasks are involved
   D. *desirable,* this method of issuing orders allows the subordinate to determine for himself the precise method of carrying out the order

1.\_\_\_

2. A lieutenant suspects that Sergeant A is supervising Patrolman B more closely and intensively than seems necessary. For the lieutenant to direct the sergeant in this situation to relax his supervision somewhat would be undesirable MAINLY because
   A. other patrolmen might suspect personal animosity between the sergeant and lieutenant
   B. he may not be fully aware of the facts in the situation
   C. the patrolman has procedures available for the correction of grievances
   D. such supervision rarely continues for any prolonged period

2.\_\_\_

3. One of the best indications of interest in the job on the part of subordinates is the fact that they ask questions. Such questions are of value CHIEFLY because they
   A. provide an excellent guide to the re-assignment of subordinates
   B. serve to enhance the status of the supervisor when he answers them
   C. indicate the efficiency of the men involved
   D. can be utilized as part of the training process

3.\_\_\_

4. A superior officer is reading orders to a group of patrolmen and observes that one of them appears to be inattentive to the orders being read. This is the first time this patrolman has appeared to be inattentive. The superior officer thereupon stops reading the orders and asks this patrolman a question about the orders. The patrolman responds with an acceptable answer. At this point it would be MOST appropriate for the superior officer to
   A. reprimand the patrolman severely then and there for his behavior

4.\_\_\_

B. continue reading the orders since the patrolman appears to have understood them
C. Continue reading the orders, but plan to surprise the patrolman at some other time when he is again seemingly inattentive in order to highlight his inattentiveness
D. emphasize to the group the necessity to be attentive

5. A patrolman informs the desk officer that he believes that a certain sergeant, whom he mentions by name, is too strict in supervising all the patrolmen, especially when compared with the supervision carried out by the other sergeants in the same command. Of the following, the BEST advice the desk officer can offer this patrolman is to
   A. suggest that this is a matter that requires a meeting with the captain
   B. remind the patrolman that the sergeant himself is often subject to severe supervision
   C. tell the patrolman that acceptance of supervision is a part of his job
   D. tell the patrolman that he will conduct his own study of the situation

6. A superior officer is newly assigned to a police unit in which a very close personal friend is already assigned as a patrolman. The superior officer knows that the entire personnel of the unit is generally aware of this close friendship. In this situation, the one of the following actions which would be MOST desirable for the superior officer to take is to
   A. avoid, as much as possible, any conversation with this patrolman so as not to create any appearance of favoritism
   B. discuss with the patrolman the ways in which they should conduct themselves so that strict impartiality will prevail
   C. suggest to the patrolman that he apply for a transfer to a different unit
   D. suspend temporarily and completely his personal friendly relationship with the patrolman while both are assigned to the same unit

7. One definition of STAFF supervision reads that it is control over the actual function which others are performing, without exercising line command over the persons who are performing the function. This situation arises MOST often in police work
   A. when a uniformed officer is performing a technical or a semi-technical task
   B. in response to police needs at an emergency of considerable magnitude
   C. in response to predictable situations which necessitate the assignment of substantial numbers of men from various commands

8. The police supervisor should realize that the performance of unpleasant duties is GENERALLY
   A. *unavoidable*, it is part of his responsibility as a leader
   B. *undesirable*, they should be avoided whenever possible
   C. *predictable*, mistakes follow an established pattern
   D. *desirable*, the self-discipline required insures supervisory growth

9. After a reprimand of a subordinate for a violation of the rules, the subordinate corrects himself and appears to perform his work acceptably. For the supervisor to remind the subordinate *occasionally* of his past violation would be
   A. *bad*, it suggests that the supervisor is devoting too much time and effort to one individual
   B. *good*, it is an indication of the use of positive discipline on a continuing basis
   C. *bad*, the original corrective action appears to have served its purpose
   D. *good*, the supervisor has the best interests of the subordinate in mind

10. Development and change of practices will characterize public administration during the next twenty years. The public administrator who is taught too specifically what to do may find that his knowledge is not applicable to the situations he eventually must face.

    With this in mind, it would be most logical for the police planner to stress LEAST the
    A. learning process itself
    B. principles of diagnosing situations
    C. basic elements of crime control programs
    D. preparation of more comprehensive procedural manuals

11. The one of the following which is LEAST characteristic of our system of civil rights is that
    A. governmental restrictions on some of these rights are forbidden because there is no constitutional authorization for their restriction
    B. judicial construction of these rights is in a state of change
    C. this system is a product of hundreds of years of political development
    D. this system eliminates the conflict between governmental authority and individual rights

12. Of the following, the one which is the CHIEF barrier to the development of professionalization for police officers throughout the country is the
    A. relatively low entrance requirements for entry into the police field
    B. relatively low salaries paid law enforcement officers despite the hazards that confront them
    C. failure by police administrators to make effective use of the probationary period to eliminate the unfit

13. Police departments have considered it desirable to establish regulations concerning the financial affairs of department members especially with respect to the payment of just debts and the borrowing of money.

   Of the following, the PRINCIPAL reason for these regulations is to
   A. prevent department members from being victimized by unscrupulous money lenders
   B. insure that the morale of department members does not suffer due to excessive borrowing
   C. prevent department members from becoming susceptible to the commission of dishonest acts because of their personal indebtedness
   D. insure that department members intelligently manage their personal financial affairs

14. A superior officer has been newly assigned to desk duty in a patrol precinct. He has noticed that some of the routine reports and forms which are submitted by several subordinate officers are incorrectly filled out.

   The one of the following which would be the BEST course of action for the superior officer to follow in this situation would be to
   A. ascertain from the commanding officer whether other superior officers have noticed these same errors and have attempted to correct them
   B. correct these errors himself and also recommend to the commanding officer that all precinct personnel be instructed in the proper completion of forms
   C. inform these subordinate officers as soon as practicable of their errors and what should be done to correct them
   D. wait until additional errors are committed and then use this opportunity to point out how they may be corrected

15. Assume that the suggestion has been made that time clocks be used in station houses to record the hours of reporting for duty by patrolmen.

   Of the following, the PRINCIPAL objection to the installation and use of such time clocks is that
   A. a roll call does not completely prevent irregularities in an attendance check
   B. time clocks involve additional clerical work for the station house personnel
   C. time clocks complicate the assignment of patrolmen to posts and details
   D. the present roll call and inspection procedures, which are necessary for other reasons, also provide a check on attendance

16. Assume that a certain lieutenant has developed the practice of handing the sergeants, without comment, brief written notes which are generally concerned with matters of routine operations. Ordinarily, this type of information is given to the sergeants verbally and informally.

The lieutenant's procedure is GENERALLY
A. *desirable;* the sergeants are less likely to misinterpret such information when it is given in written form
B. *undesirable;* the lieutenant should take advantage of such opportunities for establishing and maintaining good personal relationships with his subordinates
C. *desirable;* the lieutenant is able to avoid unnecessary conversation and can devote more time to desk duties
D. *undesirable;* giving information to subordinates in a written form encourages them to ask many clarifying questions

17. The good supervisor attempts to keep the channels of communication to and from his subordinates generally unobstructed by being open and sincere, even though the subordinates with whom he deals are often somewhat otherwise minded.

    With this in mind, a superior officer can BEST achieve fully effective unobstructed two-way communication by
    A. persisting in this behavior and developing the same qualities in his subordinates
    B. playing his role correctly and thereby setting an example
    C. taking immediate strong disciplinary measures
    D. developing mutual interests with his subordinates

17.___

18. The standardization of procedures and the proper scheduling of activities in an organization or agency should reduce old-fashioned bossing to a minimum.

    This is so PRIMARILY because
    A. it presupposes the existence of extensive rules and regulations
    B. little doubt should be left in the minds of subordinates as to what they are supposed to do
    C. It is evident that policy makers at the highest level have established reasonable work standards for those at the operating level
    D. the job situation has thus become completely impersonal

18.___

19. A lieutenants who is the commanding officer of a small departmental unit, periodically re-examines the procedures employed in his unit for the purpose of ascertaining whether any procedural changes ought to be made.

    This practice is
    A. *undesirable;* important procedural changes cannot be made solely on the initiative of the lieutenant
    B. *desirable;* the lieutenant is in the best position to immediately institute any procedural changes that he feels are warranted
    C. *undesirable;* the lieutenant should devote all his efforts to the supervision and execution of established procedures
    D. *desirable;* the lieutenant has a responsibility to attempt to improve the operations of his unit

19.___

20. Planning must be continuous at every level and in every unit of the police department even though the general planning job may be the primary concern of one person or bureau.

    The one of the following which is NOT implied by this statement is that such planning
    A. should permeate the entire organization even though it is the first responsibility of the planning officer
    B. should consider the possibility of intradepartmental conflicts arising and the need to eliminate them at lower levels before they develop
    C. is necessary when there is a lack of attention to it at the higher echelons of the department
    D. may stimulate the acceptance of responsibility for effective job performance at all levels in the organization

20.____

---

# KEY (CORRECT ANSWERS)

| | |
|---|---|
| 1. B | 11. D |
| 2. B | 12. A |
| 3. D | 13. C |
| 4. B | 14. C |
| 5. D | 15. D |
| 6. B | 16. B |
| 7. A | 17. A |
| 8. A | 18. B |
| 9. C | 19. D |
| 10. D | 20. C |

---

# TEST 2

DIRECTIONS: Each question or incomplete statement is followed by several suggested answers or completions. Select the one that *BEST* answers the question or completes the statement. *PRINT THE LETTER OF THE CORRECT ANSWER IN THE SPACE AT THE RIGHT.*

1. The one of the following situations which *BEST* illustrates unity of command in a police organization is when
   A. only one subordinate is directly commanded or supervised by each superior officer
   B. only one superior officer is in complete command of each situation
   C. only one superior officer is responsible for the job performance of subordinate officers
   D. there is a line of command which extends from the lowest to the highest supervisory officers

   1.___

2. The one of the following which, if increased, would *MOST* likely result in an increased span of control on the part of a supervisory officer is
   A. an intervening period of time required for orders to reach subordinates not actually present
   B. his ability to supervise subordinates effectively
   C. the complexity of the jobs to be performed by subordinates
   D. the effort which must be devoted to extra-departmental conferences and programs

   2.___

3. There is less of a need for specialization of police operations when the overall quality of police personnel is high *MAINLY* because
   A. a greater variety of police tasks can then be successfully performed by the individual patrolman
   B. high quality police personnel frequently possess specialized skills which they have acquired prior to police service
   C. well qualified personnel tend to develop specialized interests and abilities while performing their regular duties
   D. well qualified personnel understand the dangers of overspecialization to a police agency

   3.___

4. The existence of specialized operating units in a police organization is *MOST* justified when such a unit
   A. assists the patrol force by its use of specialized knowledge and methods
   B. assumes complete and sole responsibility for police performance in a specialized area of activity
   C. devotes an equal amount of time and effort to the duties and responsibilities of the unspecialized patrol force
   D. is relieved of any responsibility for the regular duties of the unspecialized patrol force

   4.___

5. Many supervising police officers complain that they are too often overburdened with an excess of detailed and routine work.

   The MOST practical of the following ways available to a supervising police officer to handle such a problem is to
   A. give the highest priority to the completion of this work until satisfactorily accomplished
   B. request at once the assignment of additional and better trained personnel
   C. assign such work to someone who may and can handle it
   D. apportion such work equally among members of the force

6. Objective indexes of police performance, such as crime and accident rates, provide a MOST exact comparison when comparing
   A. *different* police agencies which have similar administrative structures and problems
   B. *different* police agencies which operate in communities which have similar crime problems and are in the same population group
   C. *variations* in efficiency resulting from a change of procedure within a given police department when the change is made in only one procedure and the influence of other factors remains nearly constant
   D. *variations* in efficiency resulting from changes of procedure within a given police department when the comparison is between two successive years and the accuracy of the basic data has been clearly established

7. Crime statistics even when gathered in a scrupulously honest manner and with all due diligence, are *often* unsatisfactory MAINLY because of
   A. the lack of crimes that go unreported
   B. the lack of appropriate statistical formulas
   C. the lack of a system of classification of crimes
   D. incomplete reporting at the level of arrest

8. When internal statistical reports are used for the purpose of making evaluations of unit commands, the one of the following which is LEAST important in preparing these reports is that they
   A. be based upon observations which are true and data which are basically accurate
   B. be ready on the date established for their submission
   C. conform generally to standard directions for their preparation
   D. should reflect favorably on those officers who are making an effort to perform effectively

9. Assume that a nationwide survey reveals that a particular police administrative practice is widely used and that it is quite different from the city practice.

   The one of the following which is the MOST reasonable implication of the results of this survey is that the
   A. more widely accepted practice should be instituted in the city on a trial basis immediately

B. city practice should be evaluated in an effort to determine if it can be improved
C. city practice should be revised to conform to the more widely accepted practice
D. police problems of the city are unique and it is unlikely that any administrative changes ought to be made

10. The tasks of coordination, supervision and control are likely to become more complicated as the specialization of a police department increases.

    This statement is GENERALLY
    A. *false;* better performance of these tasks is likely to result because of the concentrated attention given to particular police problems
    B. *false;* the proportion of a total force which is specialized is too small to have any effect on these tasks
    C. *true;* the increased number of interrelationships which result from specialization are sources of potential conflict and friction
    D. *true;* the individual specialist resents direction from superior officers who are not themselves specialists

10.___

11. The supervisor who is responsible to several superiors is in an advantageous position since he has the benefit of intimate contacts with more people in higher positions.

    This statement is GENERALLY
    A. *false,* because a supervisor should not normally be directly responsible to more than one superior at the same time
    B. *true,* since the supervisor is in a position to learn more about the overall operation of the agency
    C. *false,* because there is a tendency in such a case for the supervisor to lose touch with his own subordinates
    D. *true,* since he can sometimes receive more favorable treatment for his subordinates by judicious use of such contacts

11.___

12. A large American city requires annual medical examinations of all police personnel. For the police department of the city to adopt such a procedure would be
    A. *undesirable,* chiefly because physical disabilities of an individual can be readily discovered by an examination of records covering absences and sick leave
    B. *undesirable,* chiefly because the police department of the city is uniquely large and such a program would be administratively difficult
    C. *desirable,* chiefly because it would indicate an interest by the department in an area which has a basic relevance to effective police work
    D. *desirable,* chiefly because it would make possible conformance to reasonable and acceptable medical standards of all police personnel involved

12.___

13. Assume that the suggestion has been made and adopted that all patrolmen with 20 years or more seniority be permitted to pick their details and assignments, and assume further that a substantial number of these patrolmen do pick NEW details or assignments.

    The one of the following which would be the LEAST serious of the problems created by such a situation would be the
    A. effect on the patrolmen being transferred elsewhere to accommodate these patrolmen with twenty years' service
    B. matter of settling disputes when two or more patrolmen chose the same detail or assignment
    C. possible staffing of certain departmental units with men who are not the most qualified for the work
    D. training required to fit these men for the details and assignments they chose

14. Departmental rules and regulations should try to anticipate all the situations that might arise involving behavior, and should attempt to provide specific rules to cover all such circumstances.

    This statement is GENERALLY
    A. *true;* the courteous behavior of individual officers is the most important part of a police public relations program
    B. *false;* this will establish minimum standards of courteous behavior and must necessarily discourage the development of much higher standards
    C. *true;* such specific statements in rules and regulations will serve to discourage the making of excuses for discourteous behavior
    D. *false;* there is no practical limit to the possible situations that could be encountered which involve courteous behavior

15. Rumors about critical intergroup tensions should be reported to superior officers by subordinate officers MAINLY because
    A. it indicates that the subordinate officers are fulfilling their responsibilities
    B. superior officers are in a better position to assess the danger-potential of such rumors
    C. the minority groups affected are thereby more likely to become aware of the sympathetic interest of the police
    D. subordinate officers are the best qualified to recommend remedial action because they are closest to the tensions

16. Gambling is a racket yielding large profits and these profits give a power to the least desirable elements in the community.

    The MOST dangerous implication for the police of such power is that it
    A. may be used in an attempt to corrupt law enforcement officers

B. is virtually impossible to check once it gains a foothold in a community
C. sets a bad example to impressionable youth by exemplifying the fruits of "easy money"
D. takes advantage of loopholes in the law so as to remain practically immune from the imposition of penalties

17. Over-specialization in youth work by the police is undesirable *MAINLY* because such over-specialization would lead
    A. the police to operate in areas and to adopt an approach which is not in line with proper police function
    B. to frequent changes in police programs to meet the variety of individual juvenile problems as they arise
    C. to undesirable competition among the specialized units engaged in youth work
    D. to the condoning of youthful disruptive behavior by the police

18. The decision of the Supreme Court of the United States in the case of *Mallory vs. United States*
    A. *upheld* a lower court decision which held that promptness of arraignment should be considered in determining the validity of a confession
    B. *reversed* a lower court decision which required that all confidential records of investigative agencies be subject to review by the courts
    C. *upheld* a lower court decision which made admissible as evidence statements elicited during a period of unlawful police detention
    D. *reversed* a lower court decision because the prisoner was not arraigned promptly enough following his arrest

19. The Crime Index of the revised Uniform Crime Reports for the United States includes a crime category called
    A. aggravated assault
    B. larceny under $50
    C. negligent manslaughter
    D. statutory rape

20. The one of the following crimes which had the highest clearance rate for the city last year was
    A. felonies against the person
    B. murder and non-negligent manslaughter
    C. felonies against property
    D. misdemeanors

# KEY (CORRECT ANSWERS)

1. B
2. B
3. A
4. A
5. C

6. C
7. A
8. D
9. B
10. C

11. A
12. D
13. B
14. D
15. B

16. A
17. A
18. D
19. A
20. B

---

# PREPARING WRITTEN MATERIAL

# PARAGRAPH REARRANGEMENT
## COMMENTARY

The sentences which follow are in scrambled order. You are to rearrange them in proper order and indicate the letter choice containing the correct answer at the space at the right.

Each group of sentences in this section is actually a paragraph presented in scrambled order. Each sentence in the group has a place in that paragraph; no sentence is to be left out. You are to read each group of sentences and decide upon the best order in which to put the sentences so as to form as well-organized paragraph.

The questions in this section measure the ability to solve a problem when all the facts relevant to its solution are not given.

More specifically, certain positions of responsibility and authority require the employee to discover connections between events sometimes, apparently, unrelated. In order to do this, the employee will find it necessary to correctly infer that unspecified events have probably occurred or are likely to occur. This ability becomes especially important when action must be taken on incomplete information.

Accordingly, these questions require competitors to choose among several suggested alternatives, each of which presents a different sequential arrangement of the events. Competitors must choose the MOST logical of the suggested sequences.

In order to do so, they may be required to draw on general knowledge to infer missing concepts or events that are essential to sequencing the given events. Competitors should be careful to infer only what is essential to the sequence. The plausibility of the wrong alternatives will always require the inclusion of unlikely events or of additional chains of events which are NOT essential to sequencing the given events.

It's very important to remember that you are looking for the best of the four possible choices, and that the best choice of all may not even be one of the answers you're given to choose from.

There is no one right way to these problems. Many people have found it helpful to first write out the order of the sentences, as they would have arranged them, on their scrap paper before looking at the possible answers. If their optimum answer is there, this can save them some time. If it isn't, this method can still give insight into solving the problem. Others find it most helpful to just go through each of the possible choices, contrasting each as they go along. You should use whatever method feels comfortable, and works, for you.

While most of these types of questions are not that difficult, we've added a higher percentage of the difficult type, just to give you more practice. Usually there are only one or two questions on this section that contain such subtle distinctions that you're unable to answer confidently, and you then may find yourself stuck deciding between two possible choices, neither of which you're sure about.

---

# EXAMINATION SECTION
## TEST 1

DIRECTIONS: The sentences that follow are in scrambled order. You are to rearrange them in proper order and indicate the letter choice containing the CORRECT answer. *PRINT THE LETTER OF THE CORRECT ANSWER IN THE SPACE AT THE RIGHT.*

1. Police Officer Jenner responds to the scene of a burglary at 2106 La Vista Boulevard. He is approached by an elderly man named Richard Jenkins, whose account of the incident includes the following five sentences:
   I. I saw that the lock on my apartment door had been smashed and the door was open.
   II. My apartment was a shambles; my belongings were everywhere and my television set was missing.
   III. As I walked down the hallway toward the bedroom, I heard someone opening a window.
   IV. I left work at 5:30 P.M. and took the bus home.
   V. At that time, I called the police.

   The MOST logical order for the above sentences to appear in the report is

   A. I, V, IV, II, III
   B. IV, I, II, III, V
   C. I, V, II, III, IV
   D. IV, III, II, V, I

   1._____

2. Police Officer LaJolla is writing an Incident Report in which back-up assistance was required. The report will contain the following five sentences:
   I. The radio dispatcher asked what my location was and he then dispatched patrol cars for back-up assistance.
   II. At approximately 9:30 P.M., while I was walking my assigned footpost, a gunman fired three shots at me.
   III. I quickly turned around and saw a white male, approximately 5'10", with black hair, wearing blue jeans, a yellow T-shirt, and white sneakers, running across the avenue carrying a handgun.
   IV. When the back-up officers arrived, we searched the area but could not find the suspect.
   V. I advised the radio dispatcher that a gunman had just fired a gun at me, and then I gave the dispatcher a description of the man.

   The MOST logical order for the above sentences to appear in the report is

   A. III, V, II, IV, I
   B. II, III, V, I, IV
   C. III, II, IV, I, V
   D. II, V, I, III, IV

   2._____

3. Police Officer Durant is completing a report of a robbery and assault. The report will contain the following five sentences:
   I. I went to Mount Snow Hospital to interview a man who was attacked and robbed of his wallet earlier that night.
   II. An ambulance arrived at 82nd Street and 3rd Avenue and took an intoxicated, wounded man to Mount Snow Hospital.
   III. Two youths attacked the man and stole his wallet.
   IV. A well-dressed man left Hanratty's Bar very drunk, with his wallet hanging out of his back pocket.
   V. A passerby dialed 911 and requested police and ambulance assistance.

   3._____

The MOST logical order for the above sentences to appear in the report is

    A. I, II, IV, III, V                       B. IV, III, V, II, I
    C. IV, V, II, III, I                      D. V, IV, III, II, I

4. Police Officer Boswell is preparing a report of an armed robbery and assault which will contain the following five sentences:
    I. Both men approached the bartender and one of them drew a gun.
    II. The bartender immediately went to grab the phone at the bar.
    III. One of the men leaped over the counter and smashed a bottle over the bartender's head.
    IV. Two men in a blue Buick drove up to the bar and went inside.
    V. I found the cash register empty and the bartender unconscious on the floor, with the phone still dangling off the hook.

The MOST logical order for the above sentences to appear in the report is

    A. IV, I, II, III, V                    B. V, IV, III, I, II
    C. IV, III, II, V, I                  D. II, I, III, IV, V

5. Police Officer Mitzler is preparing a report of a bank robbery, which will contain the following five sentences:
    I. The teller complied with the instructions on the note, but also hit the silent alarm.
    II. The perpetrator then fled south on Broadway.
    III. A suspicious male entered the bank at approximately 10:45 A.M.
    IV. At this time, an undetermined amount of money has been taken.
    V. He approached the teller on the far right side and handed her a note.

The MOST logical order for the above sentences to appear in the report is

    A. III, V, I, II, IV                   B. I, III, V, II, IV
    C. III, V, IV, I, II                   D. III, V, II, IV, I

6. A Police Officer is preparing an Accident Report for an accident which occurred at the intersection of East 119th Street and Lexington Avenue. The report will include the following five sentences:
    I. On September 18, 1990, while driving ten children to school, a school bus driver passed out.
    II. Upon arriving at the scene, I notified the dispatcher to send an ambulance.
    III. I notified the parents of each child once I got to the station house.
    IV. He said the school bus, while traveling west on East 119th Street, struck a parked Ford which was on the southwest corner of East 119th Street.
    V. A witness by the name of John Ramos came up to me to describe what happened.

The MOST logical order for the above sentences to appear in the Accident Report is

    A. I, II, V, III, IV                   B. I, II, V, IV, III
    C. II, V, I, III, IV                   D. II, V, I, IV, III

7. A Police Officer is preparing a report concerning a dispute. The report will contain the following five sentences:
    I. The passenger got out of the back of the taxi and leaned through the front window to complain to the driver about the fare.
    II. The driver of the taxi caught up with the passenger and knocked him to the ground; the passenger then kicked the driver and a scuffle ensued.
    III. The taxi drew up in front of the high-rise building and stopped.
    IV. The driver got out of the taxi and followed the passenger into the lobby of the apartment building.
    V. The doorman tried but was unable to break up the fight, at which point he called the precinct.

The MOST logical order for the above sentences to appear in the report is

    A. III, I, IV, II, V          B. III, IV, I, II, V
    C. III, IV, II, V, I          D. V, I, III, IV, II

7.\_\_\_\_

8. Police Officer Morrow is writing an Incident Report. The report will include the following four sentences:
    I. The man reached into his pocket and pulled out a gun.
    II. While on foot patrol, I identified a suspect, who was wanted for six robberies in the area, from a wanted picture I was carrying.
    III. I drew my weapon and fired six rounds at the suspect, killing him instantly.
    IV. I called for back-up assistance and told the man to put his hands up.

The MOST logical order for the above sentences to appear in the report is

    A. II, III, IV, I          B. IV, I, III, II
    C. IV, I, II, III          D. II, IV, I, III

8.\_\_\_\_

9. Sergeant Allen responds to a call at 16 Grove Street regarding a missing child. At the scene, the Sergeant is met by Police Officer Samuels, who gives a brief account of the incident consisting of the following five sentences:
    I. I transmitted the description and waited for you to arrive before I began searching the area.
    II. Mrs. Banks, the mother, reports that she last saw her daughter Julie about 7:30 A.M. when she took her to school.
    III. About 6 P.M., my partner and I arrived at this location to investigate a report of a missing 8 year-old girl.
    IV. When Mrs. Banks left her, Julie was wearing a red and white striped T-shirt, blue jeans, and white sneakers.
    V. Mrs. Banks dropped her off in front of the playground of P.S. 11.

The MOST logical order for the above sentences to appear in the report is

    A. III, V, IV, II, I          B. III, II, V, IV, I
    C. III, IV, I, II, V          D. III, II, IV, I, V

9.\_\_\_\_

10. Police Officer Franco is completing a report of an assault. The report will contain the following five sentences:
    I. In the park I observed an elderly man lying on the ground, bleeding from a back wound.
    II. I applied first aid to control the bleeding and radioed for an ambulance to respond.

10.\_\_\_\_

III. The elderly man stated that he was sitting on the park bench when he was attacked from behind by two males.
IV. I received a report of a man's screams coming from inside the park, and I went to investigate.
V. The old man could not give a description of his attackers.

The MOST logical order for the above sentences to appear in the report is

A. IV, I, II, III, V
B. V, III, I, IV, II
C. IV, III, V, II, I
D. II, I, V, IV, III

11. Police Officer Williams is completing a Crime Report. The report contains the following five sentences:
    I. As Police Officer Hanson and I approached the store, we noticed that the front door was broken.
    II. After determining that the burglars had fled, we notified the precinct of the burglary.
    III. I walked through the front door as Police Officer Hanson walked around to the back.
    IV. At approximately midnight, an alarm was heard at the Apex Jewelry Store.
    V. We searched the store and found no one.

    The MOST logical order for the above sentences to appear in the report is

    A. I, IV, II, III, V
    B. I, IV, III, V, II
    C. IV, I, III, II, V
    D. IV, I, III, V, II

12. Police Officer Clay is giving a report to the news media regarding someone who has jumped from the Empire State Building. His report will include the following five sentences:
    I. I responded to the 86th floor, where I found the person at the edge of the roof.
    II. A security guard at the building had reported that a man was on the roof at the 86th floor.
    III. At 5:30 P.M., the person jumped from the building.
    IV. I received a call from the radio dispatcher at 4:50 P.M. to respond to the Empire State Building.
    V. I tried to talk to the person and convince him not to jump.

    The MOST logical order for the above sentences to appear in the report is

    A. I, II, IV, III, V
    B. III, IV, I, II, V
    C. II, IV, I, III, V
    D. IV, II, I, V, III

13. The following five sentences are part of a report of a burglary written by Police Officer Reed:
    I. When I arrived at 2400 1st Avenue, I noticed that the door was slightly open.
    II. I yelled out, *Police, don't move!*
    III. As I entered the apartment, I saw a man with a TV set passing it through a window to another man standing on a fire escape.
    IV. While on foot patrol, I was informed by the radio dispatcher that a burglary was in progress at 2400 1st Avenue.
    V. However, the burglars quickly ran down the fire escape.

    The MOST logical order for the above sentences to appear in the report is

    A. I, III, IV, V, II
    B. IV, I, III, V, II
    C. IV, I, III, II, V
    D. I, IV, III, II, V

14. Police Officer Jenkins is preparing a report for Lost or Stolen Property. The report will include the following five sentences:
    I. On the stairs, Mr. Harris slipped on a wet leaf and fell on the landing.
    II. It wasn't until he got to the token booth that Mr. Harris realized his wallet was no longer in his back pants pocket.
    III. A boy wearing a football jersey helped him up and brushed off the back of Mr. Harris' pants.
    IV. Mr. Harris states he was walking up the stairs to the elevated subway at Queensborough Plaza.
    V. Before Mr. Harris could thank him, the boy was running down the stairs to the street.

    The MOST logical order for the above sentences to appear in the report is

    A. IV, III, V, I, II
    B. IV, I, III, V, II
    C. I, IV, II, III, V
    D. I, II, IV, III, V

15. Police Officer Hubbard is completing a report of a missing person. The report will contain the following five sentences:
    I. I visited the store at 7:55 P.M. and asked the employees if they had seen a girl fitting the description I had been given.
    II. She gave me a description and said she had gone into the local grocery store at about 6:15 P.M.
    III. I asked the woman for a description of her daughter.
    IV. The distraught woman called the precinct to report that her daughter, aged 12, had not returned from an errand.
    V. The storekeeper said a girl matching the description had been in the store earlier, but he could not give an exact time.

    The MOST logical order for the above sentences to appear in the report is

    A. I, III, II, V, IV
    B. IV, III, II, I, V
    C. V, I, II, III, IV
    D. III, I, II, IV, V

16. A police officer is completing an entry in his Daily Activity Log regarding traffic summonses which he issued. The following five sentences will be included in the entry:
    I. I was on routine patrol parked 16 yards west of 170th Street and Clay Avenue.
    II. The summonses were issued for unlicensed operator and disobeying a steady red light.
    III. At 8 A.M. hours, I observed an auto traveling westbound on 170th Street not stop for a steady red light at the intersection of Clay Avenue and 170th Street.
    IV. I stopped the driver of the auto and determined that he did not have a valid driver's license.
    V. After a brief conversation, I informed the motorist that he was receiving two summonses.

    The MOST logical order for the above sentences to appear in the report is

    A. I, III, IV, V, II
    B. III, IV, II, V, I
    C. V, II, I, III, IV
    D. IV, V, II, I, III

17. The following sentences appeared on an Incident Report:
   I. Three teenagers who had been ejected from the theater were yelling at patrons who were now entering.
   II. Police Officer Dixon told the teenagers to leave the area.
   III. The teenagers said that they were told by the manager to leave the theater because they were talking during the movie.
   IV. The theater manager called the precinct at 10:20 P.M. to report a disturbance outside the theater.
   V. A patrol car responded to the theater at 10:42 P.M. and two police officers went over to the teenagers.

   The MOST logical order for the above sentences to appear in the Incident Report

   A. I, V, IV, III, II
   B. IV, I, V, III, II
   C. IV, I, III, V, II
   D. IV, III, I, V, II

18. Activity Log entries are completed by police officers. Police Officer Samuels has written an entry concerning vandalism and part of it contains the following five sentences:
   I. The man, in his early twenties, ran down the block and around the corner.
   II. A man passing the store threw a brick through a window of the store.
   III. I arrived on the scene and began to question the witnesses about the incident.
   IV. Malcolm Holmes, the owner of the Fast Service Shoe Repair Store, was working in the back of the store at approximately 3 P.M.
   V. After the man fled, Mr. Holmes called the police.

   The MOST logical order for the above sentences to appear in the Activity Log is

   A. IV, II, I, V, III
   B. II, IV, I, III, V
   C. II, I, IV, III, V
   D. IV, II, V, III, I

19. Police Officer Buckley is preparing a report concerning a dispute in a restaurant. The report will contain the following five sentences:
   I. The manager, Charles Chin, and a customer, Edward Green, were standing near the register arguing over the bill.
   II. The manager refused to press any charges providing Green pay the check and leave.
   III. While on foot patrol, I was informed by a passerby of a disturbance in the Dragon Flame Restaurant.
   IV. Green paid the $7.50 check and left the restaurant.
   V. According to witnesses, the customer punched the owner in the face when Chin asked him for the amount due.

   The MOST logical order for the above sentences to appear in the report is

   A. III, I, V, II, IV
   B. I, II, III, IV, V
   C. V, I, III, II, IV
   D. III, V, II, IV, I

20. Police Officer Wilkins is preparing a report for leaving the scene of an accident. The report will include the following five sentences:
   I. The Dodge struck the right rear fender of Mrs. Smith's 1980 Ford and continued on its way.
   II. Mrs. Smith stated she was making a left turn from 40th Street onto Third Avenue.
   III. As the car passed, Mrs. Smith noticed the dangling rear license plate #412AEJ.
   IV. Mrs. Smith complained to police of back pains and was removed by ambulance to Bellevue Hospital.
   V. An old green Dodge traveling up Third Avenue went through the red light at 40th Street and Third Avenue.

   The MOST logical order for the above sentences to appear in the report is

   A. V, III, I, II, IV
   B. I, III, II, V, IV
   C. IV, V, I, II, III
   D. II, V, I, III, IV

21. Detective Simon is completing a Crime Report. The report contains the following five sentences:
   I. Police Officer Chin, while on foot patrol, heard the yelling and ran in the direction of the man.
   II. The man, carrying a large hunting knife, left the High Sierra Sporting Goods Store at approximately 10:30 A.M.
   III. When the man heard Police Officer Chin, he stopped, dropped the knife, and began to cry.
   IV. As Police Officer Chin approached the man, he drew his gun and yelled, *Police, freeze.*
   V. After the man left the store, he began yelling, over and over, *I am going to 'kill myself!*

   The MOST logical order for the above sentences to appear in the report is

   A. V, II, I, IV, III
   B. II, V, I, IV, III
   C. II, V, IV, I, III
   D. II, I, V, IV, III

22. Police Officer Miller is preparing a Complaint Report which will include the following five sentences:
   I. From across the lot, he yelled to the boys to get away from his car.
   II. When he came out of the store, he noticed two teenage boys trying to break into his car.
   III. The boys fled as Mr. Johnson ran to his car.
   IV. Mr. Johnson stated that he parked his car in the municipal lot behind Tams Department Store.
   V. Mr. Johnson saw that the door lock had been broken, but nothing was missing from inside the auto.

   The MOST logical order for the above sentences to appear in the report is

   A. IV, I, II, V, III
   B. II, III, I, V, IV
   C. IV, II, I, III, V
   D. I, II, III, V, IV

23. Police Officer O'Hara completes a Universal Summons for a motorist who has just passed a red traffic light. The Universal Summons includes the following five sentences:
    I. As the car passed the light, I followed in the patrol car.
    II. After the driver stopped the car, he stated that the light was yellow, not red.
    III. A blue Cadillac sedan passed the red light on the corner of 79th Street and 3rd Avenue at 11:25 P.M.
    IV. As a result, the driver was informed that he did pass a red light and that his brake lights were not working.
    V. The driver in the Cadillac stopped his car as soon as he saw the patrol car, and I noticed that the brake lights were not working.

    The MOST logical order for the above sentences to appear in the Universal Summons is

    A. I, III, V, II, IV
    B. III, I, V, II, IV
    C. III, I, V, IV, II
    D. I, III, IV, II, V

24. Detective Egan is preparing a follow-up report regarding a homicide on 170th Street and College Avenue. An unknown male was found at the scene. The report will contain the following five sentences:
    I. Police Officer Gregory wrote down the names, addresses, and phone numbers of the witnesses.
    II. A 911 operator received a call of a man shot and dispatched Police Officers Worth and Gregory to the scene.
    III. They discovered an unidentified male dead on the street.
    IV. Police Officer Worth notified the Precinct Detective Unit immediately.
    V. At approximately 9:00 A.M., an unidentified male shot another male in the chest during an argument.

    The MOST logical order for the above sentences to appear in the report is

    A. V, II, III, IV, I
    B. II, III, V, IV, I
    C. IV, I, V, II, III
    D. V, III, II, IV, I

25. Police Officer Tracey is preparing a Robbery Report which will include the following five sentences:
    I. I ran around the corner and observed a man pointing a gun at a taxidriver.
    II. I informed the man I was a police officer and that he should not move.
    III. I was on the corner of 125th Street and Park Avenue when I heard a scream coming from around the corner.
    IV. The man turned around and fired one shot at me.
    V. I fired once, shooting him in the arm and causing him to fall to the ground.

    The MOST logical order for the above sentences to appear in the report is

    A. I, III, IV, II, V
    B. IV, V, II, I, III
    C. III, I, II, IV, V
    D. III, I, V, II, IV

# KEY (CORRECT ANSWERS)

| | | | | |
|---|---|---|---|---|
| 1. | B | | 11. | D |
| 2. | B | | 12. | D |
| 3. | B | | 13. | C |
| 4. | A | | 14. | B |
| 5. | A | | 15. | B |
| 6. | B | | 16. | A |
| 7. | A | | 17. | B |
| 8. | D | | 18. | A |
| 9. | B | | 19. | A |
| 10. | A | | 20. | D |

21. B
22. C
23. B
24. A
25. C

# TEST 2

DIRECTIONS: The sentences that follow are in scrambled order. You are to rearrange them in proper order and indicate the letter choice containing the CORRECT answer. *PRINT THE LETTER OF THE CORRECT ANSWER IN THE SPACE AT THE RIGHT.*

1. Police Officer Weiker is completing a Complaint Report which will contain the following five sentences:  1.__
    I. Mr. Texlor was informed that the owner of the van would receive a parking ticket and that the van would be towed away.
    II. The police tow truck arrived approximately one half hour after Mr. Texlor complained.
    III. While on foot patrol on West End Avenue, I saw the owner of Rand's Restaurant arrive to open his business.
    IV. Mr. Texlor, the owner, called to me and complained that he could not receive deliveries because a van was blocking his driveway.
    V. The van's owner later reported to the precinct that his van had been stolen, and he was then informed that it had been towed.
   The MOST logical order for the above sentences to appear in the report is
   A. III, V, I, II, IV  B. III, IV, I, II, V
   C. IV, III, I, II, V  D. IV, III, II, I, V

2. Police Officer Ames is completing an entry in his Activity Log. The entry contains the following five sentences:  2.__
    I. Mr. Sands gave me a complete description of the robber.
    II. Alvin Sands, owner of the Star Delicatessen, called the precinct to report he had just been robbed.
    III. I then notified all police patrol vehicles to look for a white male in his early twenties wearing brown pants and shirt, a black leather jacket, and black and white sneakers.
    IV. I arrived on the scene after being notified by the precinct that a robbery had just occurred at the Star Delicatessen.
    V. Twenty minutes later, a man fitting the description was arrested by a police officer on patrol six blocks from the delicatessen.
   The MOST logical order for the above sentences to appear in the Activity Log is
   A. II, I, IV, III, V  B. II, IV, III, I, V
   C. II, IV, I, III, V  D. II, IV, I, V, III

3. Police Officer Benson is completing a Complaint Report concerning a stolen taxicab, which will include the following five sentences:  3.__
    I. Police Officer Benson noticed that a cab was parked next to a fire hydrant.
    II. Dawson *borrowed* the cab for transportation purposes since he was in a hurry.
    III. Ed Dawson got into his car and tried to start it, but the battery was dead.
    IV. When he reached his destination, he parked the cab by a fire hydrant and placed the keys under the seat.
    V. He looked around and saw an empty cab with the engine running.
   The MOST logical order for the above sentences to appear in the report is

A. I, III, II, IV, V
B. III, I, II, V, IV
C. III, V, II, IV, I
D. V, II, IV, III, I

4. Police Officer Hatfield is reviewing his Activity Log entry prior to completing a report. The entry contains the following five sentences:
   I. When I arrived at Zand's Jewelry Store, I noticed that the door was slightly open.
   II. I told the burglar I was a police officer and that he should stand still or he would be shot.
   III. As I entered the store, I saw a man wearing a ski mask attempting to open the safe in the back of the store.
   IV. On December 16, 1990, at 1:38 A.M., I was informed that a burglary was in progress at Zand's Jewelry Store on East 59th Street.
   V. The burglar quickly pulled a knife from his pocket when he saw me.

   The MOST logical order for the above sentences to appear in the report is

   A. IV, I, III, V, II
   B. I, IV, III, V, II
   C. IV, III, II, V, I
   D. I, III, IV, V, II

5. Police Officer Lorenz is completing a report of a murder. The report will contain the following five statements made by a witness:
   I. I was awakened by the sound of a gunshot coming from the apartment next door, and I decided to check.
   II. I entered the apartment and looked into the kitchen and the bathroom.
   III. I found Mr. Hubbard's body slumped in the bathtub.
   IV. The door to the apartment was open, but I didn't see anyone.
   V. He had been shot in the head.

   The MOST logical order for the above sentences to appear in the report is

   A. I, III, II, IV, V
   B. I, IV, II, III, V
   C. IV, II, I, III, V
   D. III, I, II, IV, V

6. Police Officer Baldwin is preparing an accident report which will include the following five sentences:
   I. The old man lay on the ground for a few minutes, but was not physically hurt.
   II. Charlie Watson, a construction worker, was repairing some brick work at the top of a building at 54th Street and Madison Avenue.
   III. Steven Green, his partner, warned him that this could be dangerous, but Watson ignored him.
   IV. A few minutes later, one of the bricks thrown by Watson smashed to the ground in front of an old man, who fainted out of fright.
   V. Mr. Watson began throwing some of the bricks over the side of the building.

   The MOST logical order for the above sentences to appear in the report is

   A. II, V, III, IV, I
   B. I, IV, II, V, III
   C. III, II, IV, V, I
   D. II, III, I, IV, V

7. Police Officer Porter is completing an incident report concerning her rescue of a woman being held hostage by a former boyfriend. Her report will contain the following five sentences:
   I. I saw a man holding .25 caliber gun to a woman's head, but he did not see me.
   II. I then broke a window and gained access to the house.
   III. As I approached the house on foot, a gunshot rang out and I heard a woman scream.
   IV. A decoy van brought me as close as possible to the house where the woman was being held hostage.
   V. I ordered the man to drop his gun, and he released the woman and was taken into custody.

   The MOST logical order for the above sentences to appear in the report is

   A. I, III, II, IV, V  B. IV, III, II, I, V
   C. III, II, I, IV, V  D. V, I, II, III, IV

8. Police Officer Byrnes is preparing a crime report concerning a robbery. The report will consist of the following five sentences:
   I. Mr. White, following the man's instructions, opened the car's hood, at which time the man got out of the auto, drew a revolver, and ordered White to give him all the money in his pockets.
   II. Investigation has determined there were no witnesses to this incident.
   III. The man asked White to check the oil and fill the tank.
   IV. Mr. White, a gas attendant, states that he was working alone at the gas station when a black male pulled up to the gas pump in a white Mercury.
   V. White was then bound and gagged by the male and locked in the gas station's rest room.

   The MOST logical order for the above sentences to appear in the report is

   A. IV, I, III, II, V  B. III, I, II, V, IV
   C. IV, III, I, V, II  D. I, III, IV, II, V

9. Police Officer Gale is preparing a report of a crime committed against Mr. Weston. The report will consist of the following five sentences:
   I. The man, who had a gun, told Mr. Weston not to scream for help and ordered him back into the apartment.
   II. With Mr. Weston disposed of in this fashion, the man proceeded to ransack the apartment.
   III. Opening the door to see who was there, Mr. Weston was confronted by a tall white male wearing a dark blue jacket and white pants.
   IV. Mr. Weston was at home alone in his living room when the doorbell rang.
   V. Once inside, the man bound and gagged Mr. Weston and locked him in the bathroom.

   The MOST logical order for the above sentences to appear in the report is

   A. III, V, II, I, IV  B. IV, III, I, V, II
   C. III, V, IV, II, I  D. IV, III, V, I, II

4 (#2)

10. A police officer is completing a report of a robbery, which will contain the following five sentences:
    I. Two police officers were about to enter the Red Rose Coffee Shop on 47th Street and 8th Avenue.
    II. They then noticed a male running up the street carrying a brown paper bag.
    III. They heard a woman standing outside the Broadway Boutique yelling that her store had just been robbed by a young man, and she was pointing up the street.
    IV. They caught up with him and made an arrest.
    V. The police officers pursued the male, who ran past them on 8th Avenue.

    The MOST logical order for the above sentences to appear in the report is

    A. I, III, II, V, IV
    B. III, I, II, V, IV
    C. IV, V, I, II, III
    D. I, V, IV, III, II

10.____

11. Police Officer Capalbo is preparing a report of a bank robbery. The report will contain the following five statements made by a witness:
    I. Initially, all I could see were two men, dressed in maintenance uniforms, sitting in the area reserved for bank officers.
    II. I was passing the bank at 8 P.M. and noticed that all the lights were out, except in the rear section.
    III. Then I noticed two other men in the bank, coming from the direction of the vault, carrying a large metal box.
    IV. At this point, I decided to call the police.
    V. I knocked on the window to get the attention of the men in the maintenance uniforms, and they chased the two men carrying the box down a flight of steps.

    The MOST logical order for the above sentences to appear in the report is

    A. IV, I, II, V, III
    B. I, III, II, V, IV
    C. II, I, III, V, IV
    D. II, III, I, V, IV

11.____

12. Police Officer Roberts is preparing a crime report concerning an assault and a stolen car. The report will contain the following five sentences:
    I. Upon leaving the store to return to his car, Winters noticed that a male unknown to him was sitting in his car.
    II. The man then re-entered Winters' car and drove away, fleeing north on 2nd Avenue.
    III. Mr. Winters stated that he parked his car in front of 235 East 25th Street and left the engine running while he went into the butcher shop at that location.
    IV. Mr. Robert Gering, a witness, stated that the male is known in the neighborhood as Bobby Rae and is believed to reside at 323 East 114th Street.
    V. When Winters approached the car and ordered the man to get out, the man got out of the auto and struck Winters with his fists, knocking him to the ground.

    The MOST logical order for the above sentences to appear in the report is

    A. III, II, V, I, IV
    B. III, I, V, II, IV
    C. I, IV, V, II, III
    D. III, II, I, V, IV

12.____

13. Police Officer Robinson is preparing a crime report concerning the robbery of Mr. Edwards' store. The report will consist of the following five sentences:
    I. When the last customer left the store, the two men drew revolvers and ordered Mr. Edwards to give them all the money in the cash register.
    II. The men proceeded to the back of the store as if they were going to do some shopping.
    III. Janet Morley, a neighborhood resident, later reported that she saw the men enter a green Ford station wagon and flee northbound on Albany Avenue.
    IV. Edwards complied after which the gunmen ran from the store.
    V. Mr. Edwards states that he was stocking merchandise behind the store counter when two white males entered the store.

    The MOST logical order for the above sentences to appear in the report is

    A. V, II, III, I, IV
    B. V, II, I, IV, III
    C. II, I, V, IV, III
    D. III, V, II, I, IV

14. Police Officer Wendell is preparing an accident report for a 6-car accident that occurred at the intersection of Bath Avenue and Bay Parkway. The report will consist of the following five sentences:
    I. A 2006 Volkswagen Beetle, traveling east on Bath Avenue, swerved to the left to avoid the Impala, and struck a 2004 Ford station wagon which was traveling west on Bath Avenue.
    II. The Seville then mounted the curb on the northeast corner of Bath Avenue and Bay Parkway and struck a light pole.
    III. A 2003 Buick Lesabre, traveling northbound on Bay Parkway directly behind the Impala, struck the Impala, pushing it into the intersection of Bath Avenue and Bay Parkway.
    IV. A 2005 Chevy Impala, traveling northbound on Bay Parkway, had stopped for a red light at Bath Avenue.
    V. A 2007 Toyota, traveling westbound on Bath Avenue, swerved to the right to avoid hitting the Ford station wagon, and struck a 2007 Cadillac Seville double-parked near the corner.

    The MOST logical order for the above sentences to appear in the report is

    A. IV, III, V, II, I
    B. III, IV, V, II, I
    C. IV, III, I, V, II
    D. III, IV, V, I, II

15. The following five sentences are part of an Activity Log entry Police Officer Rogers made regarding an explosion,
    I. I quickly treated the pedestrian for the injury.
    II. The explosion caused a glass window in an office building to shatter.
    III. After the pedestrian was treated, a call was placed to the precinct requesting additional police officers to evacuate the area.
    IV. After all the glass settled to the ground, I saw a pedestrian who was bleeding from the arm
    V. While on foot patrol near 5th Avenue and 53rd Street, I heard a loud explosion.

    The MOST logical order for the above sentences to appear in the report is

    A. II, V, IV, I, III
    B. V, II, IV, III, I
    C. V, II, I, IV, III
    D. V, II, IV, I, III

16. Police Officer David is completing a report regarding illegal activity near the entrance to Madison Square Garden during a recent rock concert. The report will contain the following five sentences:
    I. As I came closer to the man, he placed what appeared to be tickets in his pocket and began to walk away.
    II. After the man stopped, I questioned him about *scalping* tickets.
    III. While on assignment near the Madison Square Garden entrance, I observed a man apparently selling tickets.
    IV. I stopped the man by stating that I was a police officer.
    V. The man was then given a summons, and he left the area.
    The MOST logical order for the above sentences to appear in the report is

    A. I, III, IV, II, V
    B. III, I, IV, V, II
    C. III, IV, I, II, V
    D. III, I, IV, II, V

17. Police Officer Sampson is preparing a report concerning a dispute in a bar. The report will contain the following five sentences:
    I. John Evans, the bartender, ordered the two men out of the bar.
    II. Two men dressed in dungarees entered the C and D Bar at 5:30 P.M.
    III. The two men refused to leave and began to beat up Evans.
    IV. A customer in the bar saw me on patrol and yelled to me to come separate the three men.
    V. The two men became very drunk and loud within a short time.
    The MOST logical order for the above sentences to appear in the report is

    A. II, I, V, III, IV
    B. II, III, IV, V, I
    C. III, I, II, V, IV
    D. II, V, I, III, IV

18. A police officer is completing a report concerning the response to a crime in progress. The report will include the following five sentences:
    I. The officers saw two armed men run out of the liquor store and into a waiting car.
    II. Police Officers Lunty and Duren received the call and responded to the liquor store.
    III. The robbers gave up without a struggle.
    IV. Lunty and Duren blocked the getaway car with their patrol car.
    V. A call came into the precinct concerning a robbery in progress at Jane's Liquor Store.
    The MOST logical order for the above sentences to appear in the report is

    A. V, II, I, IV, III
    B. II, V, I, III, IV
    C. V, I, IV, II, III
    D. I, V, II, III, IV

19. Police Officer Jenkins is preparing a Crime Report which will consist of the following five sentences:
    I. After making inquiries in the vicinity, Smith found out that his next door neighbor, Viola Jones, had seen two local teenagers, Michael Heinz and Vincent Gaynor, smash his car's windshields with a crowbar.
    II. Jones told Smith that the teenagers live at 8700 19th Avenue.
    III. Mr. Smith heard a loud crash at approximately 11:00 P.M., looked out his apartment window, and saw two white males running away from his car.
    IV. Smith then reported the incident to the precinct, and Heinz and Gaynor were arrested at the address given.

> V. Leaving his apartment to investigate further, Smith discovered that his car's front and rear windshields had been smashed.

The MOST logical order for the above sentences to appear in the report is

- A. III, IV, V, I, II
- B. III, V, I, II, IV
- C. III, I, V, II, IV
- D. V, III, I, II, IV

20. Sergeant Nancy Winston is reviewing a Gun Control Report which will contain the following five sentences:
    > I. The man fell to the floor when hit in the chest with three bullets from 22 caliber gun.
    > II. Merriam'22 caliber gun was seized, and he wasgiven a summons for not having a pistol permit.
    > III. Christopher Merriam, the owner of A-Z Grocery, shot a man who attempted to rob him.
    > IV. Police Officer Franks responded and asked Merriam for his pistol permit, which he could not produce.
    > V. Merriam phoned the police to report he had just shot a man who had attempted to rob him.

    The MOST logical order for the above sentences to appear in the report is

    - A. III, I, V, IV, II
    - B. I, III, V, IV, II
    - C. III, I, V, II, IV
    - D. I, III, II, V, IV

21. Detective John Manville is completing a report for his superior regarding the murder of an unknown male who was shot in Central Park. The report will contain the following five sentences:
    > I. Police Officers Langston and Cavers responded to the scene.
    > II. I received the assignment to investigate the murder in Central Park from Detective Sergeant Rogers.
    > III. Langston notified the Detective Bureau after questioning Jason.
    > IV. An unknown male, apparently murdered, was discovered in Central Park by Howard Jason, a park employee, who immediately called the police.
    > V. Langston and Cavers questioned Jason.

    The MOST logical order for the above sentences to appear in the report is

    - A. I, IV, V, III, II
    - B. IV, I, V, II, III
    - C. IV, I, V, III, II
    - D. IV, V, I, III, II

22. A police officer is completing a report concerning the arrest of a juvenile. The report will contain the following five sentences:
    > I. Sanders then telephoned Jay's parents from the precinct to inform them of their son's arrest.
    > II. The store owner resisted, and Jay then shot him and ran from the store.
    > III. Jay was transported directly to the precinct by Officer Sanders.
    > IV. James Jay, a juvenile, walked into a candy store and announced a hold-up.
    > V. Police Officer Sanders, while on patrol, arrested Jay a block from the candy store.

    The MOST logical order for the above sentences to appear in the report is

    - A. IV, V, II, I, III
    - B. IV, II, V, III, I
    - C. II, IV, V, III, I
    - D. V, IV, II, I, III

23. Police Officer Olsen prepared a crime report for a robbery which contained the following five sentences:
    I. Mr. Gordon was approached by this individual who then produced a gun and demanded the money from the cash register.
    II. The man then fled from the scene on foot, southbound on 5th Avenue.
    III. Mr. Gordon was working at the deli counter when a white male, 5'6", 150-160 lbs., wearing a green jacket and blue pants, entered the store.
    IV. Mr. Gordon complied with the man's demands and handed him the daily receipts.
    V. Further investigation has determined there are no other witnesses to this robbery.

    The MOST logical order for the above sentences to appear in the report is
    A. I, III, IV, V, II
    B. I, IV, II, III, V
    C. III, IV, I, V, II
    D. III, I, IV, , II, V

24. Police Officer Bryant responded to 285 E. 31st Street to take a crime report of a burglary of Mr. Bond's home. The report will contain a brief description of the incident, consisting of the following five sentences:
    I. When Mr. Bond attempted to stop the burglar by grabbing him, he was pushed to the floor.
    II. The burglar had apparently gained access to the home by forcing open the 2nd floor bedroom window facing the fire escape.
    III. Mr. Bond sustained a head injury in the scuffle, and the burglar exited the home through the front door.
    IV. Finding nothing in the dresser, the burglar proceeded downstairs to the first floor, where he was confronted by Mr. Bond who was reading in the dining room.
    V. Once inside, he searched the drawers of the bedroom dresser.

    The MOST logical order for the above sentences to appear in the report is
    A. V, IV, I, II, III
    B. II, V, IV, I, III
    C. II, IV, V, III, I
    D. III, II, I, V, IV

25. Police Officer Derringer responded to a call of a rape-homicide case in his patrol area and was ordered to prepare an incident report, which will contain the following five sentences:
    I. He pushed Miss Scott to the ground and forcibly raped her.
    II. Mary Scott was approached from behind by a white male, 5'7", 150-160 lbs. wearing dark pants and a white jacket.
    III. As Robinson approached the male, he ordered him to stop.
    IV. Screaming for help, Miss Scott alerted one John Robinson, a local grocer, who chased her assailant as he fled the scene.
    V. The male turned and fired two shots at Robinson, who fell to the ground mortally wounded.

    The MOST logical order for the above' sentences to appear in the report is
    A. IV, III, I, II, V
    B. II, IV, III, V, I
    C. II, IV, I, V, III
    D. II, I, IV, III, V

# KEY (CORRECT ANSWERS)

| | | | | |
|---|---|---|---|---|
| 1. | B | | 11. | C |
| 2. | C | | 12. | B |
| 3. | C | | 13. | B |
| 4. | A | | 14. | C |
| 5. | B | | 15. | D |
| 6. | A | | 16. | D |
| 7. | B | | 17. | D |
| 8. | C | | 18. | A |
| 9. | B | | 19. | B |
| 10. | A | | 20. | A |

21. C
22. B
23. D
24. B
25. D

---

# REPORT WRITING
## EXAMINATION SECTION
## TEST 1

DIRECTIONS: Each question or incomplete statement is followed by several suggested answers or completions. Select the one that BEST answers the question or completes the statement. *PRINT THE LETTER OF THE CORRECT ANSWER IN THE SPACE AT THE RIGHT.*

1. Police Officer Johnson responds to the scene of an assault and obtains the following information:
   Time of Occurrence: 8:30 P.M.
   Place of Occurrence: 120-18 119th Avenue, Apt. 2A
   Suspects: John Andrews, victim's ex-husband and unknown white male
   Victim: Susan Andrews
   Injury: Broken right arm
   Officer Johnson is preparing a complaint report on the incident.
   Which one of the following expresses the above information MOST clearly and accurately?
   A. Susan Andrews was assaulted at 120-18 119th Avenue, Apt. 2A. At 8:30 P.M., her ex-husband, John Andrews, and an unknown white male broke her arm.
   B. At 8:30 P.M., Susan Andrews was assaulted at 120-18 119th Avenue, Apt. 2A, by her ex-husband, John Andrews, and an unknown white male. Her right arm was broken.
   C. John Andrews, an unknown white male, and Susan Andrews' ex-husband, assaulted and broke her right arm at 8:30 P.M., at 120-18 119th Avenue, Apt. 2A.
   D. John Andrews, ex-husband of Susan Andrews, broke her right arm with an unknown white male at 120-18 119th Avenue, at 8:30 P.M. in Apt. 2A.

1.___

2. While on patrol, Officers Banks and Thompson see a man lying on the ground bleeding. Officer Banks records the following details about the incident:
   Time of Incident: 3:15 P.M.
   Place of Incident: Sidewalk in front of 517 Rock Avenue
   Incident: Tripped and fell
   Name of Injured: John Blake
   Injury: Head wound
   Action Taken: Transported to Merry Hospital
   Officer Banks is completing a report on the incident.
   Which one of the following expresses the above information MOST clearly and accurately?
   A. At 3:15 P.M., Mr. John Blake was transported to Merry Hospital. He tripped and fell, injuring his head on sidewalk in front of 517 Rock Avenue.
   B. Mr. John Blake tripped and fell on the sidewalk at 3:15 P.M. in front of 517 Rock Avenue. He was transported to Merry Hospital while he sustained a head wound.

2.___

C. Mr. John Blake injured his head when he tripped and fell on the sidewalk in front of 517 Rock Avenue at 3:15 P.M. He was transported to Merry Hospital.
D. A head was wounded on the sidewalk in front of 517 Rock Avenue at 3:15 P.M. Mr. John Blake tripped and fell and was transported to Merry Hospital.

3. When assigned to investigate a complaint, a police officer should
   I. Interview witnesses and obtain facts
   II. Conduct a thorough investigation of circumstances concerning the complaint
   III. Prepare a complaint report
   IV. Determine if the complaint report should be closed or referred for further investigation
   V. Enter complaint report on the Complaint Report Index and obtain a complaint report number at the station house

   While on patrol, Police Officer John is instructed by his supervisor to investigate a complaint by Mr. Stanley Burns, who was assaulted by his brother-in-law, Henry Traub. After interviewing Mr. Burns, Officer John learns that Mr. Traub has been living with Mr. Burns for the past two years. Officer John accompanies Mr. Burns to his apartment but Mr. Traub is not there. Officer John fills out the complaint report and takes the report back to the station house where it is entered on the Complaint Report Index and assigned a complaint report number.
   Officer John's actions were
   A. *improper*, primarily because he should have stayed at Mr. Burns' apartment and waited for Mr. Traub to return in order to arrest him
   B. *proper*, primarily because after obtaining all the facts, he took the report back to the station house and was assigned a complaint report number
   C. *improper*, primarily because he should have decided whether to close the report or refer it for further investigation
   D. *proper*, primarily because he was instructed by his supervisor to take the report from Mr. Burns even though it involved his brother-in-law

4. Police Officer Waters was the first person at the scene of a fire which may have been the result of arson. He obtained the following information:
   Place of Occurrence: 35 John Street, Apt. 27
   Time of Occurrence: 4:00 P.M.
   Witness: Daisy Logan
   Incident: Fire (possible arson)
   Suspect: Male, white, approximately 18 years old, wearing blue jeans and a plaid shirt, running away from the incident
   Officer Waters is completing a report on the incident.

Which one of the following expresses the above information MOST clearly and accurately?
- A. At 4:00 P.M., Daisy Logan saw a white male, approximately 18 years old who was wearing blue jeans and a plaid shirt, running from the scene of a fire at 35 John Street, Apt. 27.
- B. Seeing a fire at 35 John Street, a white male approximately 18 years old, wearing blue jeans and a plaid shirt, was seen running from Apt. 27 at 4:00 P.M. reported Daisy Logan.
- C. Approximately 18 years old and wearing blue jeans and a plaid shirt, Daisy Logan saw a fire and a white male running from 35 John Street, Apt. 27 at 4:00 P.M.
- D. Running from 35 John Street, Apt. 27, the scene of the fire, reported Daisy Logan at 4:00 P.M., was a white male approximately 18 years old and wearing blue jeans and a plaid shirt.

5. Police Officer Sullivan obtained the following information at the scene of a two-car accident:
Place of Occurrence: 2971 William Street
Drivers and Vehicles Involved: Mrs. Wilson, driver of blue 1984 Toyota Camry; Mr. Bailey, driver of white 1981 Dodge Omni
Injuries Sustained: Mr. Bailey had a swollen right eye; Mrs. Wilson had a broken left hand

Which one of the following expresses the above information MOST clearly and accurately?
- A. Mr. Bailey, owner of a white 1981 Dodge Omni, at 2971 William Street, had a swollen right eye. Mrs. Wilson, with a broken left hand, is the owner of the blue 1984 Toyota Camry. They were in a car accident.
- B. Mrs. Wilson got a broken left hand and Mr. Bailey a swollen right eye at 2971 William Street. The vehicles involved in the car accident were a 1981 Dodge Omni, white, owned by Mr. Bailey, and Mrs. Wilson's blue 1984 Toyota Camry.
- C. Mrs. Wilson, the driver of the blue 1984 Toyota Camry, and Mr. Bailey, the driver of the white 1981 Dodge Omni, were involved in a car accident at 2971 William Street. Mr. Bailey sustained a swollen right eye, and Mrs. Wilson broke her left hand.
- D. Mr. Bailey sustained a swollen right eye and Mrs. Wilson broke her left hand in a car accident at 2971 William Street. They owned a 1981 white Dodge Omni and a 1984 blue Toyota Camry.

6. Officer Johnson has issued a summons to a driver and has obtained the following information:
Place of Occurrence: Corner of Foster Road and Woodrow Avenue
Time of Occurrence: 7:10 P.M.
Driver: William Grant
Offense: Driving through a red light
Age of Driver: 42
Address of Driver: 23 Richmond Avenue

Officer Johnson is making an entry in his Memo Book regarding the incident.
Which one of the following expresses the above information MOST clearly and accurately?
- A. William Grant, lives at 23 Richmond Avenue at 7:10 P.M., went through a red light. He was issued a summons at the corner of Foster Road and Woodrow Avenue. The driver is 42 years old.
- B. William Grant, age 42, who lives at 23 Richmond Avenue, was issued a summons for going through a red light at 7:10 P.M. at the corner of Foster Road and Woodrow Avenue.
- C. William Grant, age 42, was issued a summons on the corner of Foster Road and Woodrow Avenue for going through a red light. He lives at 23 Richmond Avenue at 7:10 P.M.
- D. A 42-year-old man who lives at 23 Richmond Avenue was issued a summons at 7:10 P.M. William Grant went through a red light at the corner of Foster Road and Woodrow Avenue.

7. Police Officer Frome has completed investigating a report of a stolen auto and obtained the following information:
Date of Occurrence: October 26, 1994
Place of Occurrence: 51st Street and 8th Avenue
Time of Occurrence: 3:30 P.M.
Crime: Auto theft
Suspect: Michael Wadsworth
Action Taken: Suspect arrested
Which one of the following expresses the above information MOST clearly and accurately?
- A. Arrested on October 26, 1994 was a stolen auto at 51st Street and 8th Avenue at 3:30 P.M. driven by Michael Wadsworth.
- B. For driving a stolen auto at 3:30 P.M., Michael Wadsworth was arrested at 51st Street and 8th Avenue on October 26, 1994.
- C. On October 26, 1994 at 3:30 P.M., Michael Wadsworth was arrested at 51st Street and 8th Avenue for driving a stolen auto.
- D. Michael Wadsworth was arrested on October 26, 1994 at 3:30 P.M. for driving at 51st Street and 8th Avenue. The auto was stolen.

8. Police Officer Wright has finished investigating a report of Grand Larceny and has obtained the following information:
Time of Occurrence: Between 1:00 P.M. and 2:00 P.M.
Place of Occurrence: In front of victim's home, 85 Montgomery Avenue
Victim: Mr. Williams, owner of the vehicle
Crime: Automobile broken into
Property Taken: Stereo valued at $1,200

Officer Wright is preparing a report on the incident.
Which one of the following expresses the above information MOST clearly and accurately?
- A. While parked in front of his home Mr. Williams states that between 1:00 P.M. and 2:00 P.M. an unknown person broke into his vehicle. Mr. Williams, who lives at 85 Montgomery Avenue, lost his $1,200 stereo.
- B. Mr. Williams, who lives at 85 Montgomery Avenue, states that between 1:00 P.M. and 2:00 P.M. his vehicle was parked in front of his home when an unknown person broke into his car and took his stereo worth $1,200.
- C. Mr. Williams was parked in front of 85 Montgomery Avenue, which is his home, when it was robbed of a $1,200 stereo. When he came out, he observed between 1:00 P.M. and 2:00 P.M. that his car had been broken into by an unknown person.
- D. Mr. Williams states between 1:00 P.M. and 2:00 P.M. that an unknown person broke into his car in front of his home. Mr. Williams further states that he was robbed of a $1,200 stereo at 85 Montgomery Avenue.

9. Police Officer Fontaine obtained the following details relating to a suspicious package:
Place of Occurrence: Case Bank, 2 Wall Street
Time of Occurrence: 10:30 A.M.
Date of Occurrence: October 10, 1994
Complaint: Suspicious package in doorway
Found By: Emergency Service Unit
Officer Fontaine is preparing a report for department records.
Which one of the following expresses the above information MOST clearly and accurately?
- A. At 10:30 A.M., the Emergency Service Unit reported they found a package on October 10, 1994 which appeared suspicious. This occurred in a doorway at 2 Wall Street, Case Bank.
- B. A package which appeared suspicious was in the doorway of Case Bank. The Emergency Service Unit reported this at 2 Wall Street at 10:30 A.M. on October 10, 1994 when found.
- C. On October 10, 1994 at 10:30 A.M., a suspicious package was found by the Emergency Service Unit in the doorway of Case Bank at 2 Wall Street.
- D. The Emergency Service Unit found a package at the Case Bank. It appeared suspicious at 10:30 A.M. in the doorway of 2 Wall Street on October 10, 1994.

10. Police Officer Reardon receives the following information regarding a case of child abuse:
Victim:              Joseph Mays
Victim's Age:        10 years old
Victim's Address:    Resides with his family at 42 Columbia Street, Apt. 1B
Complainant:         Victim's uncle, Kevin Mays
Suspects:            Victim's parents
Police Officer Reardon is preparing a report to send to the Department of Social Services.
Which one of the following expresses the above information MOST clearly and accurately?
   A. Kevin Mays reported a case of child abuse to his ten-year-old nephew, Joseph Mays, by his parents. He resides with his family at 42 Columbia Street, Apt. 1B.
   B. Kevin Mays reported that his ten-year-old nephew, Joseph Mays, has been abused by the child's parents. Joseph Mays resides with his family at 42 Columbia Street, Apt. 1B.
   C. Joseph Mays has been abused by his parents. Kevin Mays reported that his nephew resides with his family at 42 Columbia Street, Apt. 1B. He is ten years old.
   D. Kevin Mays reported that his nephew is ten years old. Joseph Mays has been abused by his parents. He resides with his family at 42 Columbia Street, Apt. 1B.

11. While on patrol, Police Officer Hawkins was approached by Harry Roland, a store owner, who found a leather bag valued at $200.00 outside his store. Officer Hawkins took the property into custody and removed the following items:
   2 Solex watches, each valued at           $500.00
   4 14-kt. gold necklaces, each valued at   $315.00
   Cash                                      $519.00
   1 diamond ring, valued at                 $400.00
Officer Hawkins is preparing a report on the found property.
Which one of the following is the TOTAL value of the property and cash found?
   A. $1,734     B. $3,171     C. $3,179     D. $3,379

12. While on patrol, Police Officer Blake observes a man running from a burning abandoned building. Officer Blake radios the following information:
Place of Occurrence: 310 Hall Avenue
Time of Occurrence:  8:30 P.M.
Type of Building:    Abandoned
Suspect:             Male, white, about 35 years old
Crime:               Arson
Officer Blake is completing a report on the incident.
Which one of the following expresses the above information MOST clearly and accurately?

A. An abandoned building located at 310 Hall Avenue was on fire at 8:30 P.M. A white male, approximately 35 years old, was observed fleeing the scene.
B. A white male, approximately 35 years old, at 8:30 P.M. was observed fleeing 310 Hall Avenue. The fire was set at an abandoned building.
C. An abandoned building was set on fire. A white male, approximately 35 years old, was observed fleeing the scene at 8:30 P.M. at 310 Hall Avenue.
D. Observed fleeing a building at 8:30 P.M. was a white male, approximately 35 years old. An abandoned building, located at 310 Hall Avenue, was set on fire.

13. Police Officer Winters responds to a call regarding a report of a missing person. The following information was obtained by the Officer:
Time of Occurrence: 3:30 P.M.
Place of Occurrence: Harrison Park
Reported By: Louise Dee - daughter
Description of Missing
 Person: Sharon Dee, 70 years old, 5'5", brown eyes, black hair - mother

Officer Winters is completing a report on the incident. Which one of the following expresses the above information MOST clearly and accurately?
A. Mrs. Sharon Dee, reported missing by her daughter, Louise, was seen in Harrison Park. The last time she saw her was at 3:30 P.M. She is 70 years old with black hair, brown eyes, and 5'5".
B. Louise Dee reported that her mother, Sharon Dee, is missing. Sharon Dee is 70 years old, has black hair, brown eyes, and is 5'5". She was last seen at 3:30 P.M. in Harrison Park.
C. Louise Dee reported Sharon, her 70-year-old mother at 3:30 P.M., to be missing after being seen last at Harrison Park. Described as being 5'5", she has black hair and brown eyes.
D. At 3:30 P.M. Louise Dee's mother was last seen by her daughter in Harrison Park. She has black hair and brown eyes. Louise reported Sharon is 5'5" and 70 years old.

14. While on patrol, Police Officers Mertz and Gallo receive a call from the dispatcher regarding a crime in progress. When the Officers arrive, they obtain the following information:
Time of Occurrence: 2:00 P.M.
Place of Occurrence: In front of 2124 Bristol Avenue
Crime: Purse snatch
Victim: Maria Nieves
Suspect: Carlos Ortiz
Witness: Jose Perez, who apprehended the subject

The Officers are completing a report on the incident.

Which one of the following expresses the above information MOST clearly and accurately?
- A. At 2:00 P.M., Jose Perez witnessed Maria Nieves. Her purse was snatched. The suspect, Carlos Ortiz, was apprehended in front of 2124 Bristol Avenue.
- B. In front of 2124 Bristol Avenue, Carlos Ortiz snatched the purse belonging to Maria Nieves. Carlos Ortiz was apprehended by a witness to the crime after Jose Perez saw the purse snatch at 2:00 P.M.
- C. At 2:00 P.M., Carlos Ortiz snatched a purse from Maria Nieves in front of 2124 Bristol Avenue. Carlos Ortiz was apprehended by Jose Perez, a witness to the crime.
- D. At 2:00 P.M., Carlos Ortiz was seen snatching the purse of Maria Nieves as seen and apprehended by Jose Perez in front of 2124 Bristol Avenue.

15. Police Officers Willis and James respond to a crime in progress and obtain the following information:
Time of Occurrence: 8:30 A.M.
Place of Occurrence: Corner of Hopkin Avenue and Amboy Place
Crime: Chain snatch
Victim: Mrs. Paula Evans
Witness: Mr. Robert Peters
Suspect: White male
Officers Willis and James are completing a report on the incident.
Which one of the following expresses the above information MOST clearly and accurately?
- A. Mrs. Paula Evans was standing on the corner of Hopkin Avenue and Amboy Place at 8:30 A.M. when a white male snatched her chain. Mr. Robert Peters witnessed the crime.
- B. At 8:30 A.M., Mr. Robert Peters witnessed Mrs. Paula Evans and a white male standing on the corner of Hopkin Avenue and Amboy Place. Her chain was snatched.
- C. At 8:30 A.M., a white male was standing on the corner of Hopkin Avenue and Amboy Place. Mrs. Paula Evans' chain was snatched, and Mr. Robert Peters witnessed the crime.
- D. At 8:30 A.M., Mr. Robert Peters reported he witnessed a white male snatching Mrs. Paula Evans' chain while standing on the corner of Hopkin Avenue and Amboy Place.

16. Police Officers Cleveland and Logan responded to an assault that had recently occurred. The following information was obtained at the scene:
Place of Occurrence: Broadway and Roosevelt Avenue
Time of Occurrence: 1:00 A.M.
Crime: Attempted robbery, assault
Victim: Chuck Brown, suffered a broken tooth
Suspect: Lewis Brown, victim's brother
Officer Logan is completing a report on the incident.

Which one of the following expresses the above information MOST clearly and accurately?
- A. Lewis Brown assaulted his brother Chuck on the corner of Broadway and Roosevelt Avenue. Chuck Brown reported his broken tooth during the attempted robbery at 1:00 A.M.
- B. Chuck Brown had his tooth broken when he was assaulted at 1:00 A.M. on the corner of Broadway and Roosevelt Avenue by his brother, Lewis Brown, while Lewis was attempting to rob him.
- C. An attempt at 1:00 A.M. to rob Chuck Brown turned into an assault at the corner of Broadway and Roosevelt Avenue when his brother Lewis broke his tooth.
- D. At 1:00 A.M., Chuck Brown reported that he was assaulted during his brother's attempt to rob him. Lewis Brown broke his tooth. The incident occurred on the corner of Broadway and Roosevelt Avenue.

17. Police Officer Mannix has just completed an investigation regarding a hit-and-run accident which resulted in a pedestrian being injured. Officer Mannix has obtained the following information:
Make and Model of Car: Pontiac, Trans Am
Year and Color of Car: 1986, white
Driver of Car: Male, black
Place of Occurrence: Corner of E. 15th Street and 8th Avenue
Time of Occurrence: 1:00 P.M.
Officer Mannix is completing a report on the accident. Which one of the following expresses the above information MOST clearly and accurately?
- A. At 1:00 P.M., at the corner of E. 15th Street and 8th Avenue, a black male driving a white 1986 Pontiac Trans Am was observed leaving the scene of an accident after injuring a pedestrian with the vehicle.
- B. On the corner of E. 15th Street and 8th Avenue, a white Pontiac, driven by a black male, a 1986 Trans Am injured a pedestrian and left the scene of the accident at 1:00 P.M.
- C. A black male driving a white 1986 Pontiac Trans Am injured a pedestrian and left with the car while driving on the corner of E. 15th Street and 8th Avenue at 1:00 P.M.
- D. At the corner of E. 15th Street and 8th Avenue, a pedestrian was injured by a black male. He fled in his white 1986 Pontiac Trans Am at 1:00 P.M.

18. The following details were obtained by Police Officer Dwight at the scene of a family dispute:
Place of Occurrence: 77 Baruch Drive
Victim: Andrea Valdez, wife of Walker
Violator: Edward Walker
Witness: George Valdez, victim's brother
Crime: Violation of Order of Protection
Action Taken: Violator arrested

Police Officer Dwight is preparing a report on the incident.
Which one of the following expresses the above information MOST clearly and accurately?
- A. George Valdez saw Edward Walker violate his sister's Order of Protection at 77 Baruch Drive. Andrea Valdez's husband was arrested for this violation.
- B. Andrea Valdez's Order of Protection was violated at 77 Baruch Drive. George Valdez saw his brother-in-law violate his sister's Order. Edward Walker was arrested.
- C. Edward Walker was arrested for violating an Order of Protection held by his wife, Andrea Valdez. Andrea's brother, George Valdez, witnessed the violation at 77 Baruch Drive.
- D. An arrest was made at 77 Baruch Drive when an Order of Protection held by Andrea Valdez was violated by her husband. George Valdez, her brother, witnessed Edward Walker.

19. The following details were obtained by Police Officer Jackson at the scene of a robbery:
Place of Occurrence: Chambers Street, northbound A platform
Victim: Mr. John Wells
Suspect: Joseph Miller
Crime: Robbery, armed with knife, wallet taken
Action Taken: Suspect arrested

Officer Jackson is completing a report on the incident. Which one of the following expresses the above information MOST clearly and accurately?
- A. At Chambers Street northbound A platform, Joseph Miller used a knife to remove the wallet of John Wells while waiting for the train. Police arrested him.
- B. Mr. John Wells, while waiting for the northbound A train at Chambers Street, had his wallet forcibly removed at knifepoint by Joseph Miller. Joseph Miller was later arrested.
- C. Joseph Miller was arrested for robbery. At Chambers Street, John Wells stated that his wallet was taken. The incident occurred at knifepoint while waiting on a northbound A platform.
- D. At the northbound Chambers Street platform, John Wells was waiting for the A train. Joseph Miller produced a knife and removed his wallet. He was arrested.

20. Police Officer Bellows responds to a report of drugs being sold in the lobby of an apartment building. He obtains the following information at the scene:
Time of Occurrence: 11:30 P.M.
Place of Occurrence: 1010 Bath Avenue

Witnesses: Mary Markham, John Silver
Suspect: Harry Stoner
Crime: Drug sales
Action Taken: Suspect was gone when police arrived

Officer Bellows is completing a report of the incident. Which one of the following expresses the above information MOST clearly and accurately?

- A. Mary Markham and John Silver witnessed drugs being sold and the suspect flee at 1010 Bath Avenue. Harry Stoner was conducting his business at 11:30 P.M. before police arrival in the lobby.
- B. In the lobby, Mary Markham reported at 11:30 P.M. she saw Harry Stoner, along with John Silver, selling drugs. He ran from the lobby at 1010 Bath Avenue before police arrived.
- C. John Silver and Mary Markham reported that they observed Harry Stoner selling drugs in the lobby of 1010 Bath Avenue at 11:30 P.M. The witnesses stated that Stoner fled before police arrived.
- D. Before police arrived, witnesses stated that Harry Stoner was selling drugs. At 1010 Bath Avenue, in the lobby, John Silver and Mary Markham said they observed his actions at 11:30 P.M.

21. While on patrol, Police Officer Fox receives a call to respond to a robbery. Upon arriving at the scene, he obtains the following information:

Time of Occurrence: 6:00 P.M.
Place of Occurrence: Sal's Liquor Store at 30 Fordham Road
Victim: Sal Jones
Suspect: White male wearing a beige parka
Description of Crime: Victim was robbed in his store at gunpoint

Officer Fox is completing a report on the incident. Which one of the following expresses the above information MOST clearly and accurately?

- A. I was informed at 6:00 P.M. by Sal Jones that an unidentified white male robbed him at gunpoint at 30 Fordham Road while wearing a beige parka at Sal's Liquor Store.
- B. At 6:00 P.M., Sal Jones was robbed at gunpoint in his store. An unidentified white male wearing a beige parka came into Sal's Liquor Store at 30 Fordham Road, he told me.
- C. I was informed at 6:00 P.M. while wearing a beige parka an unidentified white male robbed Sal Jones at gunpoint at Sal's Liquor Store at 30 Fordham Road.
- D. Sal Jones informed me that at 6:00 P.M. he was robbed at gunpoint in his store, Sal's Liquor Store, located at 30 Fordham Road, by an unidentified white male wearing a beige parka.

22. The following details were obtained by Police Officer Connors at the scene of a bank robbery:
Time of Occurrence:   10:21 A.M.
Place of Occurrence:  Westbury Savings and Loan
Crime:                Bank Robbery
Suspect:              Male, dressed in black, wearing a black woolen face mask
Witness:              Mary Henderson of 217 Westbury Ave.
Amount Stolen:        $6141 U.S. currency
Officer Connors is completing a report on the incident. Which one of the following expresses the above information MOST clearly and accurately?
   A. At 10:21 A.M., the Westbury Savings and Loan was witnessed being robbed by Mary Henderson of 217 Westbury Avenue. The suspect fled dressed in black with a black woolen face mask. He left the bank with $6141 in U.S. currency.
   B. Dressed in black wearing a black woolen face mask, Mary Henderson of 217 Westbury Avenue saw a suspect flee with $6141 in U.S. currency after robbing the Westbury Savings and Loan. The robber was seen at 10:21 A.M.
   C. At 10:21 A.M., Mary Henderson of 217 Westbury Avenue, witness to the robbery of the Westbury Savings and Loan, reports that a male, dressed in black, wearing a black face mask, did rob said bank and fled with $6141 in U.S. currency.
   D. Mary Henderson, of 217 Westbury Avenue, witnessed the robbery of the Westbury Savings and Loan at 10:21 A.M. The suspect, a male, was dressed in black and was wearing a black woolen face mask. He fled with $6141 in U.S. currency.

23. At the scene of a dispute, Police Officer Johnson made an arrest after obtaining the following information:
Place of Occurrence:  940 Baxter Avenue
Time of Occurrence:   3:40 P.M.
Victim:               John Mitchell
Suspect:              Robert Holden, arrested at scene
Crime:                Menacing
Weapon:               Knife
Time of Arrest:       4:00 P.M.
Officer Johnson is completing a report of the incident. Which one of the following expresses the above information MOST clearly and accurately?
   A. John Mitchell was menaced by a knife at 940 Baxter Avenue. Robert Holden, owner of the weapon, was arrested at 4:00 P.M., twenty minutes later, at the scene.
   B. John Mitchell reports at 3:40 P.M. he was menaced at 940 Baxter Avenue by Robert Holden. He threatened him with his knife and was arrested at 4:00 P.M. at the scene.

C. John Mitchell stated that at 3:40 P.M. at 940 Baxter Avenue he was menaced by Robert Holden, who was carrying a knife. Mr. Holden was arrested at the scene at 4:00 P.M.
D. With a knife, Robert Holden menaced John Mitchell at 3:40 P.M. The knife belonged to him, and he was arrested at the scene of 940 Baxter Avenue at 4:00 P.M.

24. Officer Nieves obtained the following information after he was called to the scene of a large gathering:
Time of Occurrence:   2:45 A.M.
Place of Occurrence:  Mulberry Park
Complaint:            Loud music
Complainant:          Mrs. Simpkins, 42 Mulberry Street, Apt. 25
Action Taken:         Police officer dispersed the crowd
Officer Nieves is completing a report on the incident. Which one of the following expresses the above information MOST clearly and accurately?

A. Mrs. Simpkins, who lives at 42 Mulberry Street, Apt. 25, called the police to make a complaint. A large crowd of people were playing loud music in Mulberry Park at 2:45 A.M. Officer Nieves responded and dispersed the crowd.
B. Officer Nieves responded to Mulberry Park because Mrs. Simpkins, the complainant, lives at 42 Mulberry Street, Apt. 25. Due to a large crowd of people who were playing loud music at 2:45 A.M., he immediately dispersed the crowd.
C. Due to a large crowd of people who were playing loud music in Mulberry Park at 2:45 A.M., Officer Nieves responded and dispersed the crowd. Mrs. Simpkins called the police and complained. She lives at 42 Mulberry Street, Apt. 25.
D. Responding to a complaint by Mrs. Simpkins, who resides at 42 Mulberry Street, Apt. 25, Officer Nieves dispersed a large crowd in Mulberry Park. They were playing loud music. It was 2:45 A.M.

25. While patroling the subway, Police Officer Clark responds to the scene of a past robbery where he obtains the following information:
Place of Occurrence:  Northbound E train
Time of Occurrence:   6:30 P.M.
Victim:               Robert Brey
Crime:                Wallet and jewelry taken
Suspects:             2 male whites armed with knives
Officer Clark is completing a report on the incident. Which one of the following expresses the above information MOST clearly and accurately?

A. At 6:30 P.M., Robert Brey reported he was robbed of his wallet and jewelry. On the northbound E train, two white males approached Mr. Brey. They threatened him before taking his property with knives.
B. While riding the E train northbound, two white men approached Robert Brey at 6:30 P.M. They threatened him with knives and took his wallet and jewelry.
C. Robert Brey was riding the E train at 6:30 P.M. when he was threatened by two whites. The men took his wallet and jewelry as he was traveling northbound.
D. Robert Brey reports at 6:30 P.M. he lost his wallet to two white men as well as his jewelry. They were carrying knives and threatened him aboard the northbound E train.

---

# KEY (CORRECT ANSWERS)

1. B
2. C
3. C
4. A
5. C

6. B
7. C
8. B
9. C
10. B

11. D
12. A
13. B
14. C
15. A

16. B
17. A
18. C
19. B
20. C

21. D
22. D
23. C
24. A
25. B

---

# TEST 2

DIRECTIONS: Each question or incomplete statement is followed by several suggested answers or completions. Select the one that BEST answers the question or completes the statement. *PRINT THE LETTER OF THE CORRECT ANSWER IN THE SPACE AT THE RIGHT.*

1. Police Officer Johnson has just finished investigating a report of a burglary and has obtained the following information:  
   Place of Occurrence: Victim's residence  
   Time of Occurrence: Between 8:13 P.M. and 4:15 A.M.  
   Victim: Paul Mason of 1264 Twentieth Street, Apt. 3D  
   Crime: Burglary  
   Damage: Filed front door lock  
   Officer Johnson is preparing a report of the incident. Which one of the following expresses the above information MOST clearly and accurately?
   - A. Paul Mason's residence was burglarized at 1264 Twentieth Street, Apt. 3D, between 8:13 P.M. and 4:15 A.M. by filing the front door lock.
   - B. Paul Mason was burglarized by filing the front door lock and he lives at 1264 Twentieth Street, Apt. 3D, between 8:13 P.M. and 4:15 A.M.
   - C. Between 8:13 P.M. and 4:15 A.M., the residence of Paul Mason, located at 1264 Twentieth Street, Apt. 3D, was burglarized after the front door lock was filed.
   - D. Between 8:13 P.M. and 4:15 A.M., at 1264 Twentieth Street, Apt. 3D, after the front door lock was filed, the residence of Paul Mason was burglarized.

1.___

2. Police Officer Lowell has just finished investigating a burglary and has received the following information:  
   Place of Occurrence: 117-12 Sutphin Boulevard  
   Time of Occurrence: Between 9:00 A.M. and 5:00 P.M.  
   Victim: Mandee Cotton  
   Suspects: Unknown  
   Officer Lowell is completing a report on this incident. Which one of the following expresses the above information MOST clearly and accurately?
   - A. Mandee Cotton reported that her home was burglarized between 9:00 A.M. and 5:00 P.M. Ms. Cotton resides at 117-12 Sutphin Boulevard. Suspects are unknown.
   - B. A burglary was committed at 117-12 Sutphin Boulevard reported Mandee Cotton between 9:00 A.M. and 5:00 P.M. Ms. Cotton said unknown suspects burglarized her home.
   - C. Unknown suspects burglarized a home at 117-12 Sutphin Boulevard between 9:00 A.M. and 5:00 P.M. Mandee Cotton, homeowner, reported.

2.___

D. Between the hours of 9:00 A.M. and 5:00 P.M., it was reported that 117-12 Sutphin Boulevard was burglarized. Mandee Cotton reported that unknown suspects are responsible.

3. Police Officer Dale has just finished investigating a report of attempted theft and has obtained the following information:

Place of Occurrence: In front of 103 W. 105th Street
Time of Occurrence: 11:30 A.M.
Victim: Mary Davis
Crime: Attempted theft
Suspect: Male, black, scar on right side of face
Action Taken: Drove victim around area to locate suspect

Officer Dale is preparing a report on the incident.
Which one of the following expresses the above information MOST clearly and accurately?

A. Mary Davis was standing in front of 103 W. 105th Street when Officer Dale arrived after an attempt to steal her pocketbook failed at 11:30 A.M. Officer Dale canvassed the area looking for a black male with a scar on the right side of his face with Ms. Davis in the patrol car.
B. Mary Davis stated that, at 11:30 A.M., she was standing in front of 103 W. 105th Street when a black male with a scar on the right side of his face attempted to steal her pocketbook. Officer Dale canvassed the area with Ms. Davis in the patrol car.
C. Officer Dale canvassed the area by putting Mary Davis in a patrol car looking for a black male with a scar on the right side of his face. At 11:30 A.M. in front of 103 W. 105th Street, she said he attempted to steal her pocketbook.
D. At 11:30 A.M., in front of 103 W. 105th Street, Officer Dale canvassed the area with Mary Davis in a patrol car who said that a black male with a scar on the right side of his face attempted to steal her pocketbook.

4. While on patrol, Police Officer Santoro received a call to respond to the scene of a shooting. The following details were obtained at the scene:

Time of Occurrence: 4:00 A.M.
Place of Occurrence: 232 Senator Street
Victim: Mike Nisman
Suspect: Howard Conran
Crime: Shooting
Witness: Sheila Norris

Officer Santoro is completing a report on the incident.
Which one of the following expresses the above information MOST clearly and accurately?

A. Sheila Norris stated at 4:00 A.M. she witnessed a shooting of her neighbor in front of her building. Howard Conran shot Mike Nisman and ran from 232 Senator Street.
B. Mike Nisman was the victim of a shooting incident seen by his neighbor. At 4:00 A.M., Sheila Norris saw Howard Conran shoot him and run in front of their building. Norris and Nisman reside at 232 Senator Street.
C. Sheila Norris states that at 4:00 A.M. she witnessed Howard Conran shoot Mike Nisman, her neighbor, in front of their building at 232 Senator Street. She further states she saw the suspect running from the scene.
D. Mike Nisman was shot by Howard Conran at 4:00 A.M. His neighbor, Sheila Norris, witnessed him run from the scene in front of their building at 232 Senator Street.

5. Police Officer Taylor responds to the scene of a serious traffic accident in which a car struck a telephone pole, and obtains the following information:
Place of Occurrence:    Intersection of Rock Street and Amboy Place
Time of Occurrence:     3:27 A.M.
Name of Injured:        Carlos Black
Driver of Car:          Carlos Black
Action Taken:           Injured taken to Beth-El Hospital
Officer Taylor is preparing a report on the accident. Which one of the following expresses the above information MOST clearly and accurately?
A. At approximately 3:27 A.M., Carlos Black drove his car into a telephone pole located at the intersection of Rock Street and Amboy Place. Mr. Black, who was the only person injured, was taken to Beth-El Hospital.
B. Carlos Black, injured at the intersection of Rock Street and Amboy Place, hit a telephone pole. He was taken to Beth-El Hospital after the car accident which occurred at 3:27 A.M.
C. At the intersection of Rock Street and Amboy Place, Carlos Black injured himself and was taken to Beth-El Hospital. His car hit a telephone pole at 3:27 A.M.
D. At the intersection of Rock Street and Amboy Place at 3:27 A.M., Carlos Black was taken to Beth-El Hospital after injuring himself by driving into a telephone pole.

5.___

6. While on patrol in the Jefferson Housing Projects, Police Officer Johnson responds to the scene of a Grand Larceny. The following information was obtained by Officer Johnson:
Time of Occurrence:    6:00 P.M.
Place of Occurrence:   Rear of Building 12A
Victim:                Maria Lopez
Crime:                 Purse snatched
Suspect:               Unknown
Officer Johnson is preparing a report on the incident.

6.___

Which one of the following expresses the above information MOST clearly and accurately?
A. At the rear of Building 12A, at 6:00 P.M., by an unknown suspect, Maria Lopez reported her purse snatched in the Jefferson Housing Projects.
B. Maria Lopez reported that at 6:00 P.M. her purse was snatched by an unknown suspect at the rear of Building 12A in the Jefferson Housing Projects.
C. At the rear of Building 12A, Maria Lopez reported at 6:00 P.M. that her purse had been snatched by an unknown suspect in the Jefferson Housing Projects.
D. In the Jefferson Housing Projects, Maria Lopez reported at the rear of Building 12A that her purse had been snatched by an unknown suspect at 6:00 P.M.

7. Criminal Possession of Stolen Property 2nd Degree occurs when a person knowingly possesses stolen property with intent to benefit himself or a person other than the owner, or to prevent its recovery by the owner, and when the
   I. value of the property exceeds two hundred fifty dollars; or
   II. property consists of a credit card; or
   III. person is a pawnbroker or is in the business of buying, selling, or otherwise dealing in property; or
   IV. property consists of one or more firearms, rifles, or shotguns.
   Which one of the following is the BEST example of Criminal Possession of Stolen Property in the Second Degree?
   A. Mary knowingly buys a stolen camera valued at $225 for her mother's birthday.
   B. John finds a wallet containing $100 and various credit cards. John keeps the money and turns the credit cards in at his local precinct.
   C. Mr. Varrone, a pawnbroker, refuses to buy Mr. Cutter's stolen VCR valued at $230.
   D. Mr. Aquista, the owner of a toy store, knowingly buys a crate of stolen water pistols valued at $260.

8. Police Officer Dale has just finished investigating a report of menacing and obtained the following information:
   Time of Occurrence: 10:30 P.M.
   Place of Occurrence: (Hallway) 77 Hill Street
   Victim: Grace Jackson
   Suspect: Susan, white female, 30 years of age
   Crime: Menacing with a knife
   Officer Dale is preparing a report on the incident.
   Which one of the following expresses the above information MOST clearly and accurately?
   A. At 10:30 P.M., Grace Jackson was stopped in the hallway of 77 Hill Street by a 30-year-old white female known to Grace as Susan. Susan put a knife to Grace's throat and demanded that Grace stay out of the building or Susan would hurt her.

5 (#2)

    B. Grace Jackson was stopped in the hallway at knife-point and threatened to stay away from the building located at 77 Hill Street. The female who is 30 years of age known as Susan by Jackson stopped her at 10:30 P.M.
    C. At 10:30 P.M. in the hallway of 77 Hill Street, Grace Jackson reported a white female 30 years of age put a knife to her throat. She knew her as Susan and demanded she stay away from the building or she would get hurt.
    D. A white female 30 years of age known to Grace Jackson as Susan stopped her in the hallway of 77 Hill Street. She put a knife to her throat and at 10:30 P.M. demanded she stay away from the building or she would get hurt.

9. Police Officer Bennett responds to the scene of a car accident and obtains the following information from the witness:
Time of Occurrence:    3:00 A.M.
Victim:    Joe Morris, removed to Methodist Hospital
Crime:    Struck pedestrian and left the scene of accident
Description of Auto:    Blue 1988 Thunderbird, license plate BOT-3745
Officer Bennett is preparing an accident report.
Which one of the following expresses the above information MOST clearly and accurately?
    A. Joe Morris, a pedestrian, was hit at 3:00 A.M. and removed to Methodist Hospital. Also a blue Thunderbird, 1988 model left the scene, license plate BOT-3745.
    B. A pedestrian was taken to Methodist Hospital after being struck at 3:00 A.M. A blue automobile was seen leaving the scene with license plate BOT-3745. Joe Morris was knocked down by a 1988 Thunderbird.
    C. At 3:00 A.M., Joe Morris, a pedestrian, was struck by a blue 1988 Thunderbird. The automobile, license plate BOT-3745, left the scene. Mr. Morris was taken to Methodist Hospital.
    D. Joe Morris, a pedestrian at 3:00 A.M. was struck by a Thunderbird. A 1988 model, license plate BOT-3745, blue in color, left the scene and the victim was taken to Methodist Hospital.

9.___

10. At 11:30 A.M., Police Officers Newman and Johnson receive a radio call to respond to a reported robbery. The Officers obtained the following information:
Time of Occurrence:    11:20 A.M.
Place of Occurrence:    Twenty-four hour newsstand at 2024 86th Street
Victim:    Sam Norris, owner
Amount Stolen:    $450.00
Suspects:    Two male whites

10.___

Officer Newman is completing a complaint report on the incident.
Which one of the following expresses the above information MOST clearly and accurately?
- A. At 11:20 A.M., it was reported by the newsstand owner that two male whites robbed $450.00 from Sam Norris. The Twenty-four hour newsstand is located at 2024 86th Street.
- B. At 11:20 A.M., Sam Norris, the newsstand owner, reported that the Twenty-four hour newsstand located at 2024 86th Street was robbed by two male whites who took $450.00.
- C. Sam Norris, the owner of the Twenty-four hour newsstand located at 2024 86th Street, reported that at 11:20 A.M. two white males robbed his newsstand of $450.00.
- D. Sam Norris reported at 11:20 A.M. that $450.00 had been taken from the owner of the Twenty-four hour newsstand located at 2024 86th Street by two male whites.

11. While on patrol, Police Officers Carter and Popps receive a call to respond to an assault in progress. Upon arrival, they receive the following information:
Place of Occurrence: 27 Park Avenue
Victim: John Dee
Suspect: Michael Jones
Crime: Stabbing during a fight
Action Taken: Suspect arrested
The Officers are completing a report on the incident.
Which one of the following expresses the above information MOST clearly and accurately?
- A. In front of 27 Park Avenue, Michael Jones was arrested for stabbing John Dee during a fight.
- B. Michael Jones was arrested for stabbing John Dee during a fight in front of 27 Park Avenue.
- C. During a fight, Michael Jones was arrested for stabbing John Dee in front of 27 Park Avenue.
- D. John Dee was stabbed by Michael Jones, who was arrested for fighting in front of 27 Park Avenue.

12. Police Officer Gattuso responded to a report of a robbery and obtained the following information regarding the incident:
Place of Occurrence: Princess Grocery, 6 Sutton Place
Time of Occurrence: 6:00 P.M.
Crime: Robbery of $200
Victim: Sara Davidson, owner of Princess Grocery
Description of Suspect: White, female, red hair, blue jeans, and white T-shirt
Weapon: Knife
Officer Gattuso is preparing a report on the incident.

Which one of the following expresses the above information MOST clearly and accurately?
- A. Sara Davidson reported at 6:00 P.M. her store Princess Grocery was robbed at knifepoint at 6 Sutton Place. A white woman with red hair took $200 from her wearing blue jeans and a white T-shirt.
- B. At 6:00 P.M., a red-haired woman took $200 from 6 Sutton Place at Princess Grocery owned by Sara Davidson, who was robbed by the white woman. She was wearing blue jeans and a white T-shirt and used a knife.
- C. In a robbery that occurred at knifepoint, a red-haired white woman robbed the owner of Princess Grocery. Sara Davidson, the owner of the 6 Sutton Place store which was robbed of $200, said she was wearing blue jeans and a white T-shirt at 6:00 P.M.
- D. At 6:00 P.M., Sara Davidson, owner of Princess Grocery, located at 6 Sutton Place, was robbed of $200 at knifepoint. The suspect is a white female with red hair wearing blue jeans and a white T-shirt.

13. Police Officer Martinez responds to a report of an assault and obtains the following information regarding the incident:

| | |
|---|---|
| Place of Occurrence: | Corner of Frank and Lincoln Avenues |
| Time of Occurrence: | 9:40 A.M. |
| Crime: | Assault |
| Victim: | Mr. John Adams of 31 20th Street |
| Suspect: | Male, white, 5'11", 170 lbs., dressed in gray |
| Injury: | Victim suffered a split lip |
| Action Taken: | Victim transported to St. Mary's Hospital |

Officer Martinez is completing a report on the incident. Which one of the following expresses the above information MOST clearly and accurately?
- A. At 9:40 A.M., John Adams was assaulted on the corner of Frank and Lincoln Avenues by a white male, 5'11", 170 lbs., dressed in gray, suffering a split lip. Mr. Adams lives at 31 20th Street and was transported to St. Mary's Hospital.
- B. At 9:40 A.M., John Adams was assaulted on the corner of Frank and Lincoln Avenues by a white male, 5'11", 170 lbs., dressed in gray, and lives at 31 20th Street. Mr. Adams suffered a split lip and was transported to St. Mary's Hospital.
- C. John Adams, who lives at 31 20th Street, was assaulted at 9:40 A.M. on the corner of Frank and Lincoln Avenues by a white male, 5'11", 170 lbs., dressed in gray. Mr. Adams suffered a split lip and was transported to St. Mary's Hospital.
- D. Living at 31 20th Street, Mr. Adams suffered a split lip and was transported to St. Mary's Hospital. At 9:40 A.M., Mr. Adams was assaulted by a white male, 5'11", 170 lbs., dressed in gray.

14. The following information was obtained by Police Officer    14. ____
    Adams at the scene of an auto accident:
    Date of Occurrence:   August 7, 1994
    Place of Occurrence:  541 W. Broadway
    Time of Occurrence:   12:45 P.M.
    Drivers:              Mrs. Liz Smith and Mr. John Sharp
    Action Taken:         Summons served to Mrs. Liz Smith
    Officer Adams is completing a report on the accident.
    Which one of the following expresses the above information
    MOST clearly and accurately?
    A. At 541 W. Broadway, Mr. John Sharp and Mrs. Liz
       Smith had an auto accident at 12:45 P.M. Mrs. Smith
       received a summons on August 7, 1994.
    B. Mrs. Liz Smith received a summons at 12:45 P.M. on
       August 7, 1994 for an auto accident with Mr. John
       Sharp at 541 W. Broadway.
    C. Mr. John Sharp and Mrs. Liz Smith were in an auto
       accident. At 541 W. Broadway on August 7, 1994 at
       12:45 P.M., Mrs. Smith received a summons.
    D. On August 7, 1994 at 12:45 P.M. at 541 W. Broadway,
       Mrs. Liz Smith and Mr. John Sharp were involved in
       an auto accident. Mrs. Smith received a summons.

15. Police Officer Gold and his partner were directed by the    15. ____
    radio dispatcher to investigate a report of a past bur-
    glary. They obtained the following information at the
    scene:
    Date of Occurrence:   April 2, 1994
    Time of Occurrence:   Between 7:30 A.M. and 6:15 P.M.
    Place of Occurrence:  124 Haring Street, residence of
                          victim
    Victim:               Mr. Gerald Palmer
    Suspect:              Unknown
    Crime:                Burglary
    Items Stolen:         Assorted jewelry, $150 cash, TV, VCR
    Officer Gold must complete a report on the incident.
    Which one of the following expresses the above information
    MOST clearly and accurately?
    A. Mr. Gerald Palmer stated that on April 2, 1994,
       between 7:30 A.M. and 6:15 P.M., while he was at work,
       someone broke into his house at 124 Haring Street and
       removed assorted jewelry, a VCR, $150 cash, and a TV.
    B. Mr. Gerald Palmer stated while he was at work that
       somebody broke into his house on April 2, 1994 and
       between 7:30 A.M. and 6:15 P.M. took his VCR, TV,
       assorted jewelry, and $150 cash. His address is
       124 Haring Street.
    C. Between 7:30 A.M. and 6:15 P.M. on April 2, 1994,
       Mr. Gerald Palmer reported an unknown person at
       124 Haring Street took his TV, VCR, $150 cash, and
       assorted jewelry from his house. Mr. Palmer said he
       was at work at the time.
    D. An unknown person broke into the house at 124 Haring
       Street and stole a TV, VCR, assorted jewelry, and
       $150 cash from Mr. Gerald Palmer. The suspect broke
       in on April 2, 1994 while he was at work, reported
       Mr. Palmer between 7:30 A.M. and 6:15 P.M.

16. While on patrol, Police Officers Morris and Devine receive a call to respond to a reported burglary. The following information relating to the crime was obtained by the Officers:

Time of Occurrence:   2:00 A.M.
Place of Occurrence:  2100 First Avenue
Witness:              David Santiago
Victim:               John Rivera
Suspect:              Joe Ryan
Crime:                Burglary, video tape recorder stolen

The Officers are completing a report on the incident. Which one of the following expresses the above information MOST clearly and accurately?
- A. David Santiago, the witness reported at 2:00 A.M. he saw Joe Ryan leave 2100 First Avenue, home of John Rivera, with a video tape recorder.
- B. At 2:00 A.M. David Santiago reported that he had seen Joe Ryan go into 2100 First Avenue and steal a video tape recorder. John Rivera lives at 2100 First Avenue.
- C. David Santiago stated that Joe Ryan burglarized John Rivera's house at 2100 First Avenue. He saw Joe Ryan leaving his house at 2:00 A.M. with a video tape recorder.
- D. David Santiago reported that at 2:00 A.M. he saw Joe Ryan leave John Rivera's house, located at 2100 First Avenue, with Mr. Rivera's video tape recorder.

17. When a police officer responds to an incident involving the victim of an animal bite, the officer should do the following in the order given:
   I. Determine the owner of the animal
   II. Obtain a description of the animal and attempt to locate it for an examination if the owner is unknown
   III. If the animal is located and the owner is unknown, comply with the Care and Disposition of Animal procedure
   IV. Prepare a Department of Health Form 480BAA and deliver it to the Desk Officer with a written report
   V. Notify the Department of Health by telephone if the person has been bitten by an animal other than a dog or cat.

Police Officer Rosario responds to 1225 South Boulevard where someone has been bitten by a dog. He is met by John Miller who informs Officer Rosario that he was bitten by a large German Shepard. Mr. Miller also states that he believes the dog belongs to someone in the neighborhood but does not know who owns it. Officer Rosario searches the area for the dog but is unable to find it.
What should Officer Rosario do NEXT?
- A. Locate the owner of the animal.
- B. Notify the Department of Health by telephone.
- C. Prepare a Department of Health Form 480BAA.
- D. Comply with the Care and Disposition of Animal procedure.

18. The following details were obtained by Police Officer Howard at the scene of a hit-and-run accident:
Place of Occurrence: Intersection of Brown Street and Front Street
Time of Occurrence: 11:15 A.M.
Victim: John Lawrence
Vehicle: Red Chevrolet, license plate 727PQA
Crime: Leaving the scene of an accident
Officer Howard is completing a report on the incident. Which one of the following expresses the above information MOST clearly and accurately?
   A. A red Chevrolet, license plate 727PQA, hit John Lawrence. It left the scene of the accident at 11:15 A.M. at the intersection of Brown and Front Streets.
   B. At 11:15 A.M., John Lawrence was walking at the intersection of Brown Street and Front Street when he was struck by a red Chevrolet, license plate 727PQA, which left the scene.
   C. It was reported at 11:15 A.M. that John Lawrence was struck at the intersection of Brown Street and Front Street. The red Chevrolet, license plate 727PQA, left the scene.
   D. At the intersection of Brown Street and Front Street, John Lawrence was the victim of a car at 11:15 A.M. which struck him and left the scene. It was a red Chevrolet, license plate 727PQA.

19. Police Officer Donnelly has transported an elderly male to Mt. Hope Hospital after finding him lying on the street. At the hospital, Nurse Baker provided Officer Donnelly with the following information:
Name: Robert Jones
Address: 1485 E. 97th St.
Date of Birth: May 13, 1917
Age: 73 years old
Type of Ailment: Heart condition
Officer Donnelly is completing an Aided Report. Which one of the following expresses the above information MOST clearly and accurately?
   A. Mr. Robert Jones, who is 73 years old, born on May 13, 1917, collapsed on the street. Mr. Jones, who resides at 1485 E. 97th Street, suffers from a heart condition.
   B. Mr. Robert Jones had a heart condition and collapsed today on the street, and resides at 1485 E. 97th Street. He was 73 years old and born on May 13, 1917.
   C. Mr. Robert Jones, who resides at 1485 E. 97th Street, was born on May 13, 1917, and is 73 years old, was found lying on the street from a heart condition.
   D. Mr. Robert Jones, born on May 13, 1917, suffers from a heart condition at age 73 and was found lying on the street residing at 1485 E. 97th Street.

20. Police officers on patrol are often called to a scene where a response from the Fire Department might be necessary.
In which one of the following situations would a request to the Fire Department to respond be MOST critical?
   A. A film crew has started a small fire in order to shoot a scene on an October evening.
   B. Two manhole covers blow off on a September afternoon.
   C. Homeless persons are gathered around a trash can fire on a February morning.
   D. A fire hydrant has been opened by people in the neighborhood on a July afternoon.

21. Police Officer Johnson arrives at the National Savings Bank five minutes after it has been robbed at gunpoint. The following are details provided by eyewitnesses:
Suspect
Sex:          Male
Ethnicity:    White
Height:       5'10" to 6'2"
Weight:       180 lbs. to 190 lbs.
Hair Color:   Blonde
Clothing:     Black jacket, blue dungarees
Weapon:       .45 caliber revolver
Officer Johnson is completing a report on the incident. Which one of the following expresses the above information MOST clearly and accurately?
A white male
   A. weighing 180-190 lbs. robbed the National Savings Bank. He was white with a black jacket with blonde hair, is 5'10" to 6'2", and blue dungarees. The robber was armed with a .45 caliber revolver.
   B. weighing around 180 or 190 lbs. was wearing a black jacket and blue dungarees. He had blonde hair and had a .45 caliber revolver, and was 5'10" to 6'2". He robbed the National Savings Bank.
   C. who was 5'10" to 6'2" and was weighing 180 to 190 lbs., and has blonde hair and wearing blue dungarees and a black jacket with a revolver, robbed the National Savings Bank.
   D. armed with a .45 caliber revolver robbed the National Savings Bank. The robber was described as being between 180-190 lbs., 5'10" to 6'2", with blonde hair. He was wearing a black jacket and blue dungarees.

22. While on patrol, Police Officer Rogers is approached by Terry Conyers, a young woman whose pocketbook has been stolen. Ms. Conyers tells Officer Rogers that the following items were in her pocketbook at the time it was taken:
   4 Traveler's checks, each valued at $20.00
   3 Traverler's checks, each valued at $25.00
   Cash of $212.00
   1 wedding band valued at $450.00
Officer Rogers is preparing a Complaint Report on the robbery.

Which one of the following is the TOTAL value of the
property and cash taken from Ms. Conyers?
A. $707    B. $807    C. $817    D. $837

23. While on patrol, Police Officer Scott is dispatched to
respond to a reported burglary. Two burglars entered
the home of Mr. and Mrs. Walker and stole the following
items:
   3 watches valued at $65.00 each
   1 VCR valued at $340.00
   1 television set valued at $420.00
Officer Scott is preparing a Complaint Report on the
burglary.
Which one of the following is the TOTAL value of the
property stolen?
A. $707    B. $825    C. $920    D. $955

24. While on patrol, Police Officer Smith is dispatched to
investigate a grand larceny. Deborah Paisley, a business-
woman, reports that her 1990 Porsche was broken into. The
following items were taken:
   1 car stereo system valued at $2,950.00
   1 car phone valued at $1,060.00
Ms. Paisley's attache case valued at $200.00 was also
taken from the car in the incident. The attache case
contained two new solid gold pens valued at $970.00 each.
Officer Smith is completing a Complaint Report.
Which one of the following is the TOTAL dollar value of
the property stolen from Ms. Paisley's car?
A. $5,180    B. $5,980    C. $6,040    D. $6,150

25. Police Officer Grundig is writing a Complaint Report
regarding a burglary and assault case. Officer Grundig
has obtained the following facts:
Place of Occurrence:  2244 Clark Street
Victim:               Mrs. Willis
Suspect:              Mr. Willis, victim's ex-husband
Complaint:            Unlawful entry; head injury inflicted
                      with a bat
Officer Grundig is completing a report on the incident.
Which one of the following expresses the above information
MOST clearly and accurately?
  A. He had no permission or authority to do so and it
     caused her head injuries, when Mr. Willis entered his
     ex-wife's premises. Mrs. Willis lives at 2244 Clark
     Street. He hit her with a bat.
  B. Mr. Willis entered 2244 Clark Street, the premises of
     his ex-wife. He hit her with a bat, without permis-
     sion and authority to do so. It caused Mrs. Willis
     to have head injuries.
  C. After Mr. Willis hit his ex-wife, Mrs. Willis, at
     2244 Clark Street, the bat caused her to have head
     injuries. He had no permission nor authority do so so.

D. Mr. Willis entered his ex-wife's premises at 2244 Clark Street without her permission or authority. He then struck Mrs. Willis with a bat, causing injuries to her head.

## KEY (CORRECT ANSWERS)

1. C
2. A
3. B
4. C
5. A

6. B
7. D
8. A
9. C
10. C

11. B
12. D
13. C
14. D
15. A

16. D
17. C
18. B
19. A
20. B

21. D
22. C
23. D
24. D
25. D

# POLICE SCIENCE NOTES

# BASIC FUNDAMENTALS OF INVESTIGATION OF CRIME AND CRIMINAL OFFENSES

## CONTENTS

| | | Page |
|---|---|---|
| A. | *CRIME* | 1 |
| | 1. Definition of Crime | 1 |
| | 2. Investigation of Crime | 1 |
| | 3. Proof of Crime | 1 |
| B. | *CRIMINAL OFFENSES* | 2 |
| | 1. Larceny and Wrongful Appropriation | 2 |
| | 2. Burglary and Housebreaking | 3 |
| | 3. Robbery | 4 |
| | 4. Assault | 4 |
| | 5. Murder/Homicide | 5 |
| | 6. Manslaughter | 8 |
| | 7. Maiming | 8 |
| | 8. Attempted Suicide | 9 |
| | 9. Sodomy | 9 |
| | 10. Rape and Carnal Knowledge | 9 |
| | 11. Forgery | 10 |
| | 12. Counterfeiting | 10 |
| | 13. Narcotic Violations | 11 |
| | 14. Perjury | 12 |
| | 15. Arson | 12 |
| C. | *BASIC QUESTIONS IN INVESTIGATION* | 13 |
| | 1. WHO questions | 13 |
| | 2. WHAT questions | 13 |
| | 3. WHERE questions | 14 |
| | 4. WHEN questions | 14 |
| | 5. HOW questions | 14 |
| | 6. WHY questions | 14 |
| D. | *SOURCES OF INFORMATION* | 15 |
| | I. Developing Sources of Information | 15 |

| | | Page |
|---|---|---|
| II. | Personnel Sources | 15 |
| | 1. Complainants | 15 |
| | 2. Informants | 15 |
| | 3. Witnesses | 16 |
| | 4. Suspects | 16 |
| III. | Information Sources | 16 |
| | 1. Newspapers and Periodicals | 16 |
| | 2. Department of the Army Records | 16 |
| | 3. Department of the Air Force Records | 16 |
| | 4. Department of the Navy Records | 16 |
| | 5. Treasury Department Records | 17 |
| | 6. Department of Justice Records | 17 |
| | 7. United States Postal Service Records | 17 |
| | 8. Veterans Administration Records | 17 |
| | 9. State Records | 18 |
| | 10. County and City Records | 18 |
| | 11. Private Detective Bureaus | 18 |
| | 12. Other Record Sources | 18 |

# POLICE SCIENCE NOTES

# BASIC FUNDAMENTALS OF INVESTIGATION OF CRIME AND CRIMINAL OFFENSES

## A. CRIME

1. DEFINITION OF CRIME

   A crime is an act or omission of an act prohibited or enjoined by law for the protection of the public and punishable by the state in a judicial proceeding in its own name.

   Crimes are classified according to the degree of seriousness. Under the Criminal Code of the United States, a felony is a crime for which the punishment may be death or imprisonment for more than one year. (State criminal codes contain similar or equivalent definitions.)

   Those crimes for which the maximum penalty may not exceed imprisonment for one year are classified as misdemeanors.

   The police officer is concerned with three general classes of crime:
   a. Crimes Against the Person. - Offenses that are directed primarily against the physical person of another.
   b. Crimes Against Property. - Offenses that are directed primarily against property.
   c. Crimes Against the Government. - Offenses that are primarily directed against the peace and dignity of the government rather than against the person or property of an individual.

2. INVESTIGATION OF CRIME

   To investigate a criminal offense effectively and efficiently, the police officer must be familiar with the elements of the offense. He must ascertain whether a crime has, in fact, been committed and must be cognizant of the evidence required to establish the commission of such crime.

   As a guide to the investigator, some of the major offenses, their definitions, and the elements required for proof are set forth in this section. The purpose of the suggestions given is to provide a general checklist for the investigator; the suggestions appearing under a given offense may also be used in the investigation of other crimes.

   A complete investigation requires that six basic questions concerning the crime, the subject, and the victim be answered fully. They are: Who? What? Where? When? How? Why? For subsidiary questions which may be employed to elucidate these basic questions, see Part C of this section.

3. PROOF OF CRIME

   Generally, with regard to each offense, it must be proved, beyond a reasonable doubt by competent and relevant evidence, that the offense was committed, that the accused committed it, that he had the requisite criminal intent at the time or was negligent to the required degree, and that he is a person" subject to the jurisdiction. Since only evidence which is legally admissible may be introduced in a trial, the procurement of such evidence by the police investigator is of great importance.

## B. CRIMINAL OFFENSES

1. LARCENY AND WRONGFUL APPROPRIATION

    a.  Definition. - Any person is guilty of *larceny* if he wrongfully takes, obtains, or withholds, by any means whatever, from the possession of the true owner or of any other person any money, personal property, or article of value of any kind, with intent permanently to deprive or defraud another person of the use and benefit of property or to appropriate the same to his own use or the use of any person other than the true owner.
    *Wrongful appropriation* is defined in the same way as larceny, except that the wrongful taking, obtaining, or withholding need be with intent to deprive, defraud, or appropriate only temporarily. A charge of wrongful appropriation is necessarily included in a charge of larceny.

    b.  Proof of Larceny. - The elements of proof required are:
        (1) That the accused wrongfully took, obtained, or withheld from the possession of the true owner or of any other person the property described in the specification.
        (2) That such property belonged to a certain person named or described.
        (3) That such property was of the value alleged, or of some value.
        (4) The facts and circumstances of the case, showing that the taking, obtaining, or withholding by the accused was with intent permanently to deprive or defraud another person of the use of any person other than the true owner.

    c.  Proof of Wrongful Appropriation. - The elements of proof required are the same as those required of larceny except the facts and circumstances of the case must show that the taking, obtaining, or withholding by the accused was with intent to temporarily deprive or defraud.

    d.  Suggestions. - The method of investigation of larceny and wrongful appropriation is similar to that of burglary and robbery. The investigator should determine:
        (1) The date and hour of the offense.
        (2) The description of property taken, including a complete list of items and their value.
        (3) The owner of the property, the possessor of it at the time of the offense, and the proof of ownership.
        (4) The location of the property at the time of the theft.
        (5) The complete details of how the theft was accomplished.
        (6) Who knew the location and the value of the stolen property.
        (7) Who is suspected.
        (8) The facts pertaining to the description of the suspects.
        (9) Whether the property was carried away by the thief.
        (10) Whether the thief intended to deprive the owner permanently of the property.
        (11) Whether the thief intended to deprive the owner temporarily of the property.
        (12) Whether the stolen article was personal or government property.
        (13) If the property was obtained under false pretenses, and obtain the details thereof.
        (14) All the documents and other evidence connected with the offense.

2. BURGLARY AND HOUSEBREAKING
   a. Definitions. - *Burglary* is the breaking and entering, in the nighttime, of the dwelling house of another person, with intent to commit murder, manslaughter, rape and carnal knowledge, larceny and wrongful appropriation, robbery, forgery, maiming, sodomy, or arson.
   *Housebreaking* is unlawfully entering the building or structure of another person with intent to commit a criminal offense therein. The offense is broader than burglary in that the place entered is not required to be a dwelling house.
   b. Proof of Burglary. - To constitute burglary, it must be proved that:
      (1). The accused broke and entered the certain dwelling house of a certain other person, as specified.
      (2) Such breaking and entering were done in the nighttime.
      (3) The facts and circumstances of the case (such as the actual commission of the offense) show that such breaking and entering were done with the intent to commit the alleged offense therein.
   c. Proof of Housebreaking. - To prove a charge of housebreaking, the investigator must show that:
      (1) The accused unlawfully entered a certain building or structure of a certain other person, as specified.
      (2) The facts and circumstances show that there was an intent to commit a criminal offense therein.
   d. Suggestions. - The following suggestions are presented without regard to the legal distinction between burglary and house-breaking. The purpose is to suggest courses of inquiry where a structure has been entered with criminal intent. The investigator should:
      (1) Record the address or location, and the description of the structure entered.
      (2) Note the date and hour of entry.
      (3) Search the building and immediate area carefully, if property was taken.
      (4) Determine where the owners or occupants were at the time of the crime.
      (5) Ascertain when the owners or occupants left the premises, whether all the doors and windows were secured, and where the keys were kept.
      (6) Develop information pertaining to any recent visitors to the premises. Obtain descriptions of all ostensible visitors, tradesmen, and utilities inspectors. Ascertain whether the crime was committed by someone inside or outside the premises, whether the premises were occupied at the time, whether the entry was gained by force, and, if it were an outside job, how the criminal entered.
      (7) Examine the locks to determine whether entry was effected by the picking of a lock, by the taking of wax impressions, or by the use of skeleton keys or other burglar tools.
      (8) Prepare photographs and sketches of the building, and indicate the place of entry.
      (9) Compile a complete list of the property stolen, and include detailed descriptions of any identifying data.
      (10) Describe all recovered property. Record where, when, and how it was recovered, and whether the owner identified it.
      (11) Establish whether the thief limited himself to one kind of property or whether he took a variety of items.
      (12) Ascertain whether the criminal conducted a systematic search, whether that search indicated that he possessed a knowledge of the area, and whether he knew where to look for the property.

(13) Examine the area carefully for fingerprints and their location and also examine the surrounding area for tire tracks and footprints.
(14) Record all the available details of the thief's characteristics and habits. Describe his method and system of operation.
(15) Check modus operand files to see if similar methods were employed in other burglaries.
(16) Search pawnshops and secondhand shops for loot. Check express offices for evidence of recent shipments.
(17) Describe any tools recovered at the scene. Were any tools recovered from the person of the suspect or his dwelling? Have a laboratory comparison made of any recovered tools and tool marks found at the crime scene.
(18) Obtain a complete description of any person seen loitering about the premises. Did anyone observe the criminal leaving the premises? Were any clues observed in or around the premises?

3. ROBBERY
   a. Definition. - *Robbery* is the taking with intent to steal of anything of value from the person or in the presence of another against his will, by force or violence or fear of immediate or future injury to his person or property or the person or property of a relative or member of his family, or of anyone in his company at the time of the robbery.
   b. Proof. - The elements of proof required are:
      (1) The larceny of the property by the accused, as alleged. (No proof of specific value need be determined.)
      (2) That the larceny was from the person or in the presence of the person alleged to have been robbed.
      (3) That the taking was by force and violence, or by putting in fear, as alleged.
   c. Suggestions. - Many of the suggestions included under larceny and wrongful appropriation, may be useful in the investigation of robbery. If the force employed amounted to physical violence, the suggestions outlined under assault may be used.

4. ASSAULT
   a. Definition. - An *assault* is an attempt or offer with unlawful force or violence to do bodily harm to another, whether or not the attempt or offer is consummated. An assault may consist of a culpably negligent act or omission which foreseeably might and does cause another reasonably to fear that force will at once be applied to his person. An *aggravated assault* is an assault committed with a dangerous weapon or other means of force likely to produce death or grievous bodily harm or with intent to inflict greivous bodily harm with or without a weapon. *Battery* is an assult in which the attempt or offer to do bodily harm is consummated by the infliction of such harm.
   b. Proof. - The elements of proof required are:
      (1) That the accused attempted or offered with unlawful force or violence to do bodily harm to a certain person, as alleged.
      (2) That, in the case of a consummated assault, the accused, intentionally or otherwise, did bodily harm to such person with a certain weapon, unlawful force, or violence.

c. Suggestions. - The following are suggestions for developing information on assaults:
 (1) Was a description of the assault obtained?
 (2) What was the extent of the injuries, if any?
 (3) What was the purpose of the assault?
 (4) Did the suspect make any threats prior to the assault?
 (5) What was the intent of the offender? Robbery? Murder? Rape? Manslaughter? Bodily harm?
 (6) What are the complete facts and circumstances surrounding the assault?
 (7) Did the offender employ a weapon?
 (8) How was the weapon employed?
 (9) Was any other offense committed in addition to the assault? Describe.
 (10) Was there intent on the part of the offender to inflict corporal hurt on the victim?
 (11) Was there a battery? Obtain proof, if possible.
 (12) Who else or what else was involved?
 (13) If assailant is unknown, was a complete description or portrait parle obtained?
 (14) Was the assault successful? If not, what prevented its completion?
 (15) Was assailant too drunk to entertain specific intent?
 (16) Was any weapon or other pertinent evidence left at the scene? Was a laboratory examination deemed advisable and made? Was the scene of attack photographed, and/or sketches prepared?

5. MURDER/HOMICIDE  5.\_\_\_\_

 a. The killing of a human being is unlawful when done without justification or excuse. The determination of whether an unlawful killing constitutes *murder* or a lesser offense depends upon the circumstances under which it occurred.
 (1) Justification. - A murder committed in the proper performance of a legal duty is justifiable.
 (2) Excuse. - A homicide which is the result of an accident or a misadventure in doing a lawful act or in a lawful manner which is done in self-defense is excusable.
 (3) Premeditation. - Premeditated murder is murder committed after the formulation of a specific intent to kill someone and consideration of the act intended. A murder is not premeditated unless the thought of taking a life is consciously conceived, and the act or omission by which it was taken was intended.
 (4) Intent to kill or inflict great bodily harm. - An unlawful killing, without premeditation, is also murder when the person has either the intent to kill, or intent to inflict great bodily harm.
 (5) Act inherently dangerous with wanton disregard of human life. - Engaging in an act inherently dangerous to others, without any intent to cause the death of, or great bodily harm to, any particular person, or even with a wish that death may not be caused may also constitute murder if the performance of the act shows a wanton disregard for human life.
 (6) Commission of certain offenses. - A homicide committed during the perpetration or attempted perpetration of burglary, sodomy, rape, robbery, or aggravated arson also constitutes murder, and it is immaterial that the slaying may be unintentional or even accidental.

b. Proof. - The elements of proof required are:
   (1) That the victim named or described is dead.
   (2) That his death resulted from the act or omission of the accused, as alleged.
   (3) Facts and circumstances showing that the accused had a premeditated design to kill; or intended to kill or inflict great bodily harm; or was engaged in an act inherently dangerous to others, evincing a wanton disregard of human life; or was engaged in the perpetration or attempted perpetration of burglary, sodomy, rape, robbery, or aggravated arson.
c. Suggestions. - The following are suggestions for developing evidence in murder investigations and may be of assistance in manslaughter investigations:
   (1) Obtain name, address, and organization of the deceased.
   (2) Who discovered the body what other persons were present at the scene of the crime who can identify the body of the deceased? Record names and addresses for future reference.
   (3) Question available witnesses.
   (4) Ascertain the date and exact time of the discovery of the crime.
   (5) Was the deceased alive when first found?
   (6) Describe the exact location of the body when found was the body moved before the investigator arrived and, if so, by whom, why, and what change was made in the body's position?
   (7) Describe the position and appearance of the body.
   (8) Photograph the body as found, if possible, and photograph surrounding area, where necessary.
   (9) Record the condition of the weather, the visibility, the direction and force of the wind, and the illumination afforded the scene by the sun, moon, street lamps, or other sources of light.
   (10) Arrange, if possible, to have a medical examiner or physician make a brief preliminary examination of the body before it is moved. Record his name.
   (11) With the assistance of the Medical Examiner obtain a complete autopsy report which should show the following:
      (a) List of all apparent injuries, dirt, blood, or other marks on the body.
      (b) Complete physical description of the body.
      (c) Medical opinion as to time and cause of death.
   (12) When body is moved, mark position. Search area underneath and around body.
   (13) Arrange to obtain victim's clothing and make a careful search of it. Describe in notes. Preserve and identify for use as evidence.
   (14) Conduct a thorough search of the crime scene.
   (15) Search any suspects and their residence, when necessary.
   (16) Prepare necessary photographs, sketches, and notes.
   (17) Describe the crime scene in detail.
   (18) Collect all available evidence, taking precautions to identify and preserve it.
   (19) Submit any bullets, shells, weapons, hairs, bloodstains, fingernail scrapings, empty bottles, suspicious chemicals, fingerprints, footprints, and documents to a criminal laboratory for analysis.
   (20) Search scene and victim's effects for diaries, journals, letters, addresses, telephone numbers, or other documents which may reveal information about the crime.
   (21) Record the location, color, shape, size, and density of any blood spots found; collect, preserve, and identify them.

(22) Record the location, appearance, condition, and ownership of each article of clothing found at the crime scene.
(23) What is the general appearance of the exterior and interior of the scene of the crime? In what condition are the furniture, rugs, window curtains, and articles on tables? Are there any injuries, marks, scars, stains, or other soiling of furniture, carpets, curtains, and window sills? Were telephone wires cut? Did a search of the crime scene uncover strands of hair, cloth, buttons, and cigarette butts? Were these traces left by the victim, by the murderer, or by someone else?
(24) Do the premises contain any clues as to the motive, identity, means of entry, or methods of the culprit?
(25) How did the murderer escape?
(26) Does a reconstruction and search of the route of the murderer reveal footprints, damaged vegetation, articles dropped while fleeing, or traces along the road?
(27) What are the names, descriptions, addresses, peculiarities and habits of associates of the probable murderer? Where may the murderer be found? What is the description of the vehicle he used? Was he wounded or otherwise injured? What were his probable means and direction of escape and place of rendezvous? Has a general alarm been turned in for his apprehension?
(28) Was robbery, revenge, anger, jealousy, profit, sadism, sex motives, insanity, or self-defense a possible motive for the crime?
(29) Was the crime preceded by a quarrel or assault? Who participated? Where were they at the time of the homicide?
(30) What were the character, background, habits, and haunts of the deceased, the suspects, and of their associates?
(31) Were any unguarded statements made by the witnesses and bystanders?
(32) Were the suspects armed shortly before the crime? Were they seen at or near the scene of the crime under suspicious circumstances at the time of its occurrence?
(33) What were the movements of suspects during the days preceding the crime and on the day of the crime?
(34) What were the suspects' actions and demeanor subsequent to the crime? Did they take flight or go into hiding? Did they make any false statements?
(35) What persons frequently visit the suspects at their homes and their places of employment?
(36) What are suspects' channels of communication and what information passes through them?
(37) What movements are made by suspects' associates, sweethearts, and family?
(38) From whom do they receive mail?
(39) Were weapons, ammunition, empty shells, stains or other incriminating facts disclosed by a search of the suspect's residence? From whom, by whom, and when were the weapons secured?
(40) What were the location and condition of all weapons or incriminating evidence found in the suspect's residence or office?
(41) If the suspect has been apprehended, did a search of the clothing and fingernails reveal any blood or particles which would connect him with the scene of the crime?
(42) Secure evidence of all statements by accused both before and after crime.

(43) Check all statements for truth.
(44) Obtain dying declaration of victim, if possible. List persons present, and record time declaration was made.
(45) Interview all close associates of deceased for possible leads.

6. MANSLAUGHTER

   a. Definition. -
      (1) *Voluntary manslaughter.* - An unlawful killing done in the heat of sudden passion caused by provocation, although done with an intent to kill or inflict great bodily harm, is not murder but voluntary manslaughter.
      (2) *Involuntary manslaughter.* - Involuntary manslaughter is an unlawful homicide committed with an intent to kill or inflict great bodily harm. It is an unlawful killing by culpable negligence, or while perpetrating or attempting to perpetrate an offense other than burglary, sodomy, rape, robbery, or aggravated arson, directly affecting the person. It is a degree of carelessness greater than simple negligence.
   b. Proof. - The elements of proof required are:
      (1) That the victim named or described is dead.
      (2) That his death resulted from the act or omission of the accused, as alleged.
      (3) Facts and circumstances showing that the homicide amounted in law to the degree of manslaughter alleged.
   c. Suggestions. - The investigation of manslaughter may be conducted in the same manner as homicide.

7. MAIMING

   a. Definition. - *Maiming* is the inflicting upon the person of another an injury which seriously disfigures his person by any mutilation thereof, or destroys or disables any member or organ of his body or seriously diminishes his physical vigor by the injury of any member or organ. As described above, the injury must be of a substantially permanent nature even though there is a possibility that the victim may eventually recover. However, if the injury be done under circumstances which would justify or excuse homicide, the offense is not committed.
   b. Proof. - The elements of proof required are:
      (1) That the accused inflicted upon a certain person the injury alleged.
      (2) That the injury seriously disfigured his person, or destroyed or disabled an organ or member, or seriously diminished his physical vigor by the injury to an organ or member.
      (3) Facts and circumstances showing that the accused had an intent to injure, disfigure, or disable the person.
   c. Suggestions. - The investigation of maiming is similar to the investigation of an assault. Reference may be made to the suggestions heretofore outlined relative to investigations of assaults. In addition thereto, an investigation of the offense of maiming should include:
      (1) A detailed description of the particular loss or permanent injury suffered.
      (2) A determination as to whether same was self-inflicted, or inflicted upon request of the victim.

8. ATTEMPTED SUICIDE

   a. Definition. - *Attempted suicide* is the attempt to intentionally take one's own life. It is a violation of law and may be prosecuted as such.
   b. Proof. - The elements of proof required are:
      (1) That the accused inflicted upon himself a certain injury in the manner alleged.
      (2) The facts and circumstances indicating that such injury was intentionally inflicted for the purpose of effecting his own death.
   c. Suggestions. - The investigation of attempted suicide is similar to the investigation of homicide. The investigator should arrange for psychiatric examinations and use the suggestions outlined in paragraph 5c. The motive must be established and may often be determined through the subject's associates.

9. SODOMY

   a. Definition. - *Sodomy* is defined as engaging in unnatural carnal copulation, either with another person of the same or opposite sex, or with an animal. Any penetration, however slight, is sufficient to complete the offense.
   b. Proof. - That the accused engaged in unnatural carnal copulation with a certain other person or with an animal, as alleged.
   c. Suggestions. - The crime of sodomy is difficult to prove because of the usual privacy of the offense and the scarcity of physical evidence. The report of a psychiatric examination will facilitate the action of separation from a job. In investigating the crime of sodomy, the following suggestions may prove helpful. The investigator should:
      (1) Secure factual evidence of the crime, avoid hearsay or circumstantial evidence, and procure signed statements from witnesses.
      (2) Send all physical evidence collected to the laboratory for analysis.
      (3) Obtain the results of a psychiatric examination of the offenders.

10. RAPE AND CARNAL KNOWLEDGE

    a. Definition. - *Rape* is defined as the commission of an act of sexual intercourse by a person with a female not his wife, by force, and without her consent. It may be committed on a female of any age. *Carnal knowledge* is defined as the commission of an act of sexual intercourse under circumstances not amounting to rape by a person with a female not his wife who has not attained the age of 16 years. As in rape, any penetration is sufficient to complete the offense. It is no defense that the accused is ignorant or misinformed as to the true age of the female. It is the fact of the girl's age and not his knowledge or belief which fixes his criminal responsibility.
    b. Proof. - The elements of proof required are:
       (1) That the accused had sexual intercourse with a certain female not his wife.
       (2) That the act was done by force and without her consent; or
       (3) That she had not attained the age of 16 years.
    c. Suggestions. - To develop evidence in rape and carnal knowledge investigations, the investigator should:
       (1) Note the time and place of the offense.
       (2) Record the name, age, address, employment, marital status, and family relationships of the victim.
       (3) Obtain the name, social security, organization, marital status, and family relationships of the accused. Obtain a complete description, and also consult the modus operand! file for possible leads if the accused is unknown.

(4) Procure a complete written statement from the victim.
(5) Discreetly obtain information concerning the reputation of the victim as to truth and veracity, and her reputation as to morals and integrity.
(6) Arrange for an immediate physical examination of the victim by a medical officer, for evidence of injury, sexual relationship, blood, or semen.

11. FORGERY

   a. Definition. - *Forgery* is the intent to defraud by false making or altering any signature to, or any part of, any writing which would, if genuine, apparently impose a legal liability on another or change his legal right or liability to his prejudice, or the uttering, offering, issuing, or transferring, with intent to defraud, of such a writing known by the offender to be so or altered,
   b. Proof. - The elements of proof required are:
   (1) That a certain signature or writing was falsely made or altered, as alleged.
   (2) That the signature or writing was of a nature which would, if genuine, apparently impose a legal liability on another or change his legal right or liability to his prejudice.
   (3) That it was the accused who so falsely made or altered such signature or writing; or uttered, offered, issued, or transferred it, knowing it to have been so made or altered.
   (4) The facts and circumstances showing the intent of the accused thereby to defraud.

12. COUNTERFEITING

   a. Definition. - *Counterfeiting* originally was the offense of unlawfully making currency or coin for the purpose of passing the product as true money. By statute, in the United States at the present time, it includes other closely related offenses. The proof in each case varies with the nature of the particular offense charged. Generally speaking the offense usually includes the making of any currency, coin, securities, or obligations of the United States, or of any other country; reproducing or drawing stamps, official seals, possessing such reproductions; making or possessing plates, dies, hubs, or stamps for such reproductions, and dealing in any of the foregoing.
   b. Proof. - The United States Secret Service usually assumes charge of counterfeiting cases. The police criminal investigator, however, collects as much information as possible prior to the transfer of the case. To constitute counterfeiting, it must be proved that the accused possessed, dealt in, or attempted to pass as genuine any of the contraband articles enumerated above, as alleged.
   c. Suggestions. - In the investigation of this offense, the investigator may follow the suggestions outlined for the investigation of forgery. In addition to those suggestions, the investigator should:
   (1) Compare the suspected paper money with genuine money. Ascertain the difference in the types of paper and ink as well as in sharpness and contrast. Examine all details carefully and contrast scrolls, seals, letters, numbers, portraits, and ink distribution. Often the portrait is lacking in expression, the hair lacking in detail, and is unnaturally white. If available in sufficient quantity, stack paper money in order to determine any uneven cutting.

(2) Compare counterfeit coins with genuine coins by dropping them on a hard surface and noting any differences in the ring. Note the ease with which they can be cut; whether they feel greasy, have uneven corrugated edges, or blacken upon the application of a weak nitric acid solution containing silver nitrate.
(3) Identify all the participants in transactions involving the use of counterfeit money, and the nature of their activities.
(4) Ascertain the manufacturer of the money and the source of materials.
(5) Obtain the actual engraving tools, plates, printing presses, inks, papers, molds, materials, and byproducts of the manufacturing process, or information pertaining thereto.

13. NARCOTIC VIOLATIONS
   a. Definition. - The unauthorized use, possession, sale, purchase, or receipt of narcotic drugs is a violation of the -law. The use, possession, or sale of narcotic drugs is regulated by Federal law and is enforced by the Bureau of Narcotics of the Treasury Department. The Bureau of Narcotics may request the assistance of criminal investigators in obtaining evidence of narcotic law violations.
   b. Proof. - To constitute a *narcotic violation,* it must be proved that:
      (1) The accused received, had in his possession, purchased, used, dealt in, or introduced into groups, certain narcotics as alleged.
      (2) Such acts of the accused were unauthorized.
   c. Suggestions. - It is suggested that the investigator consult the Bureau of Narcotics before taking action. The investigator should:
      (1) In the United States: Notify appropriate agency and refrain from continuing investigation until coordination has been ' established.
      (2) In foreign countries:
         (a) Determine source:
            1. Interrogation of subject
            2. Surveillance
            3. Undercover
            4. By type of drug
         (b) Determine scope of distribution:
            1. Buyers
            2. Sellers
            3. Number of persons involved
            4. Locale of sales
      (3) Handling persons under the influence of drugs:
         (a) When a person is apprehended for the suspected use of narcotics, the authorities should keep the subject under observation. He may be rational at the time of apprehension but may suddenly become violent. Quite frequently it may be advisable to secure the subject with handcuffs or other means of restraint.
         (b) A complete search should be accomplished as soon as possible after the apprehension. Suspects have been known to swallow drugs rather than have such incriminating evidence found in their possession.
         (c) Where the subject is addicted to an opiate, manifestations of withdrawal symptoms will appear between eight and twelve hours after cessation of administration of the drugs. It is advisable to keep the subject under observation by a medical officer.

14. PERJURY

   a. Definition. - *Perjury* is the willful and corrupt giving, in a judicial proceeding or course of justice, and upon a lawful oath or in any form allowed by law to be substituted for an oath, any false testimony material to the issue or matter of inquiry.
   b. Proof. - Elements of proof required are:
      (1) That the accused took an oath or its equivalent in that proceeding or course of action, as alleged.
      (2) That the oath was administered to the accused in a matter in which an oath was required or authorized by law, as alleged.
      (3) That the oath was administered by a person having authority to do so.
      (4) That upon such oath, he gave the testimony alleged.
      (5) That the testimony was material; and
      (6) Facts and circumstances that such testimony showed that the accused did not believe such testimony to be true.
   c. Suggestions. - To develop evidence in perjury investigations, the investigator should:
      (1) Identify the judicial proceedings or course of justice in which the alleged perjury was committed.
      (2) Determine that the oath or lawful substitute was duly administered to the offender by a person qualified to do so.
      (3) Secure a copy of the transcript of the testimony given by the offender. If such is not available, take statements from witnesses as to substance of testimony.
      (4) Obtain, if possible, documentary proof that the testimony given was false.
      (5) Ascertain that the testimony of the offender was material to the issue.
      (6) Determine whether the offender intentionally gave false testimony, and whether the offender was familiar with the true facts when the false testimony was given.
      (7) Determine what the offender gained by giving false testimony, or what he would have lost by giving true testimony.
      (8) Interrogate the offender and attempt to secure a statement. Even a statement of denial will be useful in developing the case.

15. ARSON

   a. Definition. - *Aggravated arson* is defined as the willful and malicious burning or setting on fire of an inhabited dwelling, or of any other structure, movable or immovable, wherein, to the knowledge of the offender, there is, at the time, a human being. *Simple arson* is the willful and malicious burning or setting fire to the property of another under circumstances not amounting to aggravated arson. In aggravated arson, danger to human life is the essential element; in simple arson, it is injury to the property of another.
   b. Proof. - The elements of proof required are:
      (1) That the accused burned or set on fire the inhabited dwelling or other structure, as alleged.
      (2) That such dwelling or structure was of value and belonged to a certain person, as alleged.
      (3) Facts and circumstances showing that the act was willful and malicious, and, if in an inhabited dwelling, facts and circumstances that the accused had knowledge there was a human being in the structure at the time.

c. Suggestions. - The following are suggestions for developing evidence in arson investigations. The investigator should:
   (1) Proceed to the scene and complete the investigation as soon as possible.
   (2) Determine who observed the fire first, and obtain an account of what was observed.
   (3) Ascertain the details concerning the point of origin and the spread of the fire.
   (4) If the fire was incendiary in origin, establish the means employed to spread it, any simultaneous ignition points, and any evidence of the use of inflammable liquids.
   (5) Confirm whether inflammable objects were normally present in the burned building.
   (6) Study all possible fire hazards in the building, and determine whether they were basic factors in the fire under investigation.
   (7) Examine the debris in the vicinity, and also charrings and ashes. Suspicious specimens should be sent to the laboratory for analysis.
   (8) Check whether there were any previous fires in the building, or attempts to start fires.
   (9) Inspect fire-extinguishing devices to see whether they have been tampered with.
   (10) Ascertain who had a personal interest in the fire, and in what manner.
   (11) Consider whether the fire originated from natural causes without human aid, whether a human being was involved directly or indirectly, or whether actual arson has been committed.
   (12) Eliminate the possibility of natural causes, such as lightning, action of the sun, explosions, animals causing an accident, spontaneous combustion, or from actions involving a human being directly or indirectly, such as faulty stoves, flues, or circuits.
   (13) Ascertain whether or not the accused had knowledge that there was a human being in the structure at the time.

### C. BASIC QUESTIONS IN INVESTIGATION

1. WHO questions

   a. WHO discovered the crime?
   b. WHO reported the crime?
   c. WHO saw or heard anything of importance?
   d. WHO had a motive for committing the crime?
   e. WHO committed the crime?
   f. WHO helped the perpetrator?
   g. With WHOM did the suspect associate?
   h. With WHOM are the witnesses associated?

2. WHAT questions

   a. WHAT happened?
   b. WHAT crime was committed?
   c. WHAT are the elements of the crime?
   d. WHAT were the actions of the suspect?
   e. WHAT do the witnesses know about the case?
   f. WHAT evidence was obtained?
   g. WHAT was done with the evidence?

h. WHAT tools were employed?
i. WHAT weapons were utilized?
j. WHAT knowledge, skill, or strength was necessary to commit the crime?
k. WHAT means of transportation was used in the commission of the crime?
l. WHAT was the motive?
m. WHAT was the modus operandi?

3. WHERE questions

   a. WHERE was the crime discovered?
   b. WHERE was the crime committed?
   c. WHERE were the suspects seen?
   d. WHERE were the witnesses during the crime?
   e. WHERE was the victim found?
   f. WHERE were the tools and weapons obtained?
   g. WHERE did the suspect live?
   h. WHERE did the victim live?
   i. WHERE did the suspect spend his leisure time?
   j. WHERE is the suspect now?
   k. WHERE is the suspect likely to go?
   l. WHERE was the suspect apprehended?

4. WHEN questions

   a. WHEN was the crime committed?
   b. WHEN was the crime discovered?
   c. WHEN was notification received?
   d. WHEN did the police arrive at the scene?
   e. WHEN was the victim last seen?
   f. WHEN was the suspect apprehended?

5. HOW questions

   a. HOW was the crime committed?
   b. HOW did the suspect get to the scene?
   c. HOW did the suspect get away?
   d. HOW did the suspect get the information necessary to enable him to commit the crime?
   e. HOW was the crime discovered?
   f. HOW did the suspect secure the tools and weapons?
   g. HOW were the tools and weapons utilized?
   h. HOW much damage was done?
   i. HOW much property was stolen?
   j. HOW much skill, knowledge, and strength was necessary to commit the crime?

6. WHY questions

   a. WHY was the crime committed?
   b. WHY were the particular tools utilized?
   c. WHY was the particular method employed?
   d. WHY are the witnesses reluctant to talk?
   e. WHY was the crime reported?

## D. SOURCES OF INFORMATION

### I. Developing Sources of Information

A source of information is any person, object, or recorded data utilized by a police investigator in the conduct of an investigation.

A successful investigation depends largely upon locating, developing, and following through on as many sources of dependable information as possible.

Investigators must know all sources of information in their working area and must constantly strive to develop new sources. Persons who are reliable sources of information should be treated with tact, diplomacy, and consideration, and every effort should be made to instill and maintain confidence and complete collaboration.

### II. Personnel Sources

1. COMPLAINANTS

A complainant is a person who notifies a law enforcement agency of an actual or suspected crime or offense. He is usually the victim, witness, or discoverer of a crime.

2. INFORMANTS

An informant is a person who openly gives information to police. The good informant is a person who can produce pertinent information when it is needed. A confidential informant is a person who confidentially provides police with information with the understanding that his identity will not be revealed.
- a. Safeguarding Identity. - Although the information gained may be furnished other investigative agencies, the identity of an informant is furnished only when absolutely necessary. To preserve secrecy, each confidential informant should be assigned a number, symbol, or fictitious name, to be used in all references to him and in official reports.
- b. Investigator-Informant Relationship. - To develop and maintain close collaboration with informants, members of an investigative office should observe the following:
- (1) Treat informants fairly.
- (2) Be scrupulously exact in all transactions.
- (3) Express appreciation for information given.
- (4) Investigate all reports or leads from informants and record them for future reference as circumstances indicate.
- (5) Secure all possible information from an anonymous informant before the conversation ends. (Anonymous persons who volunteer information by telephone rarely call twice.)
- (6) Protect the interests of the informant.
- (7) Be absolutely truthful and make no promise or commitment which cannot be fulfilled.
- (8) Make no attempt to force information from informants.

3. WITNESSES

The best source of information in any incident is the person who actually witnessed it. The investigator must make every effort to locate all witnesses to every incident, and, by thorough and detailed interview, elicit from them all possible information pertaining to the case.

4. SUSPECTS

Suspects, when properly interrogated, may be valuable sources of information.

## III. Information Sources

1. NEWSPAPERS AND PERIODICALS

Newspapers and periodicals maintain permanent files of individual news items pertaining to persons and incidents. These files are termed "morgues" and may be consulted by the investigator.

2. DEPARTMENT OF THE ARMY RECORDS

Official Department of the Army records pertaining to military personnel provide a valuable source of information for the investigator's use. Some of the agencies which maintain personnel records are:
   a. Office of The Adjutant General. - The Adjutant General maintains records of all organizations, and of officers and enlisted personnel who are or have been in the military service of the United States.
   b. Office of The Provost Marshal General. - The Office of The Provost Marshal General maintains records of all investigations conducted by criminal investigators of major crimes committed by military personnel and civilians subject to the Articles of the Uniform Code of Military Justice.
   c. Counter Intelligence Corps. - The Counter Intelligence Corps (CIC) maintains records of investigations of subversive activity within the Army, including civilians employed by the Army.
   d. Army Security Agency. - The Army Security Agency (ASA) maintains records of investigations of Army communication security violations.
   e. Office of The Inspector General. - The Office of The Inspector General maintains records of investigations conducted by inspectors general.

3. DEPARTMENT OF THE AIR FORCE RECORDS

In the Department of the Air Force, the Office of Special Investigations (OSI) maintains records of all investigations conducted on major offenses, including criminal and subversive, occurring within the Air Force.

4. DEPARTMENT OF THE NAVY RECORDS

In the Department of the Navy, the Office of Naval Intelligence (ONI) maintains records of investigations conducted by Naval Intelligence.

5. TREASURY DEPARTMENT RECORDS

   The Treasury Department has five law enforcement divisions, each maintaining files and records relative to the functions it performs:
   a. United States Secret Service. - The United States Secret Service suppresses counterfeiting and protects the person of the President and members of his family.
   b. Bureau of Narcotics. - The Bureau of Narcotics investigates violations of the narcotic laws.
   c. Bureau of Internal Revenue.
      (1) The Intelligence Unit investigates violations of Federal income tax laws.
      (2) The Alcohol Tax Unit investigates violations of the laws relating to manufacture, storage, and sale of alcoholic beverages and enforces the National Firearms Act.
   d. Bureau of Customs. - The Bureau of Customs enforces the customs laws, supervises the importation of articles into the United States, and apprehends smugglers.
   e. Coast Guard. - The Coast Guard enforces the laws of the United States in the coastal areas and navigable waters of the United States. During time of peace, this department is a branch of the Treasury Department. During time of war, it becomes a branch of the Department of the Navy.

6. DEPARTMENT OF JUSTICE RECORDS

   a. Federal Bureau of Investigation.- The Federal Bureau of Investigation (FBI) enforces all Federal violations not specifically assigned to some other Federal law enforcement agency. It maintains complete files, including an extensive fingerprint file, and a scientific laboratory for analyzing and identifying evidence.
   b. Immigration and Naturalization Service,- The Immigration and Naturalization Service has photographs, fingerprints, and brief biographies of immigrants, their residence and employment addresses, and the status of their naturalization.

7. UNITED STATES POSTAL SERVICE

   U.S. Postal Service will provide the investigator with all the information which appears on the outside of envelopes in the United States mail addressed to a particular individual. This service is known as a "mail cover" and may be continued for a specific period agreed upon by the investigator and the postal authorities. Mail may not be read except by censors or when seized pursuant to a search warrant. In securing a search warrant for mail, the investigator should confer with the local postal inspector. At military establishments, the postal officer should be consulted for assistance. Tracings of covers of envelopes may be obtained on request; however, a postal inspector, either civilian or military, should be consulted on the subject.

8. VETERANS ADMINISTRATION RECORDS

   The Veterans Administration maintains records on former members of the United States military forces.

9. STATE RECORDS

State police are responsible for investigation of violations of State laws within their respective States and maintain appropriate records. A State patrol is usually vested only with the authority of peace officers and is restricted to the enforcement of the provisions of the vehicle act and maintaining appropriate records. Some States have a central body of highly trained investigators, available to any law enforcement agency within the State to assist in the solution of criminal cases in especially designated fields of investigation. Vehicle license bureaus have a record of the issuance of license plates and drivers licenses.

10. COUNTY AND CITY RECORDS

The Sheriff's department is usually responsible for the enforcement of criminal laws and the vehicular code within a county and the maintenance of records pertaining thereto. The Bureau of Vital Statistics maintains complete records of births, deaths, marriages, divorces, changes of names, and adoptions. District attorneys' offices have records of criminals or suspected criminals and other information which may be of value. Municipal police are responsible for the enforcement of all laws and ordinances within a city or town and have established records sections.

11. PRIVATE DETECTIVE BUREAUS

Private detective bureaus conduct investigations and may serve as a source of information. However, the investigator should use discretion in discussing official cases with private detectives.

12. OTHER RECORD SOURCES

    a. Employment agencies have records of applicants and former ap-licants and a record of past employment for each individual.
    b. The American Red Cross has certain types of information of a domestic nature.
    c. The American Social Hygiene Association has information regarding vice, gambling, and liquor control.
    d. Transportation companies have records of reservations of passengers and bills of lading.
    e. Insurance company clearing houses have records on all persons who have had life insurance or fire insurance policies.
    f. Water, electric, and gas companies have records of names and addresses. They are often the first agencies to obtain such information on persons newly arrived in a community.
    g. Automobile associations are able to furnish information regarding the registration and ownership of members' automobiles and, on some occasions, past or planned trips.
    h. Hotel associations maintain files on certain types of criminals, such as bad check passers, gamblers, and confidence men. Hotels maintain registers of all persons residing at the hotels and records of valuables checked by patrons.
    i. Hospital records reveal information of past and present patients, including names, addresses, injuries, and medical histories. In some localities the law requires that certain types of wounds be reported to the police.
    j. City directories contain names, addresses, and occupations of members of families living in a city at the time the information for the directory was collected. Earlier editions will reveal past information.

k. Banks have records of past and present financial transactions with customers or former customers and may supply other general information.
l. Finance companies have records of loans which may include a considerable amount of information relative to the persons securing loans.
m. Commercial credit bureaus maintain extensive files on persons who have made use of personal credit. Information includes addresses, bank accounts, charge accounts, records of judgments, assets, and financial standing.
n. Telephone companies will furnish addresses and telephone numbers of subscribers, as well as names and telephone numbers of subscribers when addresses are known.

# ANSWER SHEET

ST NO. _____ PART _____ TITLE OF POSITION _____
(AS GIVEN IN EXAMINATION ANNOUNCEMENT - INCLUDE OPTION, IF ANY)

ACE OF EXAMINATION _____ DATE _____
(CITY OR TOWN)          (STATE)

RATING

**USE THE SPECIAL PENCIL.  MAKE GLOSSY BLACK MARKS.**

| | A B C D E | | A B C D E | | A B C D E | | A B C D E | | A B C D E |
|---|---|---|---|---|---|---|---|---|---|
| 1 | ⋮ ⋮ ⋮ ⋮ ⋮ | 26 | ⋮ ⋮ ⋮ ⋮ ⋮ | 51 | ⋮ ⋮ ⋮ ⋮ ⋮ | 76 | ⋮ ⋮ ⋮ ⋮ ⋮ | 101 | ⋮ ⋮ ⋮ ⋮ ⋮ |
| 2 | ⋮ ⋮ ⋮ ⋮ ⋮ | 27 | ⋮ ⋮ ⋮ ⋮ ⋮ | 52 | ⋮ ⋮ ⋮ ⋮ ⋮ | 77 | ⋮ ⋮ ⋮ ⋮ ⋮ | 102 | ⋮ ⋮ ⋮ ⋮ ⋮ |
| 3 | ⋮ ⋮ ⋮ ⋮ ⋮ | 28 | ⋮ ⋮ ⋮ ⋮ ⋮ | 53 | ⋮ ⋮ ⋮ ⋮ ⋮ | 78 | ⋮ ⋮ ⋮ ⋮ ⋮ | 103 | ⋮ ⋮ ⋮ ⋮ ⋮ |
| 4 | ⋮ ⋮ ⋮ ⋮ ⋮ | 29 | ⋮ ⋮ ⋮ ⋮ ⋮ | 54 | ⋮ ⋮ ⋮ ⋮ ⋮ | 79 | ⋮ ⋮ ⋮ ⋮ ⋮ | 104 | ⋮ ⋮ ⋮ ⋮ ⋮ |
| 5 | ⋮ ⋮ ⋮ ⋮ ⋮ | 30 | ⋮ ⋮ ⋮ ⋮ ⋮ | 55 | ⋮ ⋮ ⋮ ⋮ ⋮ | 80 | ⋮ ⋮ ⋮ ⋮ ⋮ | 105 | ⋮ ⋮ ⋮ ⋮ ⋮ |
| 6 | ⋮ ⋮ ⋮ ⋮ ⋮ | 31 | ⋮ ⋮ ⋮ ⋮ ⋮ | 56 | ⋮ ⋮ ⋮ ⋮ ⋮ | 81 | ⋮ ⋮ ⋮ ⋮ ⋮ | 106 | ⋮ ⋮ ⋮ ⋮ ⋮ |
| 7 | ⋮ ⋮ ⋮ ⋮ ⋮ | 32 | ⋮ ⋮ ⋮ ⋮ ⋮ | 57 | ⋮ ⋮ ⋮ ⋮ ⋮ | 82 | ⋮ ⋮ ⋮ ⋮ ⋮ | 107 | ⋮ ⋮ ⋮ ⋮ ⋮ |
| 8 | ⋮ ⋮ ⋮ ⋮ ⋮ | 33 | ⋮ ⋮ ⋮ ⋮ ⋮ | 58 | ⋮ ⋮ ⋮ ⋮ ⋮ | 83 | ⋮ ⋮ ⋮ ⋮ ⋮ | 108 | ⋮ ⋮ ⋮ ⋮ ⋮ |
| 9 | ⋮ ⋮ ⋮ ⋮ ⋮ | 34 | ⋮ ⋮ ⋮ ⋮ ⋮ | 59 | ⋮ ⋮ ⋮ ⋮ ⋮ | 84 | ⋮ ⋮ ⋮ ⋮ ⋮ | 109 | ⋮ ⋮ ⋮ ⋮ ⋮ |
| 10 | ⋮ ⋮ ⋮ ⋮ ⋮ | 35 | ⋮ ⋮ ⋮ ⋮ ⋮ | 60 | ⋮ ⋮ ⋮ ⋮ ⋮ | 85 | ⋮ ⋮ ⋮ ⋮ ⋮ | 110 | ⋮ ⋮ ⋮ ⋮ ⋮ |

Make only ONE mark for each answer.  Additional and stray marks may be counted as mistakes.  In making corrections, erase errors COMPLETELY.

| | A B C D E | | A B C D E | | A B C D E | | A B C D E | | A B C D E |
|---|---|---|---|---|---|---|---|---|---|
| 11 | ⋮ ⋮ ⋮ ⋮ ⋮ | 36 | ⋮ ⋮ ⋮ ⋮ ⋮ | 61 | ⋮ ⋮ ⋮ ⋮ ⋮ | 86 | ⋮ ⋮ ⋮ ⋮ ⋮ | 111 | ⋮ ⋮ ⋮ ⋮ ⋮ |
| 12 | ⋮ ⋮ ⋮ ⋮ ⋮ | 37 | ⋮ ⋮ ⋮ ⋮ ⋮ | 62 | ⋮ ⋮ ⋮ ⋮ ⋮ | 87 | ⋮ ⋮ ⋮ ⋮ ⋮ | 112 | ⋮ ⋮ ⋮ ⋮ ⋮ |
| 13 | ⋮ ⋮ ⋮ ⋮ ⋮ | 38 | ⋮ ⋮ ⋮ ⋮ ⋮ | 63 | ⋮ ⋮ ⋮ ⋮ ⋮ | 88 | ⋮ ⋮ ⋮ ⋮ ⋮ | 113 | ⋮ ⋮ ⋮ ⋮ ⋮ |
| 14 | ⋮ ⋮ ⋮ ⋮ ⋮ | 39 | ⋮ ⋮ ⋮ ⋮ ⋮ | 64 | ⋮ ⋮ ⋮ ⋮ ⋮ | 89 | ⋮ ⋮ ⋮ ⋮ ⋮ | 114 | ⋮ ⋮ ⋮ ⋮ ⋮ |
| 15 | ⋮ ⋮ ⋮ ⋮ ⋮ | 40 | ⋮ ⋮ ⋮ ⋮ ⋮ | 65 | ⋮ ⋮ ⋮ ⋮ ⋮ | 90 | ⋮ ⋮ ⋮ ⋮ ⋮ | 115 | ⋮ ⋮ ⋮ ⋮ ⋮ |
| 16 | ⋮ ⋮ ⋮ ⋮ ⋮ | 41 | ⋮ ⋮ ⋮ ⋮ ⋮ | 66 | ⋮ ⋮ ⋮ ⋮ ⋮ | 91 | ⋮ ⋮ ⋮ ⋮ ⋮ | 116 | ⋮ ⋮ ⋮ ⋮ ⋮ |
| 17 | ⋮ ⋮ ⋮ ⋮ ⋮ | 42 | ⋮ ⋮ ⋮ ⋮ ⋮ | 67 | ⋮ ⋮ ⋮ ⋮ ⋮ | 92 | ⋮ ⋮ ⋮ ⋮ ⋮ | 117 | ⋮ ⋮ ⋮ ⋮ ⋮ |
| 18 | ⋮ ⋮ ⋮ ⋮ ⋮ | 43 | ⋮ ⋮ ⋮ ⋮ ⋮ | 68 | ⋮ ⋮ ⋮ ⋮ ⋮ | 93 | ⋮ ⋮ ⋮ ⋮ ⋮ | 118 | ⋮ ⋮ ⋮ ⋮ ⋮ |
| 19 | ⋮ ⋮ ⋮ ⋮ ⋮ | 44 | ⋮ ⋮ ⋮ ⋮ ⋮ | 69 | ⋮ ⋮ ⋮ ⋮ ⋮ | 94 | ⋮ ⋮ ⋮ ⋮ ⋮ | 119 | ⋮ ⋮ ⋮ ⋮ ⋮ |
| 20 | ⋮ ⋮ ⋮ ⋮ ⋮ | 45 | ⋮ ⋮ ⋮ ⋮ ⋮ | 70 | ⋮ ⋮ ⋮ ⋮ ⋮ | 95 | ⋮ ⋮ ⋮ ⋮ ⋮ | 120 | ⋮ ⋮ ⋮ ⋮ ⋮ |
| 21 | ⋮ ⋮ ⋮ ⋮ ⋮ | 46 | ⋮ ⋮ ⋮ ⋮ ⋮ | 71 | ⋮ ⋮ ⋮ ⋮ ⋮ | 96 | ⋮ ⋮ ⋮ ⋮ ⋮ | 121 | ⋮ ⋮ ⋮ ⋮ ⋮ |
| 22 | ⋮ ⋮ ⋮ ⋮ ⋮ | 47 | ⋮ ⋮ ⋮ ⋮ ⋮ | 72 | ⋮ ⋮ ⋮ ⋮ ⋮ | 97 | ⋮ ⋮ ⋮ ⋮ ⋮ | 122 | ⋮ ⋮ ⋮ ⋮ ⋮ |
| 23 | ⋮ ⋮ ⋮ ⋮ ⋮ | 48 | ⋮ ⋮ ⋮ ⋮ ⋮ | 73 | ⋮ ⋮ ⋮ ⋮ ⋮ | 98 | ⋮ ⋮ ⋮ ⋮ ⋮ | 123 | ⋮ ⋮ ⋮ ⋮ ⋮ |
| 24 | ⋮ ⋮ ⋮ ⋮ ⋮ | 49 | ⋮ ⋮ ⋮ ⋮ ⋮ | 74 | ⋮ ⋮ ⋮ ⋮ ⋮ | 99 | ⋮ ⋮ ⋮ ⋮ ⋮ | 124 | ⋮ ⋮ ⋮ ⋮ ⋮ |
| 25 | ⋮ ⋮ ⋮ ⋮ ⋮ | 50 | ⋮ ⋮ ⋮ ⋮ ⋮ | 75 | ⋮ ⋮ ⋮ ⋮ ⋮ | 100 | ⋮ ⋮ ⋮ ⋮ ⋮ | 125 | ⋮ ⋮ ⋮ ⋮ ⋮ |

# ANSWER SHEET

TEST NO. _____ PART _____ TITLE OF POSITION _____
(AS GIVEN IN EXAMINATION ANNOUNCEMENT - INCLUDE OPTION, IF ANY)

PLACE OF EXAMINATION _____ DATE _____
(CITY OR TOWN)                                    (STATE)

RATING

**USE THE SPECIAL PENCIL.    MAKE GLOSSY BLACK MARKS.**

Make only ONE mark for each answer.    Additional and stray marks may be counted as mistakes.    In making corrections, erase errors COMPLETELY.